Community Action
in a Contested Society

Community Action in a Contested Society

The Story of Northern Ireland

Avila Kilmurray

PETER LANG

Oxford • Bern • Berlin • Bruxelles • Frankfurt am Main • New York • Wien

Bibliographic information published by Die Deutsche Nationalbibliothek.
Die Deutsche Nationalbibliothek lists this publication in the Deutsche National-
bibliografie; detailed bibliographic data is available on the Internet at
http://dnb.d-nb.de.

A catalogue record for this book is available from the British Library.

Library of Congress Control Number: 2016954862

Cover image: Elaine Farrell (www.elainefarrellphotography.com).

ISBN 978-3-0343-2257-7 (print) • ISBN 978-1-78707-216-9 (ePDF)
ISBN 978-1-78707-217-6 (ePub) • ISBN 978-1-78707-218-3 (mobi)

© Peter Lang AG, International Academic Publishers, Bern 2017
Hochfeldstrasse 32, CH-3012 Bern, Switzerland
info@peterlang.com, www.peterlang.com, www.peterlang.net

This publication has been peer reviewed.

Contents

Abbreviations

ACE	Action for Community Employment
BAT	Belfast Action Teams
BCA	Bogside Community Association
CFNI	Community Foundation for Northern Ireland (previously Northern Ireland Voluntary Trust – NIVT).
CNR	Catholic/Nationalist/Republican single identity community designation
CPI	Communist Party of Ireland
DHAG	Derry Housing Action Group
DSD	Department of Social Development (latterly Department of Communities)
DUP	Democratic Unionist Party
HTR	Healing through Remembering
IFB	Intermediary Funding Body for the EU PEACE Programme funds
INLA	Irish National Liberation Army
IRA	Irish Republican Army (otherwise the Republican Movement)
IRA Official	traditional IRA (ideologically left-wing)
IRSP	Irish Republican Socialist Party
LVF	Loyalist Volunteer Force (critical of the 1998 Peace Agreement)
MBW	Making Belfast Work
NICRA	Northern Ireland Civil Rights Association
NICRC	Northern Ireland Community Relations Commission (1969–1974)
NICRC	Northern Ireland Community Relations Council (1990–)
NICVA	Northern Ireland Council of Voluntary Action (previously Northern Ireland Council of Social Services – NICSS)
NIWRM	Northern Ireland Women's Rights Movement

OFMDFM	Office of First Minister, Deputy First Minister, Northern Ireland Executive
PSNI	Police Service of Northern Ireland
PUL	Protestant/Unionist/Loyalist single identity community designation
PUP	Progressive Unionist Party
RAP (NI)	Rural Action Project (1984–1989)
RCN	Rural Community Network
RTE	Radio Telefís Eireann
RUC	Royal Ulster Constabulary
SEUPB	Special EU Programmes Body to administer EU PEACE funds
SDLP	Social Democratic Labour Party
SICDG	Springfield Inter Community Development Group (later Interaction Belfast)
SLIG	Suffolk Lenadoon Interface Group
SPADs	Special Political Advisers
TSN	Targeting Social Need
UDA	Ulster Defence Association
UDP	Ulster Democratic Party
UFF	Ulster Freedom Fighters (aligned to UDA)
UKUP	United Kingdom Unionist Party
UPNI	Unionist Party of Northern Ireland
UVF	Ulster Volunteer Force
UWC	Ulster Workers' Council (1994)
VAU	Voluntary Activity Unit (Dept. of Health & Social Services, latterly Dept. of Social Development).
WEA	Workers' Educational Association

Introduction

Much has been written about Northern Ireland but the contribution of community action over the period of the Troubles is largely unrecorded. This book attempts to fill at least some of the gap by charting aspects of the kaleidoscope of that story. It primarily draws on interviews conducted with ninety-eight local activists and community development workers, in addition to eighteen statutory officials, scanning experience over the period 1969–2016. Interviewees from the community catchment are drawn in roughly equal numbers from Catholic/Nationalist/Republican (CNR) and Protestant/Unionist/Loyalist (PUL) identities. The officials are predominantly from the latter. Where quotes are used from those interviewed, they are not attributed to named individuals unless the person in question is a known public figure. This is not a concern over misrepresentation of the views expressed, but in recognition of authorial responsibility for the selection of quotes used.

The book is by necessity impressionistic given the discipline of publication word limit. Chapter 1 provides a light touch introduction to the political context of the period for readers engaging with it for the first time. As such, it can only reference and frame events and developments that warrant considerably greater study and explanation. Subsequent chapters are arranged in approximate chronological order to facilitate insight into the challenges and opportunities offered for community action and the inventiveness shown by activists that balanced on the interface between political and social developments. The final chapter, Chapter 12, highlights learning that is considered relevant for workers looking to create space in violently divided societies.

While focused on the story of Northern Ireland, there are aspects that are applicable to any contested society – the problem of closing space for either complexity or critique; the power of perception and rumour; conflicting community and/or official narratives; and the prevalence of physical threat. Community action has to develop thinking and skills to remain feasible and relevant. Similarly, while every conflict is unique, the clustering of perceived grievances and seeking a sense of security with one's 'own' will be generally recognisable. There is reference throughout this book to 'single identity' communities, which are either overwhelmingly Catholic/Nationalist/Republican or Protestant/Unionist/Loyalist; this is a short-hand signifier of a relationship to the State based on national and cultural identity, kinship and political affiliation, rather than primarily a theological identification. The bracketing of Catholic/Nationalism/Republicanism and Protestant/Unionism/Loyalism also acknowledges the heterogeneous views within these two dominant categories. However given the clumsiness of the designation, a shortened version of the description of these single-identity communities will be used throughout the remainder of the text.

The motivation for this work was observation over many years of the commitment, dedication and courage shown by many individuals that contributed to community resilience in abnormal circumstances. Some of those interviewed are no longer with us. Ann McGeeney, William (Plumb) Smith, Jeremy Harbison, David Stevens, Tom Lovett, Theresa Kelly, Fr. Matt Wallace, Hughie Smyth and Joe Wright are all remembered. My thanks to them and to all the other interviewees who generously contributed to a study that became a PhD thesis and latterly this book. Thanks also to Mary Black, Chairperson of the Community Foundation for Northern Ireland, who encouraged the venture, and to the patience of my family who lived it. The publication of this book has been supported by the generosity of the Joseph Rowntree Charitable Trust that made its own very important contribution to peacebuilding in Northern Ireland over many years. I would also like to acknowledge Elaine Farrell for her kind permission for use of the front cover photograph. Finally, thanks to John Morison, my Queens University Belfast supervisor, who at times despaired of the PhD but always said he would buy the book – John, here is the book.

Avila Kilmurray

Timeline: Northern Ireland, 1969–2015

Date	Government	Political Developments	Community Development	Community Relations	Social Policies
1969–1974	Northern Ireland Government under (i) Terence O'Neill; (ii) James Chichester-Clark; (iii) Brian Faulkner. 1972 – Direct Rule under (i) William Whitelaw; (ii) Francis Pym; (iii) Merlyn Rees. Sunningdale Executive (Jan–May 1974).	NICRA protests. Introduction of British Army (1969). Internment without Trial (1971). Establishment of Provisional IRA and UDA. Est. of SDLP, DUP and Alliance Party. Escalation in violence. Ulster Workers' Council Strike (1974).	Anti-rent increase cross-community protests. Bogside Community Association & Ardoyne Assemblies. Greater West Belfast Community Assoc. (GWBCA) & Shankill Community Council.	Northern Ireland Community Relations Commission (1969–1974) and Department of Community Relations.	Establishment of Northern Ireland Housing Executive. Belfast Areas of Special Social Need survey and review. Macrory Report on Review of Local Government (1970).

Date	Government	Political Developments	Community Development	Community Relations	Social Policies
1975–1980	Direct Rule under (i) Merlyn Rees; (ii) Roy Mason; (iii) Humphrey Atkins.	Republican and Loyalist ceasefires/feuding (1975). 'Normalisation, criminalization, Ulsterisation' – government meta-narrative. Peace People demonstrations (1976/77). Establishment of IRSP/INLA.	Establishment of CONI (Community Organisations of Northern Ireland) and UCAG (Ulster Community Action Group). Northern Ireland Women's Rights Movement and Charter (1975). Save the Shankill & Divis Protests in Belfast. Establishment of Centre for Neighbourhood Development (Belfast). Focus on Community Education. Establishment of Community Worker Research Project and Northern Ireland Voluntary Trust (NIVT) (1979).	Community Relations policy located in Dept of Education (NI). Fair Employment Agency established under Fair Employment Act (1976). Equal Opportunities Commission established.	Moyle Report on District Councils and Community Services. Coordinating Committee on Social Problems established within central government. Belfast Areas of Need (BAN) operating. Lord Melchett – Minister responsible for Education and Health & Social Services (NI). First EC Anti-Poverty Programme focus on Welfare Rights.

1981–1985	Direct Rule under (i) James Prior; (ii) Douglas Hurd.	Maze Prison Hunger Strikes – 10 republicans die. Sinn Féin enters electoral politics. UDA establish Ulster Loyalist Democratic Party (re-named Ulster Democratic Party). Irish government establish New Ireland Forum. Anglo-Irish Agreement signed resulting in Unionist protests (1985).	Protests against government austerity policies and public spending cuts. Establishment of Women's Information Day network and community-based Women's Centres. Northern Ireland Council of Social Services renamed NICVA (Northern Ireland Council for Voluntary Action). Establishment of Northern Ireland Poverty Lobby, GingerBread (NI), etc. Establishment of Women's Education Project (later Women's Resource & Development Agency) (1983).	Action for Community Employment (ACE) programme rolled out. Hurd Principles introduced.

Date	Government	Political Developments	Community Development	Community Relations	Social Policies
1986–1990	Direct Rule under (i) Tom King; (ii) Peter Brooke.	Andy Tyrie replaced as UDA Chairman (1988). Hume/Adams Talks (1988). Brooke announces Britain has 'no strategic interest' in Northern Ireland. Loyalist attacks on 'pan nationalist front.'	Obair Conference and reports over allocation of public money (West Belfast). Establishment of West Belfast Parent Youth Support Group over 'joyriding'. Second EC Anti-Poverty Programme on rural poverty (RAP) and unemployment. Establishment of Community Development Review Group. Third EU Anti-Poverty Programme in Craigavon (1989). Establishment of Springfield Inter Community Development Project (1988). Establishment of Women's Support Network (1989).	SACHR (Standing Advisory Commission on Human Rights) Report on Community Relations (1986). Establishment of CCRU (Central Community Relations Unit) within government. Funding for District Council Good Relations. Establishment of Northern Ireland Community Relations Council (1990). Establishment of Fair Employment Commission (1990).	Establishment of Belfast Action Teams (BAT) (1987). Decision to demolish Divis Flats complex. Establishment of International Fund for Ireland (IFI). Establishment of MBW (Making Belfast Work) (1988). DHSS (Dept. of Health & Social Services) circulars on community development. Londonderry Initiative (1988–2004).

1991–1995	Direct Rule under (i) Peter Brooke; (ii) Patrick Mayhew.	Use of IRA 'proxy' bombs target alleged 'collaborators'. UDA proscribed (1992). President Mary Robinson visits Belfast (1993). IRA Shankill Bomb kills 10 (1993) followed by loyalist retaliations. IRA and Loyalist ceasefires (Autumn 1994). British and Irish governments' framework document. David Trimble elected leader of Ulster Unionist Party. Violence over Loyal Order parades. White House Investment Conference to support peace process and Clinton visit.	CDRG Reports issued (1991). 'Community Work in Protestant Areas' Report (1991). Rural Community Network established. Opshal Enquiry (1992). 'Beyond Hate' conference, Derry (1992). Shankill Community Planning Convention. NIVT launches 'Weak Community Infrastucture' programme (1995). Establishment of Community Development & Health Network (1995).	Both Catholics and Protestants demonstrate increasing optimism over community relations post 1994 ceasefires. On-going community based work to alleviate interface tensions.	Era of partnership working. Establishment of Rural Development Council & RATs (Rural Action Teams). Targeting Social Need priority established by government. Robson Report on Distribution of Relative Deprivation in Northern Ireland (1994). DHSS Strategy for Support of Voluntary Sector & Community Development (1993), with establishment of VAU (Voluntary Activity Unit). EU Special Support Programme for Peace & Reconciliation (1995–1999).

Date	Government	Political Developments	Community Development	Community Relations	Social Policies
1996–2000	Direct Rule under (i) Patrick Mayhew; (ii) Mo Mowlam; (iii) Peter Mandelson. Power passed to Northern Ireland Executive (1999), which collapses, and is restored (2000).	Elections to Northern Ireland Peace Talks & Forum. IRA ceasefire breaks down (1996–1997). Belfast/Good Friday Agreement (1998) ratified by North/South referenda. Omagh Bomb planted by dissident republicans kills 31 (1998). Establishment of NI Women's Coalition (1996).	Intermediary Funding Bodies (IFBs) drawn from voluntary sector to deliver PEACE 1. Early Victims & Survivors and Political ex-Prisoner Support Groups. Growth in Restorative Justice projects.	Bloomfield Report on Victims commissioned in 1998. Northern Ireland Human Rights Commission (1999). Alex Boraine visit from South Africa and establishment of Healing through Remembering. IFI Community Bridges programme (1996).	First Compact between government and the community/voluntary sector (1998). Establishment of Department for Social Development (1999), later re-named Department of Communities. VAU re-named the Voluntary & Community Unit. EU PEACE 11 Programme (2000–2006). New TSN (1998).
2001–2005	Intermittent Direct Rule under (i) John Reid; (ii) Paul Murphy; (iii) Peter Hain.	First Minister Trimble resigns over lack of IRA decommissioning (2001), executive collapses but is restored Sept. 2001. October 2002,	Community Foundation for Northern Ireland launches Communities in Transition programme (2001). Community Evaluation NI (CENI) Report on	'A Shared Future' Policy document (2005).	'Partners for Change' DSD document, 2001–2004 commitment to build communities. HM Treasury (2002), The Role of the Voluntary &

	devolution suspended again. Ardoyne/Glenbryn interface violence (2001). Police Service of Northern Ireland replaces RUC (2001). IRA formally orders an end to its armed campaign (2005) and finalizes decommissioning of arms.			Social Capital community development indicators (2005). Establishment of BIG Lottery Fund NI (2004).	Community Sector in Service Delivery: A Cross Cutting Review (2002). 'People and Place': Neighbourhood Renewal Programme (2003).
2006–2015	Re-establishment of Northern Ireland Assembly 2007. Secretary of State (i) Shaun Woodward; (ii) Theresa Villiers. St. Andrews Agreement (2006). Sinn Féin agrees to support PSNI (2007). Dissident Republicans active. Loyalist paramilitary decommissioning (2010). Agreed devolution of justice powers to Stormont Assembly (2010).	Community Places, Community Planning project (2007). Strategic Framework for Community Development for Northern Ireland (2011). Establishment of Belfast Conflict Resolution Consortium (2007).	Independent Consultative Group on the Past Report. Four Victims' Commissioners appointed (2008), later reduced to one. 'Cohesion, Sharing & Integration' document issued (2010).		Communities Empowerment programme, North Belfast (2003–2009). Social Exclusion Strategy (2006). Areas at Risk programme (2006–2015). Re-Imagining Communities programme (2006–2009).

Date	Government	Political Developments	Community Development	Community Relations	Social Policies
		Loyalist Flags protest (2012). Stormont House Agreement (2014). Fresh Start Agreement (2015).		Establishment of Victims & Survivors' Forum (2012). TBUC (Together Building a United Community) document issued (2013). International Fund for Ireland Peace Impact Programme & Peace Walls programme.	EU PEACE III Programme (2007–2013). Rural Anti-Poverty Strategy (2009–2011). Noble Index of Multiple Deprivation (2010). Concordat between community & voluntary sector and government (2011). Social Investment Fund (2011). Review of Public Administration reduction in number of local authorities. Race Equality Strategy (2015–2025).

CHAPTER I

Politics Rules, OK!

Four decades is a long time in anybody's reckoning. Where society is riven by violent conflict it can seem an eternity. There are periods of desperation; even more times of frustration; but despite all, communities are resilient. In Northern Ireland survival was underpinned by a blended tonic of sardonic humour, self-justificatory community narratives and sheer bloody-mindedness. Over 3,500 people lost their lives; some 50,000 were bereaved or injured and an estimated 35,000 were imprisoned and/or interned for politically motivated activities. Many thousands were intimidated out of their homes and fled to 'safe' areas, invariably single-identity in nature (overwhelmingly either Catholic/Nationalist/Republican or Protestant/Unionist/Loyalist). The human cost in a society of 1.6 million etched deep scars. The abnormal became the norm, particularly in the most disadvantaged communities. Yet it was these communities that developed an incredibly vibrant civil society characterised by social activism and community action with a twist of politics.

Setting 'the Troubles' in context

Northern Ireland was established as a self-governing region in 1921 after the partition of Ireland. The southern twenty-six counties negotiated independence from Britain after a hard fought War of Independence, leaving the unionist dominated six north-eastern counties part of the United Kingdom (UK). Division was in-built from the start, given the Protestant majority of some 65 per cent, and a Catholic minority of 35 per cent. The latter were seen as potentially disloyal and subversive in a chronically insecure

northern state that struggled to even agree on a name. Officially termed
Northern Ireland, it was also known as Ulster, the North, or even 'the
occupied six counties', depending on political perspective. While overall
sovereignty remained with the Westminster Parliament in London, to all
intents and purposes the Stormont Parliament in Belfast ruled through
single party Ulster Unionist government over the period 1921–1972. Its
core remit was to protect the union with Britain by resisting the perceived
threat of a united Ireland.

Stormont relied on a battery of emergency provisions legislation, an
overwhelmingly Protestant police and Special Reserve forces, electoral
maladministration and the privileging of unionists in terms of employment
and the allocation of social housing. Periodic attempts to counter Unionist
rule through the mobilisation of cross-community working-class protest
had limited success where criticism of the state was depicted as republican
manipulation. Catholic reaction shifted along a spectrum from seeking
political reforms and community self-help on the one hand, to advocating
the unification of Ireland by force, at the other extreme. By the mid-1960s,
all three elements, together with a number of progressive Protestants, were
in the mix that gave rise to a civil rights movement. Seen as a threat to the
state, the security response was uncompromising. This, together with the
pre-existing small IRA (Irish Republican Army) and even smaller loyalist
UVF (Ulster Volunteer Force) set the stage for trouble.

The reaction to Civil Rights

NICRA (Northern Ireland Civil Rights Movement) was established in
mirror-image of the civil rights movement in America, sweeping up a
number of earlier reform initiatives, such as the Campaign for Social Justice
in mid-Ulster. It advocated non-violent action to achieve more equitable
access to voting rights, employment and services. Although if this was the
script, it was spiced with antagonism to the Unionist government; a feeling
reciprocated by Unionist Party Ministers who characterised the protesters

as a malign mix of republicanism, communism and general malcontents. This official narrative was reiterated to dissuade any Protestant sympathy for the grievances raised. The violent reaction by both the police and loyalist protesters to the civil rights marches was captured by international media to the increasing alarm of the British Government. A package of reforms was pressed on the Stormont government and British soldiers were deployed on the streets in the summer of 1969, to support the Northern Irish government in restoring law and order and to intervene in the increasingly violent clashes between Protestant and Catholic communities. By then streets in many working-class areas were protected by their own barricades and local defence structures. The period also saw a winnowing of Unionist Prime Ministers, characterised by a consistent shuffle to the right of the political centre, but never quite as far as the refusenik Democratic Unionist Party (DUP) which was fronted by the Rev. Dr Ian Paisley to oppose 'Romanising' tendencies and political sell-out.

In June 1970, the Conservative Party, under Ted Heath, was elected to power in London. Newly appointed Home Secretary, Reginald Maudling, returning from a visit to Northern Ireland, was widely reported as saying 'For God's sake bring me a large scotch. What a bloody awful country!' Arguably Ulster unionism was in need of more than a stiff drink faced with the shattering of its monolithic hold on power. The DUP was an increasingly successful electoral presence, the new SDLP (Social Democratic & Labour Party) was mopping up traditional nationalists and civil rights activists, and the Alliance Party of Northern Ireland (APNI) was bravely appealing to both Catholics and Protestants in support of moderate unionism. Outside of the formal arena, the Provisional IRA split from the Official IRA; mirrored by a split in the politically aligned Sinn Féin party. Nicknames were acquired as the Official nom-de-guerre became 'the stickies' from the self-adhesive Easter lily badges sold to commemorate the 1916 Irish Rising, in contrast to the traditional straight pins used to affix the emblems sold by the Provisionals, or the 'Provies'. A temporary truce was agreed between both groups when the British Army imposed the 'Falls Road curfew' in July 1970, confining a local Catholic community into their area for a destructive three-day house to house search. Relations between the army and the Catholic community entered into a downward spiral that reached its nadir with the introduction of Internment without Trial in August 1971 – a measure that was to have a disproportionate impact on republicans and Catholics. William Stout, a former official in the Stormont Ministry of Home Affairs, reappeared out of retirement to help plan the internment process, having the niche experience of implementing internment in the late 1950s. In what became known as 'the Flight' it was estimated that some 7,000 Catholics and 2,000 Protestants relocated in the period following internment, often hastened by a bullet in the post or an increasing sense of community discomfort.

Community 'defence' became the order of the day on both sides of the community, as work places, Orange Order lodges and public houses became the hubs for passing on 'proof' of planned republican insurrection and for the recruitment of future paramilitary activists. The loyalist UDA (Ulster Defence Association) grew exponentially to an estimated 70,000–80,000 at the height of its strength, joining the pre-existing loyalist UVF, Red Hand Commandos and the Ulster Special Constabulary Association. There was a strong whiff of 'conditional loyalty' to Britain in the air, as defence transmuted into offensive action by loyalists against Catholics, and by republicans against 'state forces' and loyalist communities. Bombing campaigns became increasingly indiscriminate in terms of targets and central Belfast experienced the first of many 'car bombs' in 1972. Attempts to counter these attacks resulted in rows of unattractive concrete bollards, known as 'dragons' teeth' closing off streets and thoroughfares. Pedestrians soon developed an intuitive 'third eye' when passing parked cars and ads in local newspapers explained how to tape up windows to minimise the risks of shattered glass splinters.

The final period of Ulster Unionist rule was marked by 'Bloody Sunday' in January 1972, when British soldiers shot dead thirteen unarmed civil rights protestors; allegations of torture (later redefined as 'inhuman and degrading treatment') of a number of republican internees; a 'rent and rates' strike in protest to 'Bloody Sunday'; and an increasingly fragmented unionism. Direct rule from London was declared in March 1972, resulting in demonstrations despite the British government objective of seeking to restore an acceptable form of devolution as soon as possible. This was to take twenty-six years and eleven secretary of states for Northern Ireland:

eight from the Conservative Party and three from the Labour Party; all were men with the exception of Mo Mowlam (1997–1999). A young UDA man participated in a mass protest against Direct Rule: 'Paisley and all were standing there ... so I thought we had political backing in the thing. And their speeches were that we will fight and we will die and all – and I left those things and you know my heart was busting – right we're going to fight'. It was noted that Ulster flags far outnumbered Union Jacks, and those Union Jacks flown by the 150,000 protestors had the words Aden, India, Cyprus, Kenya, Palestine, Malaya, Ireland, printed on them – a litany of British withdrawal.

From Direct Rule to power-sharing and beyond

Under Direct Rule executive authority was vested in the Secretary of State, supported by a Ministerial team and the Northern Ireland Office (boasting two addresses – one in London and one in Belfast). Security remained a major challenge as was the attempt to engineer political accommodation. A short-lived Provisional IRA truce was achieved through back channel negotiation in 1972, but the main emphasis was placed on the search for a political 'formula'. Hopes were raised when the Sunningdale Agreement (1973) made provision for a power-sharing Executive that featured participation by the nationalist SDLP and the Alliance Party, under the premiership of Brian Faulkner (Unionist Party of Northern Ireland). Unionist critics of the power-sharing and the cross-Border (with the Republic of Ireland) dimensions of the Agreement mobilised in opposition, focusing their attacks on the proposed Council of Ireland. The power-sharing experiment in devolved governance survived for a short five months, brought down in May 1974 by a successful Ulster Workers' Council (UWC) Strike, to the thunderous judgement of Rev. Ian Paisley that it had been 'out-flanked, out-manoeuvred and out-witted'. The Strike, which was muscled by loyalist paramilitaries, was only called off when the unionist members of the Executive resigned and the Stormont Assembly was prorogued.

Direct Rule Phase 2 began, under the new Labour Party Secretary of State, Merlyn Rees.

There was a certain sense of self-confidence within loyalism inspired by the collapse of power-sharing; leaving nationalists pondering the apparent inability of the state to face down the strikers. The state was not behind the door, however, in its continuing legal and security battle against terrorism, conducted by both covert and overt military operations, reinforced by a battery of emergency provisions. House searches peaked in 1973 when 74,556 houses were searched – many repeatedly – 20 per cent of all households in Northern Ireland. On the legislative front the Northern Ireland (Emergency Provisions) Act, 1973, listed scheduled offences (generally related to terrorist offences) to be tried by non-jury courts – the 'Diplock Courts'. The Act allowed more permissive rules concerning the admissibility of evidence; restrictions on granting bail; and increased powers of arrest. Effectively, this anti-terrorist toolkit placed the courts and the judicial system in prime position in the war being waged. The IRA, Sinn Féin, the UVF and other smaller republican groups had been proscribed; a list that was extended to include the UDA related UFF (Ulster Freedom Fighters) and the Red Hand Commandos in November 1973.

Faced with the inability to make political progress, back channel negotiation delivered a second Provisional IRA truce in December 1974, although the terms agreed were ambiguous and disputed, resulting in claim, denial and counter-claim over what had been agreed, by whom, with regard to what. The Incident Centres that appeared in republican areas to monitor the operation of the ceasefire were dubbed 'rebel hot-lines' by an outraged Ian Paisley. The more government Ministers denied contact with 'terrorists', the greater the suspicion of Unionist politicians, causing one Northern Ireland Office official to muse: 'One of the least engaging traits of British policy, as it has always appeared to foreigners, is its hypocrisy. In fact, more often than not, it is not hypocrisy at all; it is a process of double-think, whereby British governments persuade themselves that something is so because it is evident to them that it ought to be so and it would be a lot more comfortable for all concerned if it were so'. However, official double-think also provided fertile ground for longer-term mistrust.

If British soldiers were relatively safe during the ceasefire period, the same could not be said for anybody else. The number of sectarian attacks escalated, as well as internal loyalist and republican feuds. An early confrontation sparked off between the Official IRA and the Irish National Liberation Army (INLA) which together with its political wing, the Irish Republican Socialist Party (IRSP) had emerged in 1974/75. Later in the year the Official IRA broke out arms again in a feud with the Provisional IRA. Within loyalism there were both internal UDA stand-offs and shoot outs as well as feuding between the UDA and the UVF. By autumn 1975 the death of the one thousandth victim of the Troubles was marked, as the British Secretary of State declared the ceasefires null and void. There were early mutterings of alleged collusion between the security forces and loyalist paramilitaries in attacks on republicans, followed by indignant denials of any official 'blind eye' policy. The question for the British was when is a war a war?

Surveying the state of the province in his 1976 New Year message, Secretary of State Rees bid a glad farewell to the 'Year of the Criminal' and argued that 'More and more, the community as a whole has come to realise that crimes are committed for personal gain or for sectarian or functional reasons rather than for "political" motives, which were in the past misguidedly put forward as the reasons for outright criminality'. This analysis opened the door for a new government narrative – 'normalisation, criminalisation and Ulsterisation'. This macro truth-claim framed the 'Ulster problem' as the case of a normal democratic society, experiencing an unfortunately aggravated crime wave. The response was robust policing and an uncompromising criminal justice system in a society that was open for business. This message was bolstered during the 'no nonsense' imperium of Rees's successor as Secretary of State, Roy Mason. The official narrative became an art form in defining polite and acceptable discourse about the state of Northern Ireland. There were, of course, the inevitable lurking anomalies, such as ministerial references to 'defeating terrorism', however the narrative struck a certain chord with the growing public abhorrence at the scale and impact of the violence. In the summer of 1976 many thousands of people mobilised behind the Peace People (initially Peace Women) in mass rallies for peace, although a discordant message was grafittied on the wall of the Milltown Cemetery in West Belfast: 'You will not break us, Stonewall Mason!'

The politics of the prisons

Positing the concept of a 'Long War' the IRA security-proofed itself by adopting a tighter cell structure, but it was developments within the prisons that flared the warning signal that a new front was opening up. Internment without Trial had been phased out, to be replaced by a criminalisation strategy that saw the removal of Special Category status for politically motivated prisoners. This resulted in a policy of non-cooperation as republican prisoners refused to wear prison issue uniform, covering themselves instead in grey prison blankets. Many loyalist prisoners were sympathetic to this struggle but found difficulty in relating to what was seen as a republican initiative. In broader society there was a mixed response – those who sympathised with the prison protest and those who condemned it as self-imposed victimisation by convicted terrorists who had the luxury of choosing their means of protest in stark contrast to their victims. Strip searches became a routine method of security/harassment depending on one's point of view. In March 1978 republican prisoners refused to leave their cells and commenced a 'dirty protest', smearing urine and excreta on cell walls. By December an estimated 300–400 prisoners were involved in the protest. The deteriorating prison conditions were accompanied by increased street protests and attempts to fashion an 'Anti-Imperialist' unity. As the prison confrontation escalated there were attacks on prison officers, including the murder of the Deputy Governor of the Maze Prison.

The perception of security-inspired production line arrest, interrogation and sentencing procedures was aggravated by an increase in allegations of brutality used in the interrogation of detainees in police Holding Centres. A Government Commission (the Bennett Commission) reported that between September 1977 and August 1978, 2,970 people were arrested and detained for more than four hours under Emergency Provisions legislation. Although the report found that abuses had taken place, it balanced this by condemning the 'coordinated and extensive campaign to discredit the police'. More cynical local commentators sketched a cartoon with the caption 'Help a policeman, beat yourself up'. The balanced niceties of the report did little to settle the apprehension of a civil rights activist, not herself a Provisional IRA supporter: 'I wouldn't have gone to the security forces and said "I think there's semtex in that block of flats", because every man in that block of flats would have been hauled in and beaten up, and that's one of the things that stopped people ... And those sort of tactics, the nature of those terror tactics were counter-productive'. Although the counter-productive nature of much anti-terrorism strategy went unremarked, there was daily graphic evidence of the horror of terror tactics. The fireball that swept through the function rooms of the La Mon House Hotel, on the outskirts of East Belfast, caused the deaths of twelve people, many attending the Irish Collie Club dinner and a function for the Northern Ireland Junior Motorcycle Club. It proved difficult to identify many of the victims due to the severity of their burns, and dozens of others suffered horrific injuries as a result of the IRA bomb. The La Mon bombing exploded into folk memory as one of a litany of Troubles-related atrocities, although the narrative of terror and counter terror was nuanced by respective community perspectives.

With virtually no political movement, the Direct Rule agenda continued to be dominated by the dual concerns of security and inward investment in order to address spiralling unemployment. In February 1978 it was reported that over 97,000 people had packed their bags and left Northern Ireland over the previous decade. By July, the official unemployment rate stood at 13.4 per cent and rising; in response government Ministers emphasised the good industrial relations record in the region, referencing the passing of the Fair Employment Act (1976) to prevent religious discrimination in employment, over the declared opposition of the DUP and Ulster Unionist Party.

A new Conservative Party Secretary of State in May 1979 was welcomed by the less than enthusiastic headline in a local newspaper: 'Humphrey Who ...?' A colleague of Humphrey Atkins, Airey Neave

MP, had been killed by the INLA (Irish National Liberation Army) some months earlier. This attack paled in comparison to IRA attacks in August 1979, which resulted in the death of Lord Mountbatten (first cousin to Queen Elizabeth II) and members of his boating party in Sligo, on the same day as eighteen British soldiers died in roadside bombs in Warrenpoint, Co. Down. It was also on Atkins's watch that the prison 'dirty' protests escalated into a republican hunger strike in October 1980. A mediated agreement ended the strike before any deaths, but the very ambiguity of the settlement was to result in an extended hunger strike the following year. Republican prisoners issued a statement: 'We have asserted that we are political prisoners and everything about our country, our arrests, interrogations, trials and prison conditions show that we are politically motivated'. Bobby Sands was the first hunger striker to die after sixty-six days; an estimated 100,000 people attended his funeral in West Belfast. By the time the strike was called off the following October, through negotiation of a range of concessions, ten prisoners (IRA and INLA) had died. Atkins had been succeeded as Secretary of State by James Prior in September 1981, to the widely reported assessment that Belfast was the new place of political exile for those out of favour with Prime Minister, Margaret Thatcher.

The bitterness caused by the heightened prison protest was palpable. Prison officers were targeted for attack, and Ulster Unionist M.P., the Rev. Robert Bradford, was shot dead in November 1981 after it was reported that he had referred to the hunger strikers as 'subhuman vermin'. If some loyalist communities daubed wall slogans celebrating 'Bobby Sands – slimmer of the year' and 'We will never forget you Jimmy Sands', the response of many loyalist prisoners was less triumphalist. Within nationalist/republican areas riots, pickets, protests and petitions became the order of the day. Bobby Sands had been elected MP in a by-election in Fermanagh/South Tyrone prior to his death, and two fellow hunger strikers were elected to Dáil Eireann, south of the Border. Within Sinn Féin, these electoral successes were scrutinised as the long-established policy of parliamentary abstentionism came under question. The value of building broader alliances and identifying new strategies to augment the blunt instrument of the armed struggle was being considered

The growth of Anglo-Irish relations

The potential for weaving a diplomatic alignment of interests between the British and Irish governments opened up in the early years of the 1980s. On-going discussions resulted in the Anglo-Irish Agreement signed by Prime Minister Thatcher and Irish Taoiseach, Garret FitzGerald in November 1985. The Agreement committed the two governments to agree that any change in the status of Northern Ireland would only come about with the consent of the majority of the people of the state. An Inter-Governmental Conference would be established to give the Irish Government a consultative role in security, legal affairs, politics and cross-border issues and an Anglo-Irish Secretariat was to be set up in Belfast. The Agreement also confirmed that the two governments would support any future wish by the people of Northern Ireland to enter into a united Ireland. International reaction, including in the USA, was largely positive, but response nearer home verged on the apoplectic. Preaching to a congregation in his East Belfast Church, Dr Ian Paisley compared Margaret Thatcher to a 'Jezebel who sought to destroy Israel in a day'. The UDA related Ulster Freedom Fighters (UFF) declared all members of the Anglo-Irish Conference and the Secretariat as 'legitimate targets' and both the Ulster Unionist Party and the Democratic Unionist Party resigned their elected positions, causing by-elections as a proxy referendum on the Agreement, and instituted a boycott of Direct Rule Ministers. On 25 November 1985, the *Belfast Telegraph* reported an anti-Agreement rally in the centre of Belfast. The attendance estimate varied between 100,000–200,000 depending on the source, but the anger was palpable. The report continued, "'There's not even enough room to push a policeman into a flower pot", said one wee woman from Larne. You could see her point, but crushed in the middle of the crowd at the mouth of Royal Avenue last Saturday afternoon, that was about all you could see'. The slogan for the campaign against the Anglo-Irish Agreement was coined – 'Ulster Says No'. Republicans were not particularly impressed by the Agreement either, and it was left to the SDLP to maintain lonely support for the suggested deal.

The years following the Agreement saw little improvement, as sectarian assassinations, bombings and allegations of British Army 'shoot to kill' policies and under-cover operations continued. The devastating IRA bomb attack on a Remembrance Day ceremony in Enniskillen, Co. Fermanagh killed eleven people and injured another sixty three. Businesspeople and traders that supplied the British Army and the RUC were targeted by the IRA as 'collaborators' and 'part of the British war machine'. Members of the security forces remained 'legitimate targets', and an infamous pseudo road sign appeared in South Armagh – a silhouetted gunman with the legend 'Sniper at work'. The IRA also suffered its quota of causalities. In May 1987, eight members of the organisation who were preparing to attack a police station – and one civilian – were shot dead by soldiers of the SAS; the highest loss of life suffered by the IRA in any one incident. The smaller INLA was also on war footing, having gained notoriety from a number of attacks, but most memorably from an attack on worshippers in the Darkly Mission Hall in Co. Armagh, in 1983. Within loyalism there were contradictory messages. On the one hand the UDA's reinvigorated New Ulster Political Research Group, issued its 'Common Sense' document which advocated a constitutional conference, a devolved assembly and a coalition form of government, on the other, an increasing militant UFF claimed responsibility for what became colloquially known as 'Dial a Taig' – ordering taxis from companies based in nationalist areas and subsequently killing Catholic taxi drivers. Rumours of alleged collusion between loyalist paramilitaries and the British security forces continued to circulate particularly in the case of the murder of well-known Belfast solicitor, Pat Finucane. It was suggested that those targeted were being killed by loyalists in order to provide a cover of 'plausible deniability' to state forces. Various official inquiries remained mired in disappearing records and local obstructionism. Meanwhile, the 'Ulster Says No' banners that swayed in the breeze outside local authority buildings became increasingly weather worn and frayed. Discretion won through at a meeting of the small Belfast Anti-Apartheid group, when the suggestion by one member that a midnight raid might add the words '... to Apartheid' on the Belfast City Hall banner, was vetoed.

'God save Ireland': Headline in the *Economist* magazine, March 1988

Television footage of three unarmed IRA volunteers being shot dead by the SAS while on 'active service' in Gibraltar in March 1988 was the turning point for a new spiral in violence. Loyalist gunman, Michael Stone, used their funeral service to launch a grenade and gun attack on mourners, killing three people and wounding fifty others. Three days later a speeding car approached the funeral cortege of one of those killed by Stone as it wended its way through West Belfast. The two plain clothes British Army corporals in the car fired warning shots into the air when surrounded. Dragged out and severely beaten, they were taken to waste ground and shot dead. The scene was recorded by the television cameras that were covering the funeral. The reaction was instantaneous: the *Sun* newspaper headline screamed 'Scum of the Earth' and the more sober *Economist* magazine lamented 'God Save Ireland' – a play of words on a nineteenth-century patriotic song. At ministerial and senior civil service level argument paced argument between the hard security response and the feeling that something positive had to be done to prevent communities spiralling out of control. Richard Needham, the longest servicing Minister of State in Northern Ireland (1983–1992), supported the latter position, explaining the linkage between the two main government public expenditure priorities – (i) defeating terrorism and (ii) strengthening the Northern Ireland economy as 'The little known story of the economic and social war against violence and those who waged it on all sides'. A weapon in this war, introduced by an earlier Secretary of State, Douglas Hurd, was 'political vetting' – refusing public money to community-based projects with any reported involvement of paramilitaries. In a more positive vein two major regeneration programmes, with a focus on deprived urban areas, were introduced – the Belfast Action Teams (BAT) and Making Belfast Work (MBW).

Out of the headlines of political violence a number of developments laid the basis for the exploration of peaceful political progress. Weathering a split in republicanism, Gerry Adams had become President of Sinn Féin in 1983, presiding over an increasingly politically successful party.

Discussions between Adams and SDLP leader, John Hume, also facilitated the examination of options in a context made more conducive by the statement of Secretary of State, Peter Brooke (1989) that 'The British government has no selfish strategic or economic interest in Northern Ireland'. Brooke referred to the set of relationships that would inform future peace negotiations – those within Northern Ireland; North-South relations within the island of Ireland; and relations between Britain and Ireland. Informal back channel confidence building also included loyalist representatives, although there was little to reassure a despondent public faced with an upsurge of violence in the early 1990s. This included the IRA 'Shankill bomb', which killed ten people, and injured another fifty seven, in October 1993. The fact that a year later saw both IRA and Combined Loyalist Military Command ceasefires took the public by surprise. Banner headlines in local newspapers proclaimed 'It's Over'; and graffiti writers in West Belfast added 'RUC Paid Off'. Across in the Shankill loyalist graffiti responded: 'We accept the unconditional surrender of the Provisional IRA'. Within weeks British soldiers on patrol in Belfast had swapped their helmets for berets.

US President Bill Clinton supported the British and Irish governments in their determination to initiate all-party talks by February 1996, and appointed US senator George Mitchell to facilitate both this process and the thorny issue of arms decommissioning. Ending 1995 on a celebratory note, Bill Clinton switched on the Christmas tree lights in Belfast as the first serving US President to visit Northern Ireland. The mood was to darken, however, with the bombing of Canary Wharf, in the heart of London's financial district, the following February as the IRA announced its loss of patience given the British Government's precondition of arms decommissioning. Determined to proceed with the proposed talks, the government announced that elections would be held on 30 May, introducing a voting system that enabled the election of ten political parties to ensure the inclusion of the smaller PUP (Progressive Unionist Party aligned to the UVF) and the UDP (Ulster Unionist Party aligned to the UDA). The newly established Northern Ireland Women's Coalition examined the proposed system, took advice from political scientist, Sydney Elliot, and concluded that 10,000 votes (translated as 100 votes for 100 women) would see them win two seats in the peace talks. They were proved right – much to their own surprise.

When the multi-party talks opened in Stormont in June 1996, Sinn Féin was excluded. In practice they missed little as the early sittings were marked by DUP and the UKUP (UK Unionist Party) representatives hectoring and shouting their disapproval of the appointment of Senator Mitchell as chairperson. The latter wisely kept to his rooms in dignified silence, although when he attempted to actually take the chair late one evening, an ill-disciplined UKUP member leaped up to pull it physically from under him. Talks commenced but in the context of the emergence of fringe loyalist and republican paramilitary groups – the LVF (Loyalist Volunteer Force) and the Continuity IRA respectively – and a summer of violence focused around Loyal Order parades. The election of a Blair-led Labour Government the following year paved the way for a reinstatement of the IRA ceasefire, accompanied by a Sinn Féin entry to the Talks and a corresponding DUP and UKUP walk-out. Against all the odds agreement was reached in the form of the Belfast/Good Friday Agreement by April 1998, subsequently ratified by a simultaneous referendum held on both parts of the island.

The rollercoaster of political settlement

Disagreement over what to call the Agreement was matched by ill-tempered disputes over its interpretation and implementation. The power-sharing Executive provided for was suspended on four different occasions between 2000 and 2007, with Direct Rule as default mode. Crisis negotiations facilitated by the British and Irish governments were par for the course, with the US Presidency and the European Union acting as cheer leaders for compromise. Persistent issues included the nature and timing of arms decommissioning, with particular emphasis on the IRA; reform of policing; 'parity of esteem' over parades, emblems and cultural traditions; proposals for a Bill of Rights and a Civic Forum; and the zero-sum calculus of who won the peace. An underlying fault line was the lack of agreement about the causes of a conflict that the Good Friday Agreement had been crafted to end, resulting in an inability to deal with the legacies of the past. Added to the mix were the party political positioning within both unionism and nationalism/republicanism. By 2007 the DUP and Sinn Féin took over from the Ulster Unionist Party and the SDLP as the largest political parties, taking the positions of First and Deputy First Minister respectively. By 2011 the Northern Ireland Assembly and Executive celebrated its first full term in office in forty years, although the subsequent electoral period (2011–2016) required further crisis management. The optimistically named Fresh Start Agreement was concluded in November 2015.

Tensions within Stormont were reflected on the streets (and vice versa) as paramilitaries became involved in disputes over territoriality, all too often around parades and emblems, but reaching a low point when young children and their parents were on the frontline over a disputed piece of road leading to Holy Cross Primary School in the Ardoyne/Glenbryn area of North Belfast (2001–2003). Loyalist feuds also took a toll at community level initially between an anti-peace process alignment of the LVF and elements of the UFF (Ulster Freedom Fighters) in opposition to the UVF, and later between various factions of the UDA. Within republicanism the focus was on anti-peace process 'dissident' republican paramilitary groupings who as early as August 1998 signalled their dissatisfaction by planting the Omagh bomb that killed thirty-one (including unborn twins) and injured many hundreds of Saturday afternoon shoppers. Whatever the new IRA prefix (Real, Continuity or other), Sinn Féin condemned both this insurgent republican violence and alleged conspiracies hatched by remaining 'securocrats' to destroy the peace process. Whether it was reports that IRA members were training the Colombian FARC; that the IRA had a spy ring within Stormont (although a key figure was later revealed as a long term British informant); whether the IRA carried out a break-in into Castlereagh Police Station; and to what extent murders were still being directed by the IRA Army Council, were all matters of conjecture, but destabilising to an already edgy unionism. The on-going inability to deal comprehensively with the past also left both ex-combatants and victims/

survivors of violence aggrieved while laying the basis for a struggle as to whose 'truth' would prevail.

Notwithstanding the difficulties, the gains achieved were inestimable in a society that was both war weary and still bore the scars of sectarian division. Politics was back, centre stage, as an option for effecting change, and the death toll that had been a constant feature of the Troubles no longer cast the same shadow. It is true that there was a growing sense of loyalist 'loss' experienced in the perfect storm of poor socio-economic prospects and sense of threatened identity. This was demonstrated by a focus on parading, the flying of the Union Jack and determined opposition to creeping Irishness. Within the Catholic community there was an emphasis on equality, asserted with a new sense of confidence. Competing community narratives continued, although the meta-narrative of government was now increasingly home grown. If conflict transformation was an on-going project, at least peacebuilding had become a feasible objective.

Perhaps not surprisingly the drama and tragedy of politics all too often served to over-shadow developments at local community level where an equally complex story of achieving change in very difficult circumstances unfolded. Community provided space for a cacophony of voices, organisations and activities whose inherent 'messiness' carried with it a vibrancy and vitality, albeit often couched within competing frames of reference. This caused one long-term community activist to suggest: 'I think people in the end create a meaning and they work within that, and that's actually where you should go in terms of understanding where people are at and where they will move to. Because if you don't explore that framework of meaning that people have ... then you won't get the rest right'.

CHAPTER 2

Social Activism with a Twist of Politics

A young teacher recalled his sense of exuberance after participating in Derry's first civil rights march held in October 1968: 'The great energy and joy after it ... I don't think anybody felt that we were going to overthrow the state but ... the energy, the possibility of changing things here. And whatever about changing things, above all else suddenly introducing as it were colour to this place; that which had been an old grainy black and white film was now potentially technicolour'. If this was social activism with a political twist it had roots in protest community organising that had long sought out niches in the monolith of Unionist governance. Tenants' organisations existed in the mid-1930s, when the Communist Party of Ireland (CPI) supported the Tenants' Defence League in a successful rent strike in West Belfast. By the 1960s, CPI and trade union activist, Sean Morrissey, was a leading light in the Belfast Amalgamated Corporation Tenants' Association (BACTA), a deliberately cross-community coalition, whose chairman, Billy Ritchie, was from Knocknagoney in unionist East Belfast. Derry, the second city in size if not in self-perception in the North, also experienced protest agitation that was decidedly more political in nature and intent than the parallel movements of self-help community initiatives and local residents' associations. Spiced by the politicisation of events in the late sixties and early seventies, community action found itself in the eye of the storm that presented urgent needs as well as opportunities.

When grievance becomes injustice

When Derryman, Eamon Melaugh, returned home after working in England, it was to a city with legendary male unemployment and a housing crisis despaired of by the Londonderry Sanitary Officer (1968) given over one thousand houses in multiple occupancy, with as many as six or seven families sharing. Eamon advertised in the *Belfast Telegraph* and leafleted Derry City (Football) matches to recruit people to an Unemployed Action Committee. Four turned up, but undeterred the group issued regular press statements and organised direct action. Attention turned to housing issues because: 'If you got one family a house you could claim a wee victory; you could never claim a victory (with the unemployment issue) because you were never going to create a job'. It was important to set realistic demands for quick confidence-building 'wins'.

Local grievance elicited a variety of responses, including the more respectable self-help option of setting up a successful Derry Credit Union and Derry Housing Association. A survey carried out by the latter in 1967 concluded that over 1,400 families needed housing. That same year, the Foyle Hill Tenants' Association was established as the first Tenants' Association in Derry, covering the sprawling Creggan housing estate, soon to become home for 15,000 people with little local infrastructure. The immediate demands were around road safety, housing repairs and play facilities. Tenants' groups spread to other estates and small 'wins', such as the promise of a public telephone box in Shantallow, were greeted as notable victories. It was only a matter of time before the Tenants' groups came together in the Derry Central Council of Tenants' Associations to coordinate protests against threatened rent rises.

The more radical members of what by now was known as the Derry Housing Action Committee were somewhat under-whelmed by the modest tenant demands. In contrast their placards demanded: 'We want Houses, not Slums or Dilapidated Flats', when disrupting Derry Corporation meetings. Using the young Wilson family as a cause célèbre in June 1968, they blocked a main road with the caravan that the Wilsons were living in, pointing out that the family included a toddler suffering from tuberculosis.

Having been refused housing by the Corporation previously, the Wilsons were housed within the week, although eleven members of the Action Committee were brought to court and fined. The resulting publicity was grist to the mill of the campaigners but it provoked questioning of their motivation by sitting Nationalist and Unionist councillors. A Nationalist Party Alderman raised the spectre of Communist Party influence and, although denied, the whiff of political sulphur was enough to cause resignations from the committee. Undeterred, the demand of 'One family, one house' was a key demand of the civil rights movement when the Derry Action Committee welcomed a NICRA march on 5 October 1968. Those battered by the police included a Nationalist Party MP and leading Civil Rights members. The headlines in the local *Derry Journal* read: 'Batons and Barricades as Riots Rock Derry'. The initial small march of 1,500 people was repeated a month later, with 15,000 in attendance.

If the sense of injustice was stark in Derry, it tended to be more nuanced in Belfast where community activists had long experience of sectarian finger pointing. As early as 1886, an Official Enquiry into a particularly severe outbreak of sectarian rioting bemoaned the residential patterns of division which were equated with an 'extremity' of party and religious feeling. Conscious of this context the Belfast Amalgamated Corporation Tenants' Association focused on the common concern of rent increases. By 1968, a major rents war was in the offing; the following year Association members disrupted the Belfast Lord Mayor's Inaugural meeting by unfurling banners in the visitors' gallery and arguing with the Corporation members seated below. They won the postponement of the threatened increases. As in Derry, direct action activism was strengthened by the growing number of community and tenants' groups. One of the most impressive flourished in West Belfast, where the Ballymurphy Tenants' Association was established in 1963. The founding Secretary of the Association, Hugh McCormick, explained: 'At that time this place was like a leper colony, we just had to get up and fight back'. The Association became an advocate for local people and successfully represented tenants in danger of eviction or of being disconnected from essential services. It also began fundraising to build a community centre. One volunteer remembered how: 'We had parties in our houses ... to raise money for the association'. But the real key to the success of the Tenants' Association was its confidence and ability to enhance local participation with external expertise and support. Of those involved, the slight, bespectacled Frank Cahill, brought a family background of active republicanism; but the equally dominant personality of Frances McMullan (one of a dwindling number of Protestants in the area by the early 1970s) was renowned for keeping the records of the Association in the depths of her copious handbag.

By 1967, the Association had raised £5,000, recruiting its own volunteer architect (Irish language enthusiast, Sean Mackle), to design a community centre. While sub-committees worked on various issues, there was a general concern about the poor public image of the estate which forced local people to use relatives' addresses when applying for jobs. The Association retained a public relations company to work closely with a newly established Appeals Committee, which was headed by Sir Graham Larmor, a leading linen manufacturer. The message crafted was that: 'The estate has been an example of early post-war planning and suffered a reputation for hooliganism and rowdy behaviour. Considering that it had more than 3,000 children and yet absolutely no recreational facility of any kind, this is not surprising'. The local media responded positively, and by 1969, Dr H. S. Corscadden, Senior Managing Director of the Ulster Bank, agreed to act as chairman of the Community Centre Appeals Committee. Another example of lateral thinking saw the Ballymurphy Tenants' Association investing £5,000 in the Belfast Corporation's loan bond scheme in order to highlight the 'civic spirit' of the community. It encouraged the opening of a Credit Union in the estate and developed links with the Social Sciences and Planning Departments of Queen's University Belfast, where Frank Cahill became a regular guest lecturer.

Back in Derry there was a rumour that the government was considering banning Bingo Nights because every time a winner shouted 'House', it caused a rush to the streets with people asking 'Where?' The Derry Housing Action Committee led a number of homeless families to occupy the Lord Mayor's chamber on New Year's Day, 1969 after the Corporation refused approval for new housing development. Ten days later the squatters were still in occupation and Dr T. J. McHugh, a local medical doctor and former Nationalist member of the Corporation, handed them in a large refuge bin and a mop in order to: 'Assist their womenfolk in tidying up'. After six weeks of protest one of the organisers reported increased public support: 'More and more people would stop you in the street and say "Quite right, the time has come for a change".

The direct action adopted in Derry resonated with more general agitation around social issues across Ireland, North and South, at that time; the difference in Northern Ireland was the clustering of social and economic grievances with the gloss of allegations of sectarian discrimination. This raised the question of the very nature of the state itself; sharpening the demands for reform and provoking loyalist reaction. The quandary was highlighted when the Derry Guildhall played unwilling host to two events simultaneously. The DHAC squatters were barricaded into the Corporation Chamber downstairs, whilst the Rev. Ian Paisley, massed his supporters in opposition to civil rights protestors (and specifically to a planned march by the student led People's Democracy) in the Main Hall upstairs. In a commendable spirit of toleration, the Derry Citizens' Action Committee, formed after the violence of the previous October, supported Paisley's right to hold his meeting, but were unable to prevent the predictable stone throwing between opposing factions in the Guildhall Square later that evening.

Politics at centre-stage

The international media was on hand to record loyalist attacks on a People's Democracy march from Belfast to Derry in January 1969. NICRA had been critical of the march as potential 'coat-trailing', but quickly condemned the attacks and the early morning descent of the police (RUC) on the nationalist/republican Bogside area where houses were raided, wrecked and people beaten with batons. Neither the thump of batons on steel shields nor the alleged chanting of 'Fenian bastards! Fenian bastards!' proved conducive to good community relations. The next day, a Sunday, as women adjusted their headscarves and marched in protest to the police station, barricades

were erected to keep the police from entering the Bogside. The sign that was
to pass into history – 'You Are Now Entering Free Derry' – was painted
on a gable wall. The burnt out carcass of a car, forming part of a barricade,
sported the notice, 'Bunting's motor car', in wry comment on the battling
Major Ronnie Bunting, a colourful Paisleyite supporter. Rostering points
for people to join street defence committees were established in local halls
and Radio Free Derry went on air in the best traditions of the illegal Pop
Radio stations of the time; but instead of pumping out pop songs it relayed
community defence instructions from a location in Creggan. Members
of the Derry Citizens' Action Committee travelled to London to present
a petition to the British Prime Minister, while back home local communities realised that areas could effectively mobilise in self-defence when
necessary. The message spread like wildfire, as did the sense of increasing
instability of the Stormont administration which was fragmenting in the
face of demands for reform by the British government. By April 1969, the
Northern Ireland Tourist Board was warning that the ongoing civil strife
would adversely affect the tourist trade.

A new front opened up when the Dungannon Civil Rights Committee
published research into the employment practices of Dungannon Town
Council. 'Diabolical Discrimination' screamed the *Irish News* headline
when it was shown that of the fifty-nine separate occupations, totalling 367
jobs, ninety-six were held by Catholics who comprised 50 per cent of the
population of the Council area. The then Town Clerk of Downpatrick, and
later prominent public servant, Maurice Hayes remarked in his memoirs:
'When the masses start to read, the establishment is in trouble – when they
start to count, the game is up'. However there was little time to do either in
the violence that followed the Loyal Order Apprentice Boys' annual parade
in Derry in August, when inter-communal violence resulted in another
bitter confrontation between the police and the people of the Bogside,
soon to be dubbed 'the Battle of the Bogside'. Barricades were re-erected
and the art of petrol bomb making became a virtual cottage industry. So too
was the preparation of face masks and the fail-safe remedy against CS gas
irritation: buckets of water, lemon and vinegar. One local milkman found a
note on a doorstep: 'No milk today please, but leave me 200 bottles'. When
the dairy counted the cost of the confrontation it calculated that 43,000

glass milk bottles had gone missing. Trouble shifted to Belfast and other towns as the call went out to draw pressure off the hard pressed Bogsiders. It was answered as described by one young man, who later became a republican activist: 'At that stage there was the beginning of people attempting to organise, but what they were organising was barricades ... Every street had its own barricade up'. Against the sound of gunfire and the orange glow cast by burning buildings, the intimidation of those deemed 'them' rather than 'us' raised the question as to what side of the barricades people were on. A pipeline of vigilante activism was also established, recalled by a young loyalist who later graduated into the UVF: 'Paramilitaries weren't really heard of at that time, so it was vigilantism. And then that progressed into other things and it was just like a natural progression'.

By 15 August 1969 British soldiers were on the streets of Northern Ireland in support of the hard-pressed police and auxiliary forces. One newly posted soldier commented on how: 'Most of the army, officers included, hadn't much of a clue what was going on in Northern Ireland. We knew they spoke English, were white, and the media was there. I got the impression that if they'd been black or brown, and the media hadn't been there, we might have got the problem sorted out much more quickly'. As the soldiers replaced the make-shift barricades with corrugated iron and great looping rolls of barbed wire, what were to become community 'interfaces' became a permanent feature. They were serenaded by the battle of the airwaves. Radio Free Belfast spun out a mixture of pop, rebel songs, announcements to vigilantes and demands on the Stormont Government. Radio Ulster (not connected to the BBC) was forced off the air to the dying strains of 'The Sash', after it was closed down despite frantic appeals for a new home; and Peace Radio offered a five hour nightly broadcast, playing 'soft music' to 'instil peace'. The latter was appropriately located on the interface between the Protestant Shankill and the Catholic Springfield Roads. The relevant authorities declared war on them all.

In Derry, the Entertainment Sub-Committee of the Bogside Defence Association released helium filled balloons carrying messages that 'The people of Free Derry will celebrate their freedom from Unionism and their determination never to return to the grey days of the pre barricade age. Unionism was a miserable thing!' Wanderly Wagon, the Irish RTE children's programme was screened live from the Bogside and music was on offer from folk groups such as Planxty. A firework display lit up the sky on the last Sunday in August – a far cry from the *Belfast Telegraph* headline two weeks earlier: 'A red glow lit up Londonderry for miles early today as arson and bombing spread from the rebel Bogside area'. The Derry Citizens' Defence Association announced that the public houses in the Bogside would stay open, making the point: 'We haven't applied for an extension of licensing hours – we don't need to. At the moment we are a separate state and make our own rules'. The Liberation Fleadh, as it was called, was to be 'a manifestation of MASS HAPPINESS'.

Mobilising a community response

The violence of the summer necessitated a community response. A member of the Turf Lodge Tenants' Association, a TV repairman by trade, described how he helped to settle refugees streaming in from other parts of Belfast: 'When the Bombay Street (an area where people were burned out of their homes) thing blew up ... I kept my head down, I didn't want to know ... But the door rapped and this priest was standing with a child whose home had been burnt to the ground ... He didn't know where her parents were, whether they were dead or alive or where they were. So he asked me – I knew everybody because I fixed their televisions ... So at that point I went out and bought a dozen jotters and got teenagers, told them what I wanted ... And I took on 600 houses, then 1,200 ... They went and rapped at the doors ... But it so happened whenever the young people came back with the jotters the names of the parents were on it'. Not content with that, Joe set the young people another task: 'What did the people need who were playing hosts to these people ... And then we let the people know in the rest of the area what was required, blankets, kettles, pots, whatever. So there was a collection of goods. So my television van was hijacked by me and we collected all this stuff and had it distributed'. Community crisis called for common-sense organisational skills.

A young teacher, in a primary school in North Belfast, found herself in a similar situation, being drafted in by the local Parish Priest to act as secretary of a resettlement committee: 'The purpose was to rehouse these people (who had been intimidated) and to get furniture and stuff for them, and because I was a teacher ... my classroom became an advice centre'. A student volunteer, working in the increasingly segregated areas in the west of the city, noted the impact on young people: 'On a nightly basis it was the kids ... the young people were feeding off the frenzy that was beginning to happen, and there were stones flying in both directions, and then the guns appeared behind that ... I mean literally there was a pageant every night and it was the riot. It was the place to go ... It was the fear – what it fed on was the rumours that people were doing things from each other's side'. The power of rumour and the attendant fear factor fed perceptions of intimidation for those people still living in 'mixed' areas. An early study recorded the feelings of a Catholic housewife: 'When you lived in a Protestant area after '69 and you went into a shop, all the people would be having their heads together and whispering, and when you entered they stopped and there was dead silence. And nobody spoke a word till you went out'. 'Mixed' areas became increasingly uncomfortable for whichever denomination slipped below the majority watermark, resulting in a constant reconfiguration of community space.

The essentials in these circumstances became access to a telephone and means of ready transport. Tribute was paid to Denis Barritt, then Director of the Belfast Voluntary Welfare Society, a respectable and long established charitable NGO, who allowed BVWS resources to be used: 'He (Denis) allowed me to have the van and what we used the van for was to move people ... particularly Protestants from Moyard and New Barnsley over to Glencairn ... As you moved across houses were burning and people were taking their furniture out of houses and it was just war zone stuff'. One young lad whose family had to move described how people were trailing around Belfast looking for potential alternate homes to squat in: 'They hadn't got cars or anything – so you were going on word of mouth ... It wasn't that you had to go down and sign for anything, you just moved your stuff into it. Sorted things out afterwards'. The BVWS van proved very useful.

With rumour and political rhetoric running amok, the Amalgamated Corporation Tenants' Association had to work hard to maintain their cross-community support for the 'war' on rent increases. Sean Morrissey pointed out that any attempts to evict families for non-payment of the proposed increases would be actively resisted; while his colleague, Billy Ritchie, added that the money would be collected by Association representatives and lodged in a bank account pending the outcome of the campaign. The action was supported by both the Turf Lodge Tenants' Association in West Belfast, who picketed their local rent office, and by trade unionists in Shorts Aircraft factory and Harland & Wolff shipyard, in East Belfast. However, within weeks, the Association was forced to issue a statement decrying the fact that: 'Great efforts are being made in many quarters to divide Corporation tenants into sectarian camps'. With the benefit of hindsight, a leading loyalist trade unionist in Londonderry described similar pressures: 'The difficulty that all those organisations (NICRA) had in the early days was that they were very associated with republicanism and nationalism ... and of course that was feeding the Unionist politicians who used to slide up to you and say, "You can't trust them Fenian bastards, you know. It's not really a workers' movement, it's just to take you into a united Ireland" ... I've often said we were worse off than the Catholic working class. The Catholic working class could complain ... We couldn't, because we were very quickly told that if we pulled down the establishment we were heading towards a united Ireland. So we suffered our poverty in silence ... (and) played within the rules'.

With the rules increasingly up for grabs, communities started to make their own, although increasingly within the context of escalating violence as initial nationalist welcome of the British Army palled and loyalist sense of betrayal deepened. Proposed policing reforms were met with rioting in the Shankill area of Belfast; the UVF opened fire, killing Constable Victor Arbuckle, the first RUC officer to die in the Troubles. Return fire by the Army killed two local men. When trouble continued over a number of days, a 7.00 pm curfew was imposed on public houses. The shocked response was two-fold: the UVF ordered a boycott of Catholic owned public houses and the General Secretary of the Belfast & Ulster Vintners' Association complained: 'This has come as a bombshell'. Perhaps not the best turn of phrase in the circumstances.

Meanwhile British Army tactics of stop, search and question had the unforeseen consequences of alienating local communities. The raids were generally carried out at night, with soldiers making note of details like the colour of wallpaper, in order to use the information in further screening of mainly young men. The tactics adopted effectively radicalised many families as a schoolgirl in nationalist Andersonstown explained: 'Our Martin would have only been about thirteen and there was a ferocious raid on our house one time ... He was in the bunk beds up the stairs and they told him to get out of the bed, and he wouldn't ... By this stage Mrs Campbell ... the Tenants' Association woman – herself and Mrs Hanley up the street, Mrs Hall, the whole lot – everybody was in the bedroom. And I said "You're a great one to stand your ground, so stand your ground", and all the rest of it. And the soldier was going ballistic ... And all the women were going hysterical ... They'd (the soldiers) actually beaten me up out in the back garden five minutes earlier ... so I was angry at this stage. The funny thing was right in the middle of it Martin says to me, "Geraldine come over here ... Will you for fuck sake get them women out of here, I've no clothes on" ... The only reason he wouldn't get out of the bed was not that he was being staunch – he'd no clothes on'. Nevertheless the point was made, where there was a need the Tenants' Association women rallied round, hysterical or not.

Community reaction varied depending on shifting circumstances. People responded to immediate need, but there was also a variety of reactions to the ongoing violence. The North Belfast Fellowship Committee garnered Catholic, Protestant and Jewish support to provide services for older residents in a number of neighbourhoods across the complex sectarian jig-saw of their area; over in Ballymurphy, women came out to link arms across the street in an attempt to stop young people attacking soldiers in the aftermath of a June 1970 weekend of mayhem. The previous May, the Irish Congress of Trade Unions (ICTU) had cancelled its annual May Day Parade for fear it might contribute to street tension; but this was not enough to prevent five hundred workers being intimidated out of employment in Harland & Wolff shipyard. In the calmer setting of South Belfast, Catholic and Protestant clergy formed the Ballynafeigh Peace Committee; although US evangelist, Arthur Blessit, sailed closer to the wind when he insisted on dragging a seven foot high cross through the streets of the Shankill/Falls interface.

Doing it for themselves: Community resilience

A renewed focus on community self-help was evident in ever-innovative Ballymurphy. There, local Catholic priest and social activist, Fr. Des Wilson, invited fellow cleric and well-known advocate of cooperative development, Fr. McDyer, to speak at a meeting in the Community Centre. McDyer drew on his experience in Glencolmcille in Co. Donegal, arguing that if the people of any community were to succeed it must be through their own resources, drive and collectivist thinking. Whether he shared with his audience the threat used with his Glencolmcille congregation of being held guilty of mortal sin if they failed to support the proposed cooperative ventures, is not recorded. However the seeds were laid of a new approach that was to spread.

By April 1971, a group of local people decided to establish the Ballymurphy Enterprise CoOp. The contribution of a local woman, Catherine Reynolds, who was seeking occupational support for her disabled daughter, and Quaker activist, Daphne Robinson, resulted in the setting up a community-based cottage industry. After a number of meetings, and a canvass of local interest, it was agreed to develop the 'Rock Knitwear Association', involving twenty women and an order book for hand knitted Aran sweaters to be retailed through War on Want. More women were engaged in making lampshades, and men were invited to use the wood turning and metal work facilities at the local St. Thomas's Secondary School. The initial funding for the venture came when Daphne Robinson opened her handbag and placed a £20 note on the table. By July, the *Irish News* carried an article sub-titled: 'These Goods can carry a "Made in Ballymurphy" Tag'.

The initiative was envisaged as a Workers' Cooperative, profit-making but not about private gain. Despite a series of financial uncertainties and difficulties, the committee purchased second hand machinery to equip a production unit in a local house. A more ambitious venture established the Whiterock Industrial Estates Ltd in the Upper Springfield. This originated in earlier negotiations to take over a redundant Oil Filling Station to be turned into shops and small enterprises. One such was Whiterock Pictures, a laminating and picture framing workshop. Inspired by McDyer's description of developments in Co. Donegal, it was decided to purchase twelve acres of farm land, at a cost of £12,000, to establish an industrial estate in the area. It was hoped to create 1,000 jobs through forty workshop units. A deposit of £1,000 was secured and lodged for the land as fundraising began in earnest. The Stormont Department for Development assisted in providing infrastructure for the site and the Joseph Rowntree Charitable Trust offered a grant of £15,000 – a major investment at that time. Local fundraising took the form of the issue of a Loan Bond of £1 per bond. Development work was carried out and community involvement grew. Coinciding with these ventures, West Belfast also celebrated the opening of the first Naiscoil and Bunscoil (Irish language nursery and primary schools) that had long been the dream of its small Irish language community.

Community action in Lenadoon, in West Belfast, was a response to conditions resulting from population displacement. Houses were wrecked when the Protestant population moved out of the area to be replaced by Catholics moving in from East Belfast. A People's Cooperative responded to the need for urgent housing repairs. A resident explained: 'Lenadoon was a no-go area in 1971, so you got no services, no housing, no power, nothing like that, and what happened was there was a number of people actually got together that had skills, and they sort of formed a People's Coop to do repairs to people's houses'. Meanwhile activities were developing apace on the adult education front when Fr. Des Wilson rented and opened Springhill Community House, with the declared intention of providing space for people and ideas: 'People needed space in which to be free'. The largest room held some fifteen people; and the facility also offered the attraction of a public telephone in an area where telephones were at a premium. Des Wilson reflected on the learning: 'A very big lesson was that anytime that we, or anybody else, sat round a table – no matter who we were, people in the district or people outside it – sat round a table and said, "This is what we're going to do for the people", it didn't work. It had a very much better chance of working if the people were there listening to one another'. Another hub was opened by the legendary Mother Teresa of Calcutta and her nuns, some two doors down from Springhill Community House. Four sari clad Indian nuns worked with local children and adults, developing their programme of community activities in between gun battles and parents' frantic search for teenagers 'lifted' by the British Army until expelled as a result of a dispute with local clergy.

Cross-community support for local activism around issues of housing and unemployment was provided by a newly established Northern Ireland Research Institute. The Institute had been set up with financial support from two UK based Quaker charitable foundations to carry out action-research into socio-economic conditions and provide supportive training to local groups. This small, early 'Think Tank' was community responsive. Planner and Institute affiliate, Ron Weiner, helped the Andersonstown & Suffolk Industrial Promotions Association to complete a social survey of their area. Some months later he produced a 'Do-It-Yourself Guide: Community Self-Survey' and offered training for activists who wanted to undertake surveys in their own areas. One young woman found that given restricted resources, necessity became the mother of invention: 'In the pre-computer days Ron had very innovatively designed a thing whereby you got a graph paper, and for people you ticked a square on the graph paper … so then you had a square for ten little ticks – so you could say, so many people there were in a category'. When applied in a community survey in the Turf Lodge area the returns showed (i) a very young population – 60 per cent under the age of eighteen years; (ii) a very high density of population – 78 per cent of households had five or more members; and (iii) a 38 per cent unemployment rate compared to the then Northern Ireland average of 7 per cent. The research laid the basis for local advocacy which resulted in government response. A Resources Committee, composed of representatives from both statutory agencies and the Whiterock Industrial Estates committee, was established. Efforts to address unemployment were hindered by heightened fears about the dangers of travelling to work outside immediate single identity areas due to the rising toll of sectarian attacks and assassinations.

Across the peace line, community action in the loyalist/unionist Shankill was mobilised in opposition to the proposed redevelopment of this area of extended families and established neighbourhoods. By 1972, community activists on the Shankill were aware of official plans to build fifteen-storey blocks of flats, as well as a new urban motorway system that would cut a swathe through inner Belfast. A public inquiry into the planned motorway drew vigorous representation by community groups, such as the Sandy Row Redevelopment Association. This was an issue that continued to rumble on over a number of years. However the newly mobilised community activism also invited questioning by more established groups – a tension that was particularly evident within unionist/loyalist communities. In East Belfast, the WRVS (Women's Royal Voluntary Service) and the Boys' Brigade came together to set up the East Belfast Youth Council, which later had a formative role in the newly established East Belfast Community Council. In North Belfast a new Community Council was set up with representatives from sixty-seven voluntary and statutory agencies, under the chairmanship of Col. Barney Filor. The question of what was under whose influence, and with whose authority, was to persist as new organisations were formed and groups took it upon themselves to speak for 'their' community. In South Belfast, it was members of the Ballynafeigh Branch of the Loyalist Association of Women who took direct action by occupying an old school to create a youth centre for young loyalists. They complained that the teenage members of the local Tartan gangs (young loyalists that wore tartan trimmings in memory of three Scottish soldiers killed by the IRA) were being constantly harassed by the security forces and expressed the hope that the new centre would take the youngsters off the streets and out of mischief.

But mischief held its own fascination for a sixteen-year-old from Sandy Row: 'I remember getting a bus up to go rioting in the Shankill. I was just fascinated by rioting. Fascinated just by the Troubles itself and I remember my mother saying "You're not getting out", and me climbing over the wall and getting a bus up. I remember standing in burning buildings in Cupar Street, Dover Street, and all that'. There was a fascination with the chaos of the time, but also a sense of bemusement as one contemporary commentator described women on the Shankill shaking their heads at the

flight of Mrs So-and-So, who they had lived beside and possibly worked
with in a local factory.

The rise of the People's Assemblies

The early years of the 1970s showed limited progress on the political front,
but two nationalist/republican areas took it upon themselves to design their
own forms of participative democracy. Activists in Ardoyne (North Belfast)
and the Bogside (Derry) considered how best to place community action
on a democratic footing. Ethnographic researcher, Frank Burton, lived in
Ardoyne in 1972, while researching his study 'The Politics of Legitimacy:
Struggles in a Belfast Community'. He described a neighbourhood of thirty
two streets, with 2,220 houses inhabited by over 11,000 people, in a tightly
packed one quarter of a square mile. This was an area that saw itself as virtually besieged and consequently as responsible for its own survival. Both
Burton, and the much later Ardoyne Commemoration Project, charted
the development of the 'People's Assembly', established in November 1971.
Burton wrote that: 'The Council is a type of community soviet and is a
fascinating example of an attempted self-government at the local level'. At
its inception it distributed a non-violent, but clearly, republican manifesto.
The structure of the Assembly was explained in which everyone over the
age of eighteen in the area had a vote, and the Assembly members were
elected on the basis of street level representation. Street committees were
composed of eight men and eight women; as well four boys and four girls.
From these committees half of each category was elected by street poll
to sit as representatives of their street on the Assembly, and to join the
Assembly Sub-Committees – Justice, Development and Welfare – and its
two Coordinating Committees. The Welfare Committee, composed mainly
of women, was thought to be particularly effective. The Justice Committee
largely monitored the activities of the British Army; and the Development
Committee concerned itself with redevelopment and housing issues. The
Assembly, which could have up to 300 delegates, also developed its own

set of procedures, with members being instructed to table their items of business in advance so that Order Papers could be compiled.

The story is told that one of the first acts of the People's Assembly was to coordinate a peaceful protest about the lack of street lighting in the area; the lights having either been shot out or smashed. At a pre-arranged time, on the night of 2 December, 1971, everyone in the district placed a light outside their homes in protest. By coincidence, a matter of minutes earlier, a number of IRA men (including Ardoyne men, Martin Meehan and Tony 'Dutch' Doherty) had broken out of Crumlin Road jail, just a hop and a skip down the Crumlin Road from Ardoyne. The light display was misinterpreted by the astonished military as an almost instantaneous demonstration of communal celebration of the jail break. At a political level, the Provisional IRA recognised the Ardoyne Assembly as a legitimate source of authority in the area. Again, Burton reported: 'To some extent, although I could not gauge how much, the IRA was represented on the Council through street committees. What was clear was that the Community Council (Assembly) was not a front organisation for the IRA. The British Army's general harassment of some of the Community Council leaders seemed to imply that they were "plain clothes" IRA men. As it was, the Community Council boasted several bitter opponents of the IRA, including members of the clergy, who featured quite prominently in the committee work'.

The Ardoyne People's Assembly representatives met with government Ministers, civil servants, the British Army, and generally liaised with external agencies on behalf of the area. However, by the summer of 1972, a flurry of letters posted in the *Irish News* reflected a growing controversy between the Assembly and a local Catholic priest. The Assembly Press Officer condemned the level of intimidation experienced in the area and claimed that the British Army was bowing to UDA (Ulster Defence Association) demands. He also expressed disappointment that a three week republican truce had broken down. Fr. Aquinas, the priest in question, condemned the IRA and exhorted local parishioners to close their doors to paramilitaries and to make their views known to the members of the People's Assembly. In a subsequent missive to the *Irish News*, the Assembly Press Officer reprimanded the priest for 'his

efforts to use the People's Assembly to support his own particular opinion', arguing further that 'The People's Assembly has never at any time
given unqualified support to the IRA'. Another letter, two days later,
signed 'Republican – Ardoyne', supported the priest's condemnation
of the Provisional IRA, although Burton suggests that this might have
been written by a supporter of the Official IRA who, by that time, were
at odds with the Provisional IRA. The continuing controversy clearly
contributed to the gradual waning of local participation in the street
committees notwithstanding the previous efficiency of the Assembly's
work and its ability to produce and distribute fortnightly newssheets.
Communication was particularly important in supporting community
resilience during times of uncertainty.

The Bogside Community Association that emerged in Derry faced
similar controversies to those in Ardoyne but managed to survive over a
longer period of time. An individual involved remembered it as, in part,
a reaction to community disgust over Bloody Sunday, where: 'People talk
about empowerment and so on ... (but) what does it actually mean? So this
notion of getting involved – I had never heard of, or thought of, community
development before. The notion of forming a community association for
that area, and people taking control of their own lives really appealed to
me. So myself and others helped to organise an election, a write-in populist
election at Easter 1972 ... (The ideas came from a mixture of things) Three
strands – there was myself who said "What is this community stuff?" Denis
Bradley (a local priest) talked a bit about it. Martin McGuinness (Sinn Féin)
talked a bit about it, and then we had heard a bit of what was happening
in Dublin'. The Dublin model involved a progressive psychiatrist, Ivor
Browne, who helped set up the Irish Foundation for Human Development,
which, in turn, supported a community action initiative in Ballyfermot, a
deprived area of Dublin. The mantra of the Foundation was 'Create, acti-
vate, motivate'. Browne's interest in Derry was piqued by Bloody Sunday
and, matured after an exchange visit between Dublin and Derry. Browne
subsequently persuaded the Bank of Ireland to contribute £2,000 per year
through his Foundation, which would fund a Community Organiser for
the Bogside area. He asked Eamonn Deane and Denis Bradley to identify
a likely candidate for the job. They did. Larger than life, local man, Paddy

Doherty, who had returned from working on a construction site in the West Indies, agreed to take the post.

The *Derry Journal* takes up the story in April, 1972. 'Improving Area's Facilities will be Community Association's Aims – Bogside "Corporation" Will be Chosen next Week'. It explained how 6,000 people, over the age of eighteen, would be invited to participate in a 'write-in' election based on an US system. The area was divided into twelve districts, and each district would elect one representative. There would be no official candidates as such, but anybody could write in the name of the person in their district that they wanted to represent them. If the person with the greatest number of nominations from the area declined the position, then the person with the next highest vote would be offered the post. In addition to the twelve elected district representatives, there was provision for another seven people to be co-opted in an advisory capacity to the Assembly. The organisers emphasised that the Association's aims were neither political nor military, but purely social in nature.

Political reaction to the initiative was swift. At its Easter commemoration ceremony, the Official IRA advocated a policy of organising 'street committees' to ensure that local people had control of their own areas, and promised that they would be rolling out this proposition over the following weeks. The political wing of the Official IRA, the Republican Clubs, then queried the mandate of the Bogside Community Association organisers, raising questions about the people behind the initiative. Tenants' Associations in both the Bogside and Creggan complained that they had not been consulted about the idea. The headlines in the *Derry Journal* of 11 April reported 'Heavy Polling in Bogside Election', as the door-to-door collection of votes returned a participation rate in some areas as high as 95 per cent, with an overall turn-out of 74.6 per cent (4,500 out of 6,000 voters). In another intervention, Daithi O'Connell, speaking in the Bogside on behalf of the Provisional IRA national leadership, said that his organisation was planning to launch a community government in the Bogside and Creggan areas which was supported by community leaders. The same day, a statement by the Derry Citizens' Central Committee (established in 1968) expressed their opposition to Daithi O'Connell's pronouncement, and held that John Hume (SDLP) 'as the only elected representative should have the right to make decisions on behalf of the people who elected him'. Political one up-man-ship was alive and well.

Eamonn Deane, returning early from his honeymoon to help organise the election, recalled the prevailing controversy: 'There was a lot of interest in it, there was a lot of opposition to it ... The local Tenants' Association said "We've been doing this for years and you bastards come along and ignore us" – which we did. We did have some sort of consultation, but it was patronising. You know, we hadn't just ignored them, we had been unaware of them. And then the elections threw up twelve people ... and they in turn co-opted others – the co-options were very safe people for the most part; churchmen (and so forth). Within a couple of years of that, the Bogside Community Association had a parliament of over 160 delegates, who met regularly – once a month'. While Eamonn had been away, local curate Fr. Denis Bradley had come under considerable pressure: 'A very prominent man came to see me, I'll never forget it ... and he said "You will be responsible for the burning of Derry – this town will burn to the ground and you will be the person responsible" ... and it was from Hume's party it came ... The SDLP weren't really a political party – they were still a movement, and there was a battle for supremacy, and I think I was being told, you're getting in the way of this, right? ... Or you're setting up people who will look like politicians as an alternative to something, or whatever ... And the interesting thing was I thought ... you're wrong'. John Hume himself was in America, but despite his absence was elected onto the Assembly; he later refused to accept the seat. Like Eamonn Deane, Denis Bradley remembers those who were elected as being all men: 'It was a strange mixture of some of those that I would have called the conservative Catholic advisers, to right across, you know, more left-wingish people. Not terribly young mind you'. With support from the Irish Foundation for Human Development, and the Community Studies Unit in University College Dublin, the Bogside Community Association opened an office which was later transferred to a caravan in the Bogside, adjacent to the old gasyard.

The ongoing war of words continued between the Official Republican Movement and the Provisionals over street committees and People's Election's respectively. By June 1972, it was clear that the latter's attempt to hold 'Free Derry Elections' had been given up as a bad job. A statement issued by the Derry Comhairle Ceanntair (Area Committee) of Sinn Féin announced that elections would be postponed because 'Voters were not well enough instructed in PR'. The Official IRA was distracted by the pickets and protests of local women in response to their killing of an off-duty British soldier, Derryman Ranger Best, while visiting his family in the city. Over 2,000 people marched in protest; nine days later the Officials declared an indefinite ceasefire, although at times this was rather loosely interpreted. The Bogside Community Association also issued a statement which acknowledged the widespread desire for a just peace: 'There is a limit beyond which a community should not be asked to go, particularly when there seems to be reasonable ground for negotiating a just peace'. This ground all too often turned into a quagmire during the course of the conflict.

Despite the multi-faceted political pressures, the programme of work set by the Bogside Community Association was formidable. External expertise was drawn in and a distinguished consultant planner, Geoffrey Copcutt, volunteered his services to help produce a Development Plan for the area. The participative approach adopted included the imaginative tactic of discussing planning issues with the audience attending a show that noted Abbey Theatre (Dublin) actress, Siobhan McKenna, staged for the Community Association. The suggestion of an All-Ireland Community Conference to be held in Derry had to be placed on the long finger given pressing conflict-related issues. In a considered missive the BCA posed a number of questions for the community about the oppressive behaviour of British soldiers; the continuing policy of internment; the treatment of prisoners while in custody, but also concerning the role of rumour and the spread of local criminality. It asked – Why do we not accept the right of others to hold opinions we do not like? In conclusion, it was held: 'It is our deep seated conviction that so long as there are reasons to ask any of these questions, our community can never achieve even the limited goals of this, it's Association ... Our demands must be directed within, as well as without, the community'. This was a courageous statement given the political pressures of the time.

It was during this period that Paddy Doherty, as the BCA organiser, made overtures to the new loyalist structures in the Waterside area of Londonderry. Glenn Barr, a UDA advisor, responded to the overtures, appreciating the importance of networking with the 'other side': 'In those early days that was when Paddy Doherty and myself first met, and we were aware very much of Paddy. But during the No-Go days (when the Army and police were excluded from local communities) Paddy came up to Irish Street and the barricades to talk peace; and he was arrested (by the UDA) and he tells the story himself you know. They were going to shoot him, and I was sent for of course, and came up and talked them out of it, you know. He often tells the story of this fellow (who) came in, this handsome fellow came in and says he gives them political advice. He gives them more than political advice – they all stand to attention and saluted. And he tells the story about me saving his life, and I keep saying "Will you for God sake stop telling that story, it doesn't go down too well in some quarters, you know. Some people have never forgiven me for saving you"'. Paddy corroborated this account, although with some choice descriptive asides. He agreed to keep the lines of communication open and telephone numbers were exchanged. In turn, Paddy was to fulfil a similar role when necessary, negotiating the return of British soldiers or individuals under interrogation, from the fastness of the Bogside, where possible. Doherty was less impressed with a British Army 'community relations' exercise in the nearby Brandywell. This 'getting-to-know-the-people' operation involved soldiers calling door to door asking for the names, ages and religion of each resident in the house. It was stopped after protests from the BCA.

The Bogside Community Association reaffirmed its mandate with the election of a new Assembly in April 1973. On this occasion there was a 77 per cent turn-out, resulting in six of the outgoing representatives being re-elected and three replaced. Two major strategic reports were produced: the first 'An Approach to a Strategy for Derry and the North-West', and the second criticising the legal aid system. A submission was made to the Londonderry Development Commission Area Plan and the Association carried out a 'People's Critique' of a Bogside Amenity Plan. The BCA, together with the Creggan and Foyle Hill Tenants' Associations, negotiated the right to have representatives present during army searches of the homes of residents that requested their support. This monitoring role proved to be a dubious privilege as one weary BCA activist suggests: 'We had negotiated with them (the British Army) an agreement that whenever there were house raids and arrests then ... an elected member of the BCA could be present and could protect people's rights and so on. What usually happened was that the elected member of the BCA was also scooped ... I remember one week of my life I was arrested twenty-eight times, and "Not you again" type of thing ... And then you'd get a particularly vindictive officer in charge and he'd say, "I'll sicken that bastard there with rules and regulations". And then you'd get people on our side saying "You know they can ask you the following questions – here's the only answers that you're bound by law to give". You could see them muttering – "I'll get that smart-ass out of the way"'. However for all the frustrations there were the small victories. Another member of the BCA recalled an army major, who he described as 'the most effective British Officer in Derry', because he was responsive and low key. After representations were made concerning the behaviour of soldiers during house raids, he 'instructed his men to wear plimsolls – they crept through the night and tapped on doors'. Wearing plimsolls or boots, the British Army was active and by August they had carried out seventy-eight house raids, and made sixty-three arrests, over one month in the areas covered by the Creggan and Foyle Hill Tenants' Associations.

By summer 1974, the Bogside Community Association was implementing a new two-tier electoral system in an attempt to increase local participation in the organisation. There was to be a BCA Council as well as an Executive Committee. The Bogside area was divided into thirty neighbourhoods, each electing five people to the Council; resulting in a Council of 150 representatives. The individual topping the poll in each neighbourhood area was automatically a member of the Executive Committee. However although efforts were made to extend involvement, debate still simmered over the nature of representation and accountability, particularly between a number of pre-existing tenants' associations and the all-encompassing BCA. The new BCA organiser reflected on the composition of the Council: 'The Bogside was a very broad based community in that there were people from all sorts of walks of life in it – so you could have elected on to your Council from that area your local chemist alongside an unemployed labourer, your local Provo alongside your local priest. You did literally have whatever within the Catholic, Nationalist community in Northern Ireland, and they were all thrown together ... And we also saw the significance in a symbolic way; we knew the city's symbolic significance, and we were playing that at times to get resources'.

One repository of resources was the then Department of Community Relations. The Permanent Secretary of the department suggested that the BCA's request for funding should be scrutinised 'very carefully' given changes in its voting procedures. He warned of 'certain developments ... which may make the Association less deserving of financial assistance in the future'. This implicit negativity drew on a confidential note put into the system by NIO (Northern Ireland Office) man, Michael Oatley, which claimed that seven of the BCA Executive Committee members were Provisional Sinn Féin members or sympathisers. In a subsequent meeting between Direct Rule Minister, Lord Donaldson, and three representatives of the Derry Peace Women, the BCA was described as under the 'control of extremists and Sinn Féiners'. Although one of the ladies had been elected to the BCA Executive Committee, she suggested that 'moderates ... needed much courage to stand up for one's convictions in these circumstances'. The Minister commended the women and noted his appreciation of the contribution that community associations which were working well could make. He lamented the fact that 'Unfortunately these did not include the Bogside'. The Minister undoubtedly was also cognisant of reports filed by the HQ 8th Infantry Brigade, Londonderry on the outcome of the BCA elections which concluded that 'The P.I.R.A. and Official IRA have infiltrated a previously innocuous organization'. This would have been news to Eamonn Deane who in his Progress Report to the Council, argued that 'Above all else a community association must be above party politics and divisionalism, and must be geared towards the good of all the people'. He enumerated the number of news-sheets distributed to each house; the organisation of the Easter Festival; the purchase of a derelict factory building by Derry Development Enterprises Ltd, for a cooperative community employment project; the development of a Community Games; and the introduction of an adult education programme in the Bogside. The aim was to make self-help and self-determination meaningful at neighbourhood level. Deane's Progress Report to his Council was filed, alongside the warnings from Laneside (a Northern Ireland Office base in Co. Down) and the Londonderry based British Army regiment. Notes of private and confidential discussions between departmental officials expressing their concerns about the political complexion of the BCA were also on file.

Away from the tetchiness of Stormont officials, representatives of the Bogside Community Association joined with other community activists, from across the political divide in Derry, to alleviate sectarian conflict. Meetings were held in a community house that acted as a base for Paddy Doherty. An community representative from the loyalist Wapping Community Association commented: 'We met solely for community needs and community action, and I would say that Eamonn Deane, and people like that, actually saved the city from going over the brink, because we were able to meet and discuss, and we knew one another. And when things were really bad we could have phoned up and said "Look, can you do something on your side to try and get this sorted out and reduce the tension?" It did good work ... It was a very strong inter-community action at that time. It certainly saved this city'. The importance of regular contact and communication between communities was of inestimable value, although for obvious reasons it was rarely reported on; nor was there comment on the local paramilitary linkages that were essential for community activists to deliver for 'the other side'. But if these issues were successful by being managed quietly, the music of the Dubliners, the Chieftains and the Horslips continued to ring out at the benefit concerts organised by the BCA. Planxty performed its unique fusion of traditional Irish and rock music, countering the irritating clatter of low circling army helicopters. But this was nothing to the craic of the regular neighbourhood dances and forays across the Irish Border for a night of entertainment. One young black rioter, who was loosely associated with the Official IRA, raised eyebrows when he mentioned that he had to change his shirt before going across the border in case the soldiers would recognise him. As one of the very few young black men in the Bogside at that time, his fellow rioters felt that it was more than the colour of his shirt that might mark him out. The British Army also had to adapt to changed circumstances. A favoured tactic in dealing with riots was to despatch a box formation of soldiers, accompanied by two banner men who unfurled their banner with the words 'Stop or we will open fire'. Previously stationed in Aden (Yemen) the wording on the banner carried by the Gloucestershire Regiment was still in Arabic, making little sense to Belfast locals. A less ambiguous message was relayed by the Officer in Command (OC) who threatened to shoot petrol bombers on sight.

CHAPTER 3

Community Relations and Community Development: The Cuckoo or the Nest?

Community relations featured in the 1969 British reform package for Northern Ireland. A new Stormont ministry was nominated to house it and a Northern Ireland Community Relations Commission established as an arm's length body to implement it. The Board of the Commission included members drawn from both Catholic and Protestant backgrounds. Local government official, Maurice Hayes, was appointed Chairperson, noting that his Board were reasonably safe appointees of a neutral political hue. Hayes himself expressed surprise when the new Minister, Robert Simpson, asked him whether he was 'a good Catholic', later explained as due to official fears that a lapsed Catholic, an agnostic, or even a communist, might be appointed by mistake. Hayes was concerned that the Commission might simply be a sop to British public opinion or a cloak of convenience for an administration that was beyond reform. In the event, much of the debate was over the nature of community relations work and its relationship to community development. Welshman, Hywel Griffiths, was appointed as Director and the Commission opened its doors in December 1969. It worked over a period of five years, falling victim to the Sunningdale power-sharing Executive in 1974. It existed during an intensely political period which saw a growth in community activism.

Breathing life into the Commission

The community development strategy championed by Hywel Griffiths was based on his experience in post-colonial Africa. He believed in building community confidence and leadership as a pre-requisite to positive community relations. This phased approach was based on the hope, described by Hayes: 'That the great constitutional and ideological issues that divided people could be put on hold while communities got on with the ordinary business of living. In this way, too, trust, a delicate plant, might begin to take root and flower, providing a basis for exchanges on the more fundamental matters in the future'. Graffiti on the walls of North Belfast suggested that the constitutional issues had staying power: 'We shall never forsake the blue skies of freedom for the grey mists of an Irish Republic' – it warned. Despite this political weather warning the Community Relations Commission designed a community development framework, recruiting Community Development Officers (CDOs) from a wide variety of backgrounds. An in-service training facility, linked with local universities, was put in place and a research facility established. One of the newly appointed staff members outlined how: 'Maurice did the political stuff and Hywel really grounded the team in an understanding of what a team was, on community development practice, and brokered in international understanding ... And we argued the bit out ... we had hellish rows ... But we all gained a huge amount from the guy in terms of the training that was set up; the wisdom of developing a very strong team, and an understanding of community development across a wide spectrum of people who otherwise probably would have worked in total isolation from one another, with their own agendas'. It was Griffiths' intention to locate the CDOs in neighbourhood offices serving a population of some 15,000. Each office would be staffed by a qualified Community Development Leader, supported by a maximum of two other workers drawn from the local area. This geographically dispersed strategy would be coordinated from the central Commission headquarters. The Commission also supported some early 'wins' by making small grants to local community ventures. Children's summer schemes were particularly favoured in the hope of offering alternatives to rioting.

The concept of community development promoted through the Commission was very different from the grievance driven direct action espoused by existing tenants' associations. According to the Commission: 'Community development is a process ... not confined to any specific social, economic, political or cultural application. Rather it is a process which enables individuals and communities to use their own talents and growth potential to create a society in which individuals and communities have access to resources adequate to meet the needs as identified at local level. In short, the process attempts to bring the control of resources closer to the problems as identified by the communities themselves, and, equally importantly, also enables statutory and governmental agencies to be more effective and meaningful in the services which they provide to the community'. The emphasis on the social and economic chimed with the then Unionist Prime Minister's understanding of the Troubles: 'Who can reasonably doubt that the disorders we have seen in Belfast and elsewhere, are due in no small part to the social evils which stem from bad housing? Whatever their differences this is something which the Shankill shares with the Falls, and it must be our aim to offer them alike something better'. Adopting the term 'areas of special social need', Chichester-Clark encouraged projects that could deliver short-term results in order to inspire confidence. The fact that he was also preoccupied with the happier question of how to celebrate the fiftieth anniversary of Northern Ireland, with a 'Come to Ulster Year' in 1971, indicated a certain distance from reality on the streets.

When Northern Ireland Labour Party member, David Bleakley, succeeded Simpson as Minister for Community Relations, he rejected Maurice Hayes's proposal that the ministry should be dissolved in favour of a dedicated Community Relations Unit within the Prime Minister's office. Hayes argued the importance of community relations being at the heart of government. He shared his broader vision at a public meeting in Derry: 'Out of better communities will come better community relations ... Our job must be to humanise the bureaucracy to make it aware of the needs and desires and aspirations and sensitivities of individual small people'. Effective bureaucracy may have been low on the local list of priorities where it was not unknown for the sparrows to splutter in the Derry air given the whiff of CS gas used against rioters.

An increased awareness of the importance of rights flittered across many communities, but was particularly prevalent in those of a nationalist/republican complexion. Both local research into socio-economic conditions and information provided by independent advice services supported community activism. Legal Advice Centres were set up in local neighbourhoods and law students were encouraged to cut their professional teeth by volunteering. A Northern Ireland branch of the UK-based CPAG (Child Poverty Action Group) challenged official policies and decision-making. A Ballymurphy woman described how rights grew legs: 'There was a manager in the Corporation Street office (Social Security office) then and he was giving money back rather than giving it to the people who were entitled to it. So it started from there ... It was discovering that people were entitled to those things ... Somebody found a rule book which said you were entitled to it, so every time somebody said "No you're not entitled to it", we said "Yes we are because – and if we don't get what we are entitled to, we're going to do something about it" ... so there was an awful lot of protesting going on all the time'. Another woman active on housing issues reflected: 'I suppose some of those issues did definitely come from the Civil Rights Movement, and the right then to things like facilities ... And people would gather at the drop of a hat for anything and you could have called a protest about anything.++++++' She added that if local participation showed any signs of flagging the whisper was put about that compensation might be available, enticing people to meetings in droves. They were then mobilised for the next campaign.

When it came to asserting political rights, however, things were more difficult as a NICRA activist found after her family had to move from a loyalist area: 'We just squatted in this desperate house – no hot water, no bathroom, nothing ... It was the last house before you hit the grounds of the Royal Victoria Hospital where the British Army had a base ... and faced down the street in which people used to come at night and fire down at the Brits ... And we used to sit on the floor, behind the settee watching television ... We got raided on a fairly regular basis ... and we got a phone in the house and people used to come when their sons were lifted, and they wanted to know what happened to them ... There used to be people sitting on chairs in the hall waiting for us' These informal hubs of information and support were invaluable, although in this case her mother's strategy of piously squirting the front door step with Lourdes holy water from a plastic bottle to 'stop the Brits from raiding' proved to be less than effective. Both NICRA and the Association of Legal Justice (ALJ) were kept busy: making enquiries; taking statements; raising abuses of human rights and organising protests.

Community activism developed along parallel lines to community development but differed in emphasis. Within the Community Relations Commission new CDOs were schooled in community development. The framing received offered a context for the work emphasising: 'An enabling role ... Looking at the direction which people might want to take'. This focus on empowerment was reflected in six indicators: (i) the promotion of awareness of community and individual needs; (ii) the identification and development of resources internal and external to communities required to meet those needs; (iii) the growth of confidence and ability of individuals and communities to tackle community problems through self-help; (iv) the development of local leadership and encouragement of that leadership to work with their communities to ensure that adequate resources are made available to tackle community problems; and (v) the promotion of awareness on the part of statutory and voluntary agencies that individuals and communities have a right to be involved in the way services are provided and to participate in the sharing of resources. If this approach was radical rather than revolutionary, then the final indicator (vi) cooperation and an efficient working relationship between statutory agencies, voluntary bodies and local communities – highlighted partnership rather than confrontation.

The team of ten CDOs were located in Derry (two people covering Strabane as well); three in Dungannon (to include Newry and Armagh) and five in the Greater Belfast area. In addition to their area remit, each CDO was allocated a specific thematic function (e.g. community associations, cooperatives, etc.). The regular team meetings used a case study approach where, in the words of one of the officers: 'We used case studies to see what impact our intervention was having on particular areas and to see was there some potential for change ... So the idea of the nature of change was going to be determined not by us, but by the people who were experiencing it ... So that whole philosophy of community development was, I thought, very helpful for getting an understanding of what I was trying to do'. Time for reflection, however, was at a premium given the external pace of events.

'Armoured cars and tanks and guns ...'

A popular song in republican areas in the autumn of 1971 expressed solidarity with 'the men behind the wire', the internees who were scooped during the introduction of Internment without Trial. There was an upsurge in violence and intimidation in the immediate aftermath, drawing the Community Relations Commission into emergency response mode. The relocation of those intimidated was one of the largest movements of population in Western Europe, at that time, since World War II. The resulting segregation effectively reinforced 'single-identity' community configuration in Belfast and urban areas across Northern Ireland. Maurice Hayes was appalled: 'To many Catholics internment appeared not as a carefully planned and executed military operation against the IRA, but as a punitive expedition against their community ... Of all the stupid things the government could do this probably was the worst'. The Commission maintained its team of CDOs on the ground to help deal with the community fall-out, establishing an Information Centre at its Belfast headquarters. This was staffed around the clock, to gather and disseminate as accurate information as possible. The destructive impact of wildfire rumours had to be scotched; information was needed for families enquiring about arrested relatives; transport had to be made available to help people move; and advice services were at a premium. Belfast Corporation buses were suspended for fear that they would be hijacked to build local barricades. Hayes recounts a vignette on the resilience of accepted norms when he received a phone call from Dr John Robb, a surgical registrar in the Royal Victoria Hospital in West Belfast, volunteering his services in whatever capacity might be useful. According to Hayes, Robb said: 'He had just come from a medical staff meeting at the Royal, in the middle of a battle zone, with the city going up in flames all around, which had spent two hours debating whether or not to fly the Union flag on the Falls Road façade of the hospital in honour of Princess Anne's birthday'. Even the Association of Licenced Vintners declared the closure of all public houses for fear of further fuelling the conflict.

For its part, the Commission CDOs struggled to make sense of their role, with one describing how: 'Things broke down in 1971, (and) as a team we thought the Commission should come out directly to oppose this infringement of human rights ... There was a lot of tension ... There was a decision made to become a relief organisation and we set up advice centres in different places and became a conduit of information ... There were resource centres for blankets and for food requirements and all of that logistical stuff that was going on ... So we dropped all the community development related stuff and started to work on emergencies for about three months'. For some this was the Commission's finest hour, although one of the quandaries faced was the pressing needs in Catholic areas, and the fear that in responding to these the Commission would leave itself open to the all too ready accusation of sectarian partiality. There were also arguments over how explicit the Commission could be in its criticism of government policy. A considered statement was issued urging politicians to commence peace talks and: 'To replace internment as soon as possible by the normal process of law'. It was further suggested that '30,000 jobs will do more to reduce conflict than 30,000 soldiers and will be cheaper in the long run'. For his part, the Minister of Community Relations resigned, blaming the alienation of the Catholic community on internment at a time when their political cooperation was vital. Meanwhile as bombs became a daily occurrence, the headquarters of the Community Relations Commission suffered collateral damage from an explosion in the underground car park of their headquarters. Although Maurice Hayes was confident that there was nothing personal to the attack, he recorded grumpily that he had been – 'Blown twenty feet across the room by the bomb, and forty degrees to the political right'.

Negotiating space for community development

One of the initiatives supported by the Commission was a Community Development Forum: 'To give those professionally engaged in community development in Northern Ireland a chance of exchanging ideas, experience and a chance to see themselves as a part of a total approach to Northern Ireland's problems'. Clearly, the weasel word 'holistic' was yet to be discovered. The Forum met monthly to examine the principles and processes involved in community development, as well as collecting and disseminating information and identifying issues that required further research and/or action. Within the Commission itself a number of issues and approaches were considered and discussed. The use of community conferences to encourage reflection on community development practice was encouraged at local level to enable people to express their views independently of elected politicians. The more radical proposal that local people should have an input into Commission policy making was deferred. Another matter of concern was the role of recently established community relations branches within the British Army and the police. CDOs warned about the confusion that might arise between their work and that of security force personnel given the understandable sensitivities among many community activists about the army. Eventually it was agreed that some contact should be maintained, but this should be as informal and distant as possible. A North Belfast CDO drew the short straw as the liaison point – not helped by the fact that his army contact was a Major Wildblood.

Even at this early stage the differential pace of community development in Catholic and Protestant areas was noted. For the latter, the traditional course of redress for grievances was through elected political representatives or ministers of religion. This remained true despite complaints that many of these individuals belonged to the 'fur coat brigade'. As one local activist explained: 'For a long, long time Protestants felt that if you want to do something then you went to the people responsible. You went to the church, the reverend, your local councillor ... There was the whole authoritarian thing in the Protestant community'. There was also suspicion about the motivation of outsiders: 'At the start of the Troubles, in Moyard, you got a whole group of people who came from Queens University who wanted to help all the people in the area, and the Protestant people were very suspicious of them, because they thought they were just these do-gooders, and what was it to do with them; they weren't living in the area – they go home, all the usual stuff. But they forgot, so do the politicians all go home after everything happened; they've done it all along'. This reaction was in marked contrast to the nationalist community in Ballymurphy, literally a stone's throw away from Moyard.

Community Relations Commission officers experienced the reservations of loyalist communities knocked outside their accustomed comfort zones – 'I think the defensiveness of the Protestant community was always there and the side about how somehow they'd been sold something about their relationship with the state which they had to guard. And people coming in to sort of say well actually you can do something for yourself, or take action on your own behalf, was a bit of an anathema, and it created huge barriers about why are you here and an underlying suspicion'. There was also the risk that the Commission itself was seen as part of the reform measures that Catholics had been seen to win as a result of their rioting, whinging and violence. It was not unknown for the CRC to be called 'the Catholic Rights Commission'; while the language of community action and community development could all too easily be presented as synonymous with agitation and subversion. This bundle of issues was further fuelled by a deepening antagonism between the Commission and the Ministry of Community Relations, with efforts to expand the remit of the former being seen by departmental officials as potentially reducing their standing. The Commission passed a motion expressing its frustration: 'The view of the Minister that all good should be seen to be done by the government, and that community relations be seen as an extension of the government's PR and patronage system, is not one that the Commission can share'. This strongly worded statement sat in the Ministry in-tray over the 1971/1972 Christmas season.

By the end of February 1972, the statement was joined by Maurice Hayes's resignation letter hard on the heels of 'Bloody Sunday' in Derry. Three reasons were offered – (i) the fact that security policies had alienated almost the whole Catholic community; (ii) the failure of the politicians to engage with this community; and (iii) the lack of any real sense of urgency shown in the necessary radical restructuring of political and social institutions in Northern Ireland. With the benefit of hindsight he argued – 'Established institutions must ... be prepared to change, to attract and accommodate the participation of people and to provide a realistic and practical alternative to violence as a means of producing social change'. Hayes saw little indication that this was happening.

Negotiating space for community development in local communities remained difficult. Describing his first day on the job, one CDO was thrown in the deep end: 'I was given the areas of North and West (Belfast), Glencairn. I'd just been given my areas that morning and the phone rang an hour later and there were 125 workers intimidated in Glencairn ... These were building site workers ... and my job was to try and get the workers back on again. I had discussions with the leaders of the Protestant workers and the Catholic workers ... We tried things like if we weren't going to get them back on could we get them some sort of redundancy payment. I mean the employer wasn't giving them any redundancy because they were saying the site's open, you can go back on, and so that brought you into the whole realm of sort of lobbying with MPs ... Through that I got to know people like Andy Tyrie and Tommy Herron (UDA)'. Gathering and maintaining contacts was very important for the CDOs, although the result could be uncomfortable at times as this Catholic CDO remarked wryly: 'I knew them all, and I used to go up to meetings with Andy Tyrie up in Glencairn, and he used to slap me on the shoulder, "Not too many of your sort up here". And that was always a way – you know – of, fine I want to talk about, but we're letting you know how the land lies ... We know who you are and we know about you and so on'. When faced with issues such as intimidation, Griffiths was not behind the door in intervening directly despite some reservations expressed by members of his team about a man who had cut his teeth in post-colonial African state-building.

CDOs outside of Belfast also faced ongoing emergencies. The community development office in Dungannon was blown to smithereens by a van bomb. One of the officers admitted that she hadn't realised the significance of basing their office in the old local authority building: 'I remember you had to go upstairs to it ... And I remember being told that many a good person had been thrown down those steps'. If the office was poorly located, a picture in the *Belfast Telegraph* of the devastated premises featured a teddy bear hanging forlornly in the wreckage; the bear, adorned in team colours, belonged to a CDO, who was an avid football supporter. The Dungannon team took to meeting in the town's sole hotel before it, in turn, was bombed. A third base in the outlying village of Moy was also destroyed before they returned to the much battered Dungannon. On a positive note one of the officers acknowledged that the periodic lack of an office base by necessity facilitated outreach, although efforts to build relationships with the Protestant community remained difficult. A delegation of Moygashel residents walked around the square in Dungannon three times before finally deciding to attend a pre-arranged meeting in the Commission office. The caution shown was in marked contrast to people that the Commission staff met through informal networking: 'We met a lot of people and you really did more work in the evening as they were sitting there having a drink'. Ideas flowed and relationships flourished in informal settings, but this had to be balanced with an awareness of the community composition of those involved.

The intersectionality of community development and community relations work remained high on the Commission agenda. Maurice Hayes had deconstructed popular community relations definitions and approaches in an early edition of 'Community Forum', the house journal of the Commission. He identified the cross-community contact approach to better relations; the attribution of sectarian sentiment solely to those living in poor social and economic circumstances; prioritisation of funding for shared cross-community initiatives; and the privileging of purely consensual approaches to problem-solving. Instead he argued the importance of informed public leadership to take personal responsibility for 'outing' sectarian attitudes, systems and structures.

Greater West Belfast had already taken the initiative to structure cross-community organising given both the community infrastructure and pre-existing networks of local activists. The West Belfast Residents' Conference, facilitated by a Commission Officer, had a Steering Committee of representatives from loyalist and nationalist areas. Thirty five Tenants' Associations, Residents' Groups and Ratepayers' Association attended meetings, together with the Redevelopment Sub-Committee of the Shankill Community Council. Loyalist serial activist, contrarian and secretary of the Greater West Belfast Community Association, Sammy Smyth, warned that the Association should not be seen as a 'peace' committee simply because of its cross-community composition. When the First Annual Report of the Greater West Belfast Community Association was published individual area reports referred to a street theatre sketch on the work of the 'Neglectutive' (a play on the Housing Executive); the publication of a report 'Death of a Community' on redevelopment; a lecture on the Urban Motorway plans by Queen's University Professor, Cliff Moughtin, entitled, 'The Best Soil for Motorways is to be found in Working Class Districts'; the non-violent obstruction of a Housing Executive office in Highfield and an overnight sit-down protest in the Housing Executive office in the Shankill Road. This, alongside the standard round of community discos, summer schemes, pensioners' lunches, delegations to Ministers, and regular letter writing that was the stuff of community action.

As Sammy Smyth demanded community input into formal decision-making processes, there was ample evidence of intra-community networking between social activists and the plethora of paramilitary organisations and political parties. A word here or there on various grapevines was not unknown, as in the cross-community campaign against plans for the urban motorway. Hector McMillen, of the Sandy Row Redevelopment Association, complained: 'We don't think the planners care about people. All they seem to care about is roads'. The Greater West Belfast Community Association supported this campaign, as did the unlikely coalition of loyalists and the Official IRA. The latter issued a press statement with the ominous warning that dossiers had already been compiled on the various company directors who were likely to benefit from the construction of the motorway which 'is being forced on the working-class areas of Belfast'. Despite its ceasefire, this 'defence and protect' mode of the Officials may have left Mr McMillen with some explaining to do in his local area. On another occasion when a UDA man suggested that the raised section of the motorway could provide a useful staging post from which to shoot into republican areas, he had to be quietly reminded that republicans might have the same idea vis-à-vis loyalist areas. A more plaintive plea came from a retired soldier whose Sandy Row home suffered serial collateral damage from the large number of bombs at the nearby Europa Hotel (peripatetic home of the international press), who argued that his racing pigeons were living in better conditions than he was, given the perceived official policy of neglect of the area in order to ease the motorway plans.

The 'Cosmetic' campaign

British Army involvement in community relations continued to generate controversy within the Community Relations Commission. The so-
called 'Cosmetic' campaign was alive and well with cheery photographs
of a new playground in the Catholic Short Strand area, built by 12 Field
Squadron 23 – Engineer Regiment. The media coverage of the opening
occurred a week prior to Operation Motorman which ended the 'No-Go'
paramilitary control of local areas with considerable violence. By 1973 individual 'hearts and minds' projects were overseen by military Community
Relations Officers and Civil Liaison Officers (CLOs) who liaised between
the Army and the civil authorities. The latter were mainly civil servants
seconded from the Ministry of Community Relations. One of the many
Commission discussion papers on the subject complained that: 'Perhaps
most disturbing feature of these developments has been the establishment
of Community Relations coordination committees established on the basis
of police districts. These committees are essentially security committees
engaging themselves in "community development"'. The Commission staff
brought their misgivings about the 'Hearts and Minds' campaign to meetings of the independent Community Development Forum. A report was
compiled on the 'Role of the Army in the Community'. Working Party
members felt that this role should be strictly limited and placed within the
context of security issues. It also referred to the widespread suspicion of
army motivation evident in many communities and raised concerns about
the lack of basic community work skills that resulted in army personnel
adopting an overly directive approach. The problem of lack of continuity,
given the rotation of regiments, was flagged up as was the use of Social
Needs funding for army projects.

Within local neighbourhoods, notwithstanding the difficulties,
there were ongoing contacts with the army in order to lodge complaints;
as a source of necessary resources; or, where they were seen as 'our boys'.
Newspaper reports on the army 'Hearts and Minds' campaign were often
enthusiastic. One regiment took things one step further with 'Operation
Playground', planned with almost comic opera punctiliousness by a Major

Smith. The objective was to build play grounds, establish playgroups and train local people of 'good character' in the 'Catholic enclaves of Unity and New Lodge and the Protestant districts of Tiger Bay and Duncairn Gardens' in North Belfast. Regular activities were to be provided for children. The outcome of the plan would be that: 'children (could) walk in safety and troops to patrol on foot'. The good Major outlined how a babysitting group would serve each street, and each high rise flat complex, run by local mothers, grandmothers and pensioners. He suggested that 'normally retired servicemen' could be paid a small wage as play centre caretakers. The initiative, it was felt, would help 'the decent people of the area (to) control affairs and oust the gunmen and terrorists'. Op Playground was to be a joint military, RUC and civil project, with a Community Relations Officer and a project NCO appointed to oversee developments and maintain local communications. Stakeholders were prioritised as – (i) the good people, family men and women, mothers over thirty and pensioners; (ii) the children, concentrating on the under-eights; and (iii) the friendly local shops, as these, with the 'pubs', are centres of local chatter – arguably an admirable list in terms of neighbourhood networking. The Major's memo was appended with maps; lists of Play Centre First Aid box contents; outline plans for the play facilities, with admonishments that equipment should be inspected for health and safety purposes as well as to ensure that it could not be used in riot situations. The area Commission CDO presented a rather different perspective: 'The army were absolutely ruthless in the things they did, for instance they came up with a plan for the New Lodge. Major Smith's plan for the New Lodge we called it – and we'd have a Youth Centre there and a Community Centre there, and Play Ground there, and so on, and everything was cut, pat and dried. And then whenever there had been seven or eight people shot a couple of weeks before, and I decided to cross reference the places where people were shot with the facilities, and it turned out what they had (done), it was imposing community facilities between so-called IRA firing points'. This more critical lens was shared by many in the local communities, leaving Major Smith's plan to be deferred with the redeployment of the 40 Cdo. RM Regiment.

   While the Major Smith plan was an unusually comprehensive approach, the role of the army Community Relations Officer was more often fielding complaints about poor street lighting; smashed windows or the behaviour of their fellow soldiers during house searches or when on patrol. This gave rise to inevitable contradictions as described by a local activist: 'I mean the local Major came in, and he would be very understand-ing about our problems, and would have knocked the shit out of you the next day'. On a lighter note, the vicissitudes of a well-intentioned army community relations exercise between the Divis Flats (Lower Falls) and the Lower Shankill, was described by a youth worker from the Shankill: 'He (the Community Relations Officer) ... decided he would put in the newsagents this wee thing (ad) for a community relations night across the peace line ... And if there was one thing the army knew how to do it was to feed people, so everybody went for a good feed. And we had people come from Divis Towers and we had people went from the Shankill. But to him a sing song meant, you know, "Roll out the Barrel", and all of those songs. So he asked me to get a pianist – terribly posh; and the pianist, she started playing all these tunes; and then this wee woman wanted to sing from the Shankill, and she got up and she decided she would give us "The Sash". And I'm standing thinking this thing is going to disintegrate in a minute. And this wee woman from the Falls, she says "I want to sing" ... and she sang "Kevin Barry". And then another wee woman from the Shankill decided to sing and she was singing about three Scottish soldiers that had been murdered, and then somebody got another one in reply from Divis ... At the end of the night these women from the Shankill decided they wanted to close with "The Queen", and then I thought "Oh, Jesus" ... So he (the Community Relations Officer) said in a month's time what about having another community relations night, only cut out the sing song. But then I knew if anybody had said "sixty-nine" in Bingo, somebody would have said "nineteen" in front of it, or "sixteen" – you know, 1916, and I thought I think you better leave it for a while'. Whatever about the local complica-tions, activities termed community relations were wide-ranging.

As early as 1970, peace activist and journalist, Bob Overy was calling for urgent discussion about the involvement of the British Army in com-munity relations work. The controversy was taken up in the social affairs magazine 'Fortnight', with Hywel Griffiths joining the fray in 1974 to argue that the rationale for the security forces' involvement in community work had nothing in common with the philosophy or approach of the Community Relations Commission. He described the lines of reporting established for Civil Liaison Officers, which he believed fed back into Brigade Headquarters and into the Cabinet Office, in effect ensuring that 'the Cabinet can have a sensitive line to the outreaches of its administration'. Local relationships were not helped by the billeting of British Army units in local schools and community facilities, nor the fact that the Commission had to protest at the arrest of some of its CDOs. One recounted his experience: 'Well I got arrested and beaten up by the army ... We were actually talking about forming a co-op ... to make playground equipment and we heard this bang outside the door, and Jimmy (a local community activist) jumped up to open the door and the next thing the army kicked it in ... Dragged him and me out. Stood us up against the wall, and they had a rubber bullet gun stuck between my (eyes). Split my lip, you know, hit me ... And I remember looking down the barrel of the rubber bullet gun, you know, and it's funny the things that go through your head – I wondered if the bullet came out straight or twisted, and you were very, very, very calm ... There's some form of an almost icy cold. Sort of first sign of being terrified ... And then the next thing the Colonel arrived, and "Sorry old chap that this had to happen to you" ... But that was the sort of thing the hard army did ... and no matter what the army did, it was right'. Efforts to get the army to admit liability for the assault proved unsuccessful. If the good cop, bad cop approach (or in this case soft regiment, hard regiment as epitomised by the Green Howards and the Paras) was understood by local communities, the Commission was less than impressed and compiled a confidential internal report on the arrest and detention of CDOs (May 1973).

At a more modest level, a British Army Major from A Company 1, Cheshire Regiment used the Ballymurphy community newsletter, 'Spotlight', to address local concerns about wild dogs. Writing a letter to the paper he offered to 'put the dogs out of their misery ... But would like to feel it was with the consent of the majority of residents. Perhaps your paper would canvass opinion?' Local response went unrecorded, but at least the offer was made and undoubtedly 'the dogs in the streets' were the first to know of it.

The denouement

If relations between the Community Relations Commission and its government department were somewhat strained, it was the advent of the pioneering power-sharing Northern Ireland Executive in 1974 that administered the coup de grace to what was viewed by a number of civil servants as a cuckoo in the nest of its Ministry. Hywel Griffiths had departed by mid-1972 to the post of Professor in Social Administration in the New University of Ulster, leading one CDO to remark that after his departure the Board of the Commission displayed more interest in 'the tea and cakes' community relations contact work rather than community development. The power-sharing arrangement itself emerged out of negotiations that followed the June 1973 Assembly elections. Brian Faulkner (leader of the new Unionist Party of Northern Ireland) took up office as Premier in an Executive that included the SDLP and Alliance Party Ministers. This experiment in devolved government survived for five months, during the course of which SDLP representative, Ivan Cooper, was Minister for Community Relations. Two months into the post Cooper was extolling the importance of investing in local community centres, given that this encouraged 'responsible local participation in community affairs'. Cooper proceeded to celebrate his fourth month in office by announcing the abolition of the Community Relations Commission. His justification was that power-sharing provided a new relationship between government and local people, consequently there was no longer need for an independent agency and that services delivered by the Commission could more appropriately be managed directly by government departments. He promised that an Advisory Council would be established to replace the Commission, composed of District Councillors, community activists and people with an insight into community relations. The reform of local government would offer an opportunity to mainstream the 'pioneering' community development fieldwork activities of the Commission; while grant-making, research and publications functions would be subsumed into the Ministry for Community Relations.

Discontent amongst a number of unionist political representatives and community organisations supported the ministerial decision. The

Ballysillan Joint Tenants' Association Council, in Upper North Belfast, complained about the allocation of Commission funding, arguing that its area had not received a fair share. A statement alleged that the Commission officers in the area were 'exclusively Roman Catholic', and called on the responsible Minister to set up an enquiry into the matter to – 'Expose the Commission as a front for Roman Catholic propaganda'. Frank Millar, the local Unionist Party Assembly member, supported this demand. Over the course of the debate it became clear that there was unhappiness about the views expressed by the local Commission CDO in an interview with the BBC. The best advice for community workers seemed to be to say the least possible in public to avoid alienating local opinion-formers.

The Commission fieldwork team was also arguably guilty of tactical error when they circulated a discussion paper 'Community Development and Community Relations, some Proposals', which both criticised their Board and called for more resources, while demanding greater independence and grass-roots representation; failing this, they sought the creation of a new independent agency to promote community development. Although some of these criticisms may have been justified in the light of the failure to replace a CDO in the Shankill area and potential watering down of Commission reports, but it was not the time to hand additional ammunition to departmental officials. Outside the Commission there was an increasingly strong lobby for local area resourcing (such as funds for a full-time Coordinator for the GWBCA) rather than expanding the Commission's remit.

The fall of the power-sharing Executive in May 1974 offered little hope of reprieve for the Commission, when Direct Rule Minister, Lord Donaldson, confirmed the decision to disband the agency. Attention now focused on what might replace it. Proposals for the establishment of Community Development Councils were favoured by the Community Development team within the Commission itself. From his university base, Professor Griffiths lobbied for the establishment of a Regional Resources Institute (within a university and grant-aided by the government for three years), with the Institute managing Community Resource Centres, in Belfast and Derry respectively, that would be independent and responsive to local need. There was little support for any proposal offered by the Professor among civil servants that he had previously alienated.

Two conferences were convened in the Institute of Continuing Education, Magee College, in Derry. An initial meeting on 'Politics and Community Action' brought together scores of community activists from both sides of the community across the province. Tom Lovett, one of the organisers, recalled: 'We must have had about 150 people ... I mean it established links between people that lasted for years'. One of the main questions debated was whether community action needed a complementary political strategy, and if so, what this might be. The Derry conference agreed – (i) that a community development agency should be set up with similar grant-making powers to the Community Relations Commission; (ii) community development projects should have access to annual grants; (iii) community development projects should have access to research facilities; (iv) that a distinction should be made between community development projects and neighbourhood groups, with the latter having responsibility for grass roots community work; and (v) that a major community education project should be established in conjunction with relevant higher education bodies.

The second three-day conference hosted in Magee College, took place in August, under the title: 'Community Action – The Way Forward'. The chairperson of the conference Steering Committee was the previous Amalgamated Corporation Tenants' Association leader, Sean Morrissey. The seventy, or so, community groups represented agreed on the importance of effective cross-community coordination. After a keynote address delivered by Paddy Doherty, from Derry, a discussion took place on the role of paramilitaries within the community setting. Eleven conference resolutions were passed, ranging from a call for the end of internment to demanding a comprehensive community development programme. Again, the emphasis was on the establishment of an independent agency with representation from community organisations. Arguments were made in favour of setting up independent Law Centres in Northern Ireland and for community radio. It was agreed that a Steering Committee would take forward the recommendation for the structuring of an organisation to represent, as fully as possible, all the community groups across the province.

The conference was not without controversy, particularly when a Derry participant, Gordon Hagerty, queried whether the participation was representative. In response to shouts of 'Why?', Mr Hagerty replied 'It is a job to find a Protestant here'. The chairperson called on all the Protestants in the room to stand up. When fewer than twenty people stood up the question was asked: 'Why are they in a minority here when they are in a majority in Northern Ireland?' Grasping a piece of chalk, the ever ebullient Paddy 'Bogside' wrote on the blackboard: 'Where are the Protestants?'

As community discussions continued, the Ministry of Community Relations was busy developing its own scenarios. A Northern Ireland Office Press Notice stated that the government had reviewed the whole machinery of community development and decided that what was required was a tripartite alliance of community groups, local government and central government agencies. The importance of community associations and self-help groups working in close cooperation with local authorities was underlined. In passing it was pointed out that the work undertaken to date at local level had been very necessary, but that it was primarily community development, not community relations. Further consideration of how the proposed tripartite relationship would work would pass into MOG ('machinery of government') for more detailed elaboration. The continued remit of the Ministry's own Community Relations representatives was restated as being a point of liaison between local communities, the security forces, and both central and local government, enhanced by allowing them the power 'to move resources for the benefit of the community'. The wheels of MOG continued to grind through the autumn. In the event, the Department of Community Relations was merged with the Department of Education, in the stated interest of bringing together responsibilities for education, recreation, culture, youth and social facilities. A tentative expression of interest by the Department of Health & Social Services to frame community work as part of social work (i.e. 'dealing with the social problems of families and communities as well as those of individuals') was rejected, although the latter could provide assistance to voluntary organisations and community groups involved in the field of community care. The Permanent Secretary for Community Relations, Mr Slinger, also had the satisfaction of dismissing Professor Griffiths' proposed Institute of Community Development: 'On the subject of Professor Griffiths' proposed Institute, I find myself unclear as to where he is trying to get to. I would support an independent body whose clear function was to advise and help government to deal with community problems. If, however, and I speak with some feeling about our experience of the Community Relations Commission in earlier days, we are talking of an independent body which is to act completely independently with the community groups and without very much reference to central government or the elected District Councils, then I would have considerable reservations'. In other words, independence of the system was suspect.

The warning flagged up by a civil servant adviser, Ken Bloomfield, that: 'It is clear that many of the local groups are suspicious of the motivation of some District Councils ... not without reason'. was ignored. By July 1975, the Moyle Report of the Joint Working Party on Sporting and Recreation Provision of District Councils extended the role of the Councils from that of providing recreation and community centres to allow them to employ Community Service Officers. The Moyle Report, named for the then Minister, also made provision for a Standing Advisory Conference of Community Associations. The Minister praised the 'Many new groups of people anxious to help their local community to assert its identity and to improve its physical and environmental in various ways. It is these groups to which the statutory services must reach out because their help will be invaluable in building a better community'. The key, however, was to forge a direct relationship between community groups and government without independent intermediary agencies blurring the appropriate appreciation of statutory support provided.

Community relations was given a desk in the Department of Education, which based in its North Down headquarters was characterised by a senior civil servant as: 'Education were ... separated not only geographically, but in thinking from much of the civil service ... You had the odd individual there who was trying very hard (to promote community relations) and you know, they were stuffed into a branch or a division simply because they had to be watered and housed somewhere – but no interest in what they were doing'. It was to take a decade and more before the societal challenge of community relations was dusted down and considered in any serious manner. In the interim, community relations became constrained by the physicality of the growing number of 'peacewalls', across which community groups jealously eyed up developments in each other's areas. An article in the *Andersonstown News* was illustrative: 'Now it is 1975 and the Shankill Leisure Centre is designed. Construction will soon commence. The Whiterock Leisure Centre has been cancelled but the Shankill one is to go ahead. It's tough luck for the people of Ballymurphy and Turf Lodge, but then Catholics are used to being losers'. Highlighted by an increased awareness of territoriality, the politics of Tweedledum-and-Tweedledee resource allocation was evident.

Life beyond officialdom

For many activists the travails of the Community Relations Commission were irrelevant. Socialist direct action became the order of the day in the early 1970s, when Republican Club members (associated with the Official IRA) began a campaign of 'people's initiatives' that ranged from commandeering a bus on the Falls Road and abolishing fares on what was now dubbed 'a people's bus', to invading a Christian Brothers' secondary school in West Belfast to present a list of 'pupils' demands'. During the three hour occupation the balaclava-camouflaged teenagers burnt the stock of school canes. Not to be outdone Derry had 'the people's stool' – a modest, wooden bench that a local wag had inscribed with tongue-in-cheek socialist graffiti arguably 'taking a hand' out of the 'People's Shops' which the Official Republican Movement was promoting. In West Belfast, Provisional Sinn Féin activists supported the People's Co-op, which had been operating in Andersonstown since 1972. Although many of these developments owed more to individual activists than central political direction, initiatives continued. The *Andersonstown News* was established as a community newspaper that later grew into a sustainable media group and the Black Taxi movement also demonstrated staying power. Recycled London black taxis became a ubiquitous feature on the Falls and Shankill Roads, offering people cheap fares in shared taxis, that could be flagged down along a set route. The venture addressed both public transport needs and the challenge of creating jobs for released internees. The appearance of second – and even third – hand black taxis joined the military jeeps and other traffic that wended their way along the two symbolic thoroughfares. The UVF launched the service in the Shankill, emphasising that the taxi drivers would be providing a service at a reasonable price and that anyone attempting to interfere with them would be 'dealt with'. By this stage, the Falls Road service had been operating successfully for a period of time, although rumours were circulating that the drivers had to pay 'road rent' to the Provisional IRA. UVF spokesman, Capt. William Johnston, announced that there would be no black taxi charge for pensioners on production of their concessionary pass card.

If this was political action with a community twist the impact of violence continued to be felt. There was rarely a consistent single community view about the activities of 'the boys', the local defenders and part-time paramilitaries, as opinion shifted depending on the prevailing circumstances. One young woman shuddered: 'All I recall from those days (the early '70s) really was a feeling of going out into the darkened streets ... (the feeling) of terror. You could nearly taste it in the air, you could nearly feel it. It was absolute, stark intimidation and terror, and feeling very much abandoned and defenceless with no security whatsoever ... For those who were trying to find a community development or a political – you know a peace process, political process – it was nigh impossible, and you were on a hiding to nothing, and you were a lone voice'. On the other side of the divide a young man whose family supported the Northern Ireland Labour Party explained: 'There was this temptation to be like all the rest, to ensure that the thinking that your father, or your own thinking in fact, wasn't revealed'. Local graffiti sent out an unequivocal message in North Belfast: 'Don't be Vague, Shoot a Taig (Catholic)'; more than adequately answered by West Belfast graffiti: 'God made Catholics, but the armalite made them equal' – a reference to the high velocity guns that became a favoured weapon of the IRA.

As communities turned their eyes inwards, fearing to venture far due to sectarian assassinations and 'drive-by' shootings, there was a growth industry of informal Social Clubs, offering drink and a sense of identity often aligned with specific political and/or paramilitary persuasions. Targets themselves, club and pub fortification became an art form; breeze block holding porches were fitted with cameras, double doors, security men and electronic buzzers to gain entrance. Once inside the visitor was subjected to careful scrutiny by regulars through the back bar mirror. Clubs were also community knowledge hubs, recycling rumour and suspicion to reinforce community protocols that were breached at personal risk. 'Tarring and feathering', more horrific in practice than in description, became a feature of the rough justice meted out locally, particularly to young women who dated British soldiers that were warned by graffiti: 'Soldier Dolly Beware' and 'Touts Out'. Doffing a cap to the idea that justice must be seen to be done IRA statements explained how 'a sentence' passed on the respective offender had been duly carried out in pursuit of revolutionary morality. The UDA in Londonderry went one further reporting that three men were arraigned in front of a UDA court charged with the crime of impersonating UDA members. The case was heard by a hooded UDA Major; prosecuted by a hooded UDA officer, and the accused were defended by an UDA officer of their choice – also hooded. One of the accused was found not guilty; another sentenced to sweep the streets in the local housing estate, and the third forced to do physical training in the street.

If the refrain of the song 'Whatever you say, say nothing' was appropriate, life adapted out of necessity. For those 'from the other side' it was all too easy to misinterpret what was going on behind 'their' barricades. When two Protestant sisters walked out one warm summer evening, they heard numbers being called on the other side of a barricade in the nearby nationalist/republican area. 'That's them ones training', whispered one. In reality it was a game of bingo in full swing between people sitting at their doorsteps. Similarly, a Shankill Road youth worker organising a summer camp caused raised eyebrows when making the vote of thanks to those who helped: 'I had to get up and thank the police for giving their canvas and their tentage ... And I had to thank the local paramilitaries for sleeping out to guard the tentage'. The local church minister was not amused. Across in West Belfast, Springhill Community House launched a community theatre with Fr. Des Wilson recalling: 'It was great to hear people laughing at the military and laughing at that nonsense. Because there was a war on – it was part that people shouldn't feel inferior again, so the theatre was very important from that point of view'. The theatre group involved local people, but also the Chairperson of the Shankill Community Council, a woolly haired Church of Ireland cleric from south of the Border. Brain Smeaton double-jobbed as Chairperson of the Greater West Belfast Community Association, and with wayward energy scuttled between the Council; political discussions in Andy Tyrie's UDA headquarters; the People's Theatre in Ballymurphy; and a Youth Club ('the Nic') on the Shankill. The People's Theatre featured 'Thompson in Tir na nÓg', a comic tale of a true blue loyalist who mistakenly finds himself in the fabled 'Land of Youth', and the ensuing attempts of the inhabitants (a collection of legendary Irish figures) to find out if he is an Irish hero. After considerable misunderstandings the Orangeman is dispatched out of Tir na nÓg, and peace reigns once again. The rationale for the People's Theatre was that neither money nor big buildings were needed to have a theatre of your own. Meanwhile even the walls were talking to walls, and graffiti 'No Pope Here!' was answered by graffiti 'Lucky old Pope!'.

CHAPTER 4

Politics and Community Action: A Delicate Balance

Maurice Hayes was surprised to see the stocked crates of Guinness when he visited the civil service college at Sunningdale in December 1974. The light dawned when the Sunningdale Agreement was announced some weeks later. The New Year edition of the *Irish News* trumpeted: 'The historic first meeting of the Northern Ireland new Executive at Government Buildings, Stormont'. The Ulster Workers' Council (UWC) Strike brought down this exercise in power-sharing five months later, in a coup that avoided the name. The Ulster Workers' Council was a pot pourri of loyalism and unionism that included trade unionists from key industrial sectors dominated by Protestant workforces (electricity, gas and fuel distribution), together with paramilitary organisations and a dolly mixture of unionist politicians. They gelled around fears over a proposed Council of Ireland which introduced an Irish dimension, but also objected to power-sharing. The UWC Strike was launched on 15 May 1974, with the declared objective of consigning the Agreement to the dust bin of history.

Glenn Barr, by then an elected Assembly member, UDA confidante and Chairman of the Strike Committee, explained how paramilitary activists organised pickets alongside collecting and distributing food supplies in their areas. Barr spoke about how: 'People talk about this "brilliant planning". The "brilliant planning" went on from hour to hour, and we were responding on many occasions to what other people were doing. We just went along day to day and that's how the whole thing ran'. As electricity supplies dwindled, a planned march back to work that was staged by the official Trade Union Movement, attracted only limited support.

Initial uncertain community reaction was followed, depending on which proverbial foot one kicked with, by resignation, enthusiasm or anger. The smoke from barbeques wafted on both sides of the peace walls. In the Shankill: 'Everybody had the barbies on the street, and the barbeques, you know – it was a collective thing. You supplied the potatoes, somebody else supplied the meat – or the meat was sometimes extracted from vans that were hijacked ... But it was always the women that were manning them'. West Belfast was a mirror image: 'Colin Glenn Bacon factory was on the Suffolk Road at the time. They hijacked anything that moved ... Barbeques were the fashion ... the first time in their lives that people knew what a barbeque was ... We drew up rotas'. Organising area supplies became an important community duty, with self-service hijackings a default fall-back. One enterprising group attracted local wrath after hi-jacking butter and ice-cream from a van: 'They started to charge people two pounds for a pound of butter ... So we thought we'll teach these bastards a lesson ... So we set two blow torches and started melting the lot'. The importance of community solidarity was forcibly underlined.

The Secretary of State went on television to declare that there could be only one government, just as women on the Shankill demanded the closure of public houses. They argued that if the men were not going to work, then there would be no drink. The following day, the men retaliated by issuing their own ultimatum: if there was no beer for the men, then there would be no bingo for the women. In passing judgement the UWC Strike Committee decided that public houses would close as they were not deemed an essential service; an edict that did not apply to bingo clubs, although bookmakers (betting shops) were caught in the sweep. This judgement was later amended to allow pubs and clubs to open from 6.00pm. Loyalist women in Londonderry were having none of it, flour bagging the customers of bars that remained open. In republican areas public houses reported a brisk trade.

Ignoring the pleas of his nationalist colleagues, Brian Faulkner resigned as Premier collapsing the power-sharing Executive around him. Three days prior to this, an ill-advised broadcast by Prime Minister, Harold Wilson, angered the Unionist population who interpreted his characterisation of the UWC strikers as 'spongers' on the British tax-payer, as a general attack on unionism. Many flaunted slivers of sponge on their coat lapels and an exhilarated Glenn Barr exclaimed: 'I thought great stuff. This is fantastic. We'll make him an honorary member of the UDA after this ... Anything after that and we couldn't go wrong'. In loyalist areas bonfires blazed long into the night celebrating the fall of the Executive. In contrast, while republicans had been dismissive of the Sunningdale Agreement, nationalists pondered the implications of the loyalist strike. Maurice Hayes, appointed a civil service adviser after his service with the Community Relations Commission, offered a nuanced assessment: 'Catholics could bring down Stormont by refusal to be governed; Protestants held an effective veto over any proposed alternative'. It was back to the constitutional drawing board.

With the power-sharing Executive crumbling around him, Direct Rule Secretary of State, Merlyn Rees, pondered how the phased release of internees might be facilitated by community-based reintegration programmes. A cross-community selection of community and trade union activists were invited to meet with Minister of State, Stan Orme, to discuss options, although proposals later foundered in the confusion of the politics of the time and related paranoia.

Just because you're paranoid …

People at community level quickly realised the truth that being paranoid did not mean that 'they' were not out to get you. As early as 1971, British Army Brigadier, Frank Kitson, published his book 'Low Intensity operations', which focused on methods to counter armed opposition to the state, including 'psy-ops' (psychological operations); the collection and use of intelligence information; and the disruption of opposition movements. The book registered good sales in Northern Ireland where Kitson was blamed, or credited, with inspiring the black arts of counter-intelligence and surveillance. Detailed local information was collated on boys from the age of twelve, and girls over fourteen years, much of it drawn from the stop, search and questioning of young people; in effect an exercise in alienation. A covert Military Reconnaissance (also known as Reaction) Force (MRF) was established to supplement army operations.

The need for intelligence to feed coordinated political understanding was seen as important. A senior civil servant described the Secretary of

State as: 'The king pin – governor, prime minister, commander-in-chief, negotiator, arbiter, host, all rolled into one'. However the institutional knowledge of civil servants was also critical, as when one had to brief a new Secretary of State on the Loyal Order, the Apprentice Boys of Derry – 'I had to point out that these were not apprentices, these were not boys, and many of them did not come from Derry'. Eventually a Policy Coordinating Committee (PCC) was established to 'reconcile inter-departmental conflict and look at inter-departmental issues', given that the Secretary of State was bombarded with advice from the Northern Ireland Office, intelligence agencies, the security forces, Northern Ireland government departments, and, of course, the Cabinet Office in Downing Street.

The Northern Ireland Office (NIO), for its part, operated on a number of fronts, described by one retired NIO official as – the Political Section, the Security Section and a third section: 'The funny people'. There were reported sightings of the 'funny people' in the attic offices of Stormont Castle and in the considerably more salubrious Laneside, a large and desirable residence in Hollywood which housed a number of people whose work teetered on the cusp of their official job descriptions. Commenting, with the benefit of hindsight, a NIO Permanent Secretary reflected – 'I didn't think the IRA could absolutely be beaten because there had to be a political settlement of one kind or another ... In the meantime I thought it could be contained. My own view is that if you're dealing with a terrorist organisation at some remove you always ought to have a dialogue going because the basic problem about terrorism is that it's very difficult to snuff out ... We can't go around shooting everybody we think is a terrorist ... We are, after all, a parliamentary democracy, and we did behave throughout as such, which is a very, very important point. But if a political situation made it possible, one should never discount the need to have dialogue, although one should be extremely careful and extremely clear about what you were trying to do if you did'. This approach was to be operationalised, in a variety of ways.

One unforeseen side effect of the work of the 'Funny Section' was described by Col. Robin Eveleigh in his study on 'Peacekeeping in a Democratic Society' (1978). When an army battalion commander found himself blindsided by lack of official information concerning NIO contacts, he set up his own 'political intelligence unit' to discover current government and NIO policy. He might have usefully scanned the guest lists for dinner at Laneside to round off his enquiries. Other accounts (including one by McDonald & Cusack in 'Loyalists') refer to two men turning up to a poorly attended housing action meeting wearing casual trousers and tweed jackets. They maintained a low profile until an army Community Relations Officer walked in. To the consternation of some, and the amusement of others, the two men snapped to attention in the presence of the officer. These often comical accounts were soured by the more sordid details of the real undercover war, fought on all sides with teeth, claws and not a small degree of courage. For those caught in the no-man's land of this war it was a shifting and frightening place; as suspicions heightened, community activists – particularly 'outsiders' or those off-side with local certainties – could pay the cost. One retired British soldier, known locally as Nick the Brit, was assassinated by republicans when working as a Youth Worker in Ardoyne. The accusation of being an informer or an agent was a potential death sentence, and the power of rumour, or misinformation, could be deadly.

The small, highly motivated staff of the Northern Ireland Research Institute were caught up in the accusatory crossfire. A local community activist remembered them as: 'The brightest people we had ever met, they were unbelievable ... They had come from different places but their connection was left-wing politics ... They were live wires, they came in and within days they had done things that we were spending years making connections ... They made the connections between community action on the ground, academic research and administration, and ... they took it to a different level'. In its support for self-help activism the Institute worked with people on both sides of the community divide, adopting a class analysis to complement an understanding of the conflict. One such activist confirmed how: 'They were able to work alongside us as community workers ... They were also doing the political work with the Provos and the churches ... They were very open'. However, the sensitive issue of policing, and possible community alternatives, proved to be the downfall of the Institute. An Institute associate, Gill Boehringer, drafted a paper which suggested replacing the security remit of the RUC with locally based policing structures capable of developing and maintaining an integrated 'social defence programme'. It was proposed that this should include

District Councils as well as tenants' organisations, redevelopment committees, 'Peoples' Assemblies and vigilante groups'. Media reports unsettled
both politicians and policy makers. The concept of community policing
was already divisive, as the Bogside Community Association found to
its cost when it held a community referendum on the issue. Boehringer
came under attack from two unlikely media sources – the *Sunday Times*
and *Republican News*. The latter dubbed the Northern Ireland Research
Institute as a front for the British Army and the CIA, an accusation that
was vigorously denied. An Institute statement concluded: 'To the best of
our knowledge the allegations made against us do not originate from the
Provisional IRA but from a group of individuals whose motives are not
clear to us'. The question of who was who, and who carried what weight
was often a moot point. In this case it served to destroy a very effective
community support structure as a number of the Institute associates had
to leave Northern Ireland for fear of physical attack.

Meanwhile the staple elements in community programming continued
to organise children's summer schemes, housing protests, youth provision and
community newsletters. Organisations associated with paramilitary organisations raised funds to subsidise their prisoners' welfare. A brisk trade in
prison-made handicrafts supplemented the income streams derived from less
orthodox sources. One UDA member, born in the West Indies, had joined
after a friend was killed in an IRA bomb. When he was arrested for bank
robbery during a fundraising sortie, he queried the identification given that
he had been masked. The police detective arresting him replied that he had
forgotten to wear gloves. Black UDA operators were a rarity in Mid-Ulster.

Analysing the UWC Strike

As victors of the successful UWC strike, Andy Tyrie, UDA Chairman and
leading member of the Strike Council acknowledged: "74 woke me up to
what was going on and we needed an alternative. We needed to look at
what was going on here regarding government and politics, housing and

everything else ... and we were looking for alternatives ... We spent a load of time talking to people ... Things were different after the '74 strike ... People wanted answers; they wanted to know who they were, what they were'. There were reports (some true, some not) of loyalists meeting republicans and gatherings organised to include the most unlikely assortment of participants. In many cases core facilitation was provided by a small group of former Community Relations Commission CDOs. A CRC neighbourhood office, in North Belfast, became a networking hub newly branded as the Northern Ireland Community Development Centre. It was staffed by Florence, the unflappable administrator, and the 'two Joes' – Joe Camplisson and Joe Mulvenna. Both ex-CDOs engaged in conversations (often muttered) with activists wearing a variety of loyalist and republican hats and caps. The Centre focused on conflict resolution, drawing a distinction between conflict resolution and community development: 'It's one or the other in terms of the strategy. The community development strategy calls for a low level engagement but the conflict resolution approach ... is high profile, facilitating movement across the table'. The contact work was at least partially built on the relationship forged between UDA Chairman, Andy Tyrie and Joe C.

There had been efforts to minimise the impact of violence on local communities over a period. Tyrie used Camplisson to seek assurances from the IRA concerning the safety of Protestants in certain areas of the North. Joe explained: 'If the IRA were to do this and that, then he, Andy Tyrie would be able to move in a way that would prevent the pressures on Catholic communities in South-East Antrim ...' – where the minority Catholic community was particularly vulnerable. The agreement reached provided for identifiable contacts and an exchange of telephone numbers in order to establish an effective back channel communication. This was activated in 1975 when two UDA men were kidnapped and the blame placed on republicans. Threatened UDA retaliation was averted when IRA assurances of non-involvement were accepted; it later became known that the men had been killed by the UVF. Tyrie saw the contacts established during this period as small but important steps. He was acutely conscious of the deniability of the intermediaries to avert any accusations that the UDA were talking directly to republicans.

Loyalists had been involved in a cross-community residential, held in Port Salon (Co. Donegal), in September 1974, where community activists were joined by academics, churchmen and individuals with an understanding of the thinking of various republican and loyalist paramilitary groups. One participant suggested: 'If Stormont had been able to debate at this level there would have been no trouble'. In addition to the carefully negotiated agenda, the choice of music during the evening was helpful. Tom Lovett, from Magee College Derry, noted how: 'It melted the ice – you got people telling jokes, you got people singing, it got them to feel that in many respects they began to feel that they were the same sort of people – and that was important'. The traditional Irish céili music was supplemented by a Derry musician rendering the Orange anthem, 'The Sash', in Gaelic. Three days before this meeting the UDA instructed its supporters to boycott right-wing British National Front rallies against the IRA. In this post UWC strike period Tyrie's role was particularly important in creating space for political analysis. An internal loyalist three-day conference, which excluded unionist politicians, was organised to discuss the way forward. This show of independence rankled.

As the UDA considered its position, one of those involved highlighted the constraining nature of the Northern Ireland state: 'Most of the people who held office, even the civil servants, were ex-soldiers or sailors, or whatever it was, held commissions. The same with the politicians here – so you almost had a military structure the right whole way through here. And with a military structure you generally hand the whole thing back up, it just goes right up the line ... We didn't know how to use the power and the authority we had at the time'. A number of diverse initiatives were given the go-ahead: Harry Chicken pioneered the establishment of the Ulster Community Action Group (UCAG); talks continued with British officials in Laneside; and the decision was taken to engage in external diplomatic missions. One involved Harry Chicken, Glenn Barr and Tommy Lyttle travelling with a trade delegation to Libya in order to dissuade the Libyan leader, Col. Gadhafi, from supporting the IRA. On their return, the UDA men were summoned to Laneside to be reprimanded by a senior Foreign Office official. In fact, Libyan offers of financial support for political development in the North had already been refused by the UDA.

Not to be ignored, the UVF journal, 'Combat', reported on the support that the East Antrim Loyalist Front was giving to community projects in Monkstown, Rathcoole, Carrickfergus and Larne, with a loyalist co-op opening in Rathcoole to supply household goods at reduced prices. Action against local hooliganism and intimidation was promised; and advice services and evening classes were referenced in Carrickfergus and Newtownabbey. Despite these developments, experience on the ground was still scarred by sectarian killings, bombings and intimidation. In some small number of cases an enforced change of housing brought improvement – 'We squatted in a flat in Springmartin. Now the flat itself was beautiful; we moved out of a little two-up, two-down house, no such thing as hot water, bathroom, none of that. We moved into a most beautiful flat that had everything. My mother thought she had landed in Hollywood ... It even had a red telephone in the hall'. The downside was that Springmartin was located on an interface with Catholic West Belfast, consequently: 'Outside the estate was a dump ... The army was billeted in Springmartin at that time, in the school ... We couldn't even get the bins emptied because we were so near the peace line they would refuse to come to empty the bins ... The Housing Executive collected the rents from Springmartin from a safe distance'. It was these conditions that motivated two local women to set up the Springmartin Action Group.

The 1975 ceasefires and the 'rebel hotlines'

The delicate shuttle diplomacy conducted by Protestant clergymen, initiated by the Irish Council of Churches representative Rev. William Arlow, facilitated an IRA ceasefire in the winter of 1974/75. This was duly denounced by the Rev. Ian Paisley: 'Mr Arlow has drunk the heady wine of ecumenism so deeply that his mind is in a stupor and his eyes are blind to the plain unadulterated facts'. It was left to the British government and the Republican Movement to quibble over what were 'the facts'. As government ministers denied direct contact with 'terrorists', unionist politicians

became increasingly apprehensive. By summer 1975, Catholic soldiers stationed in Ballymurphy were able to march in formation to attend Sunday
Mass in the local parish church. An IRA ceasefire had been confirmed and
hotlines established between Sinn Féin offices and the British administration for ease of communication – local Incident Centres branded by Rev.
Ian Paisley as 'rebel hotlines'. A school girl volunteered in a West Belfast
centre: 'It was a very old building and there were lots of floors in it and
there were these tiny little attics ... I was up on the floor with this great big
phone linked to Whitehall and basically I had to sit by this phone in case
it rang ... and of course I'd got five minutes training for this job ... We were
the main Centre and we had to log incidents. So if a soldier was hassling
somebody in Ballymurphy, or whatever, we had to make a note of that
and then it had to be checked out ... But I always remember this one time
this thing came in from the British Army about the dogs in Turf Lodge
and Ballymurphy giving them a very hard time; and I remember just being
cheeky and ... contacting them and saying our dogs were not responsible.
Because all the messages were our such and such were not responsible, or
whatever it was ... I got the head bit off me for sending it'.

The respite in confrontation between the IRA and the British Army
allowed space for internal republican feuding, with the Official IRA (formally on ceasefire) squaring up against the INLA (Irish National Liberation
Army), and subsequently against the Provisional IRA. Things were little
better within loyalism, where there was both internal UDA feuding and
clashes between the UDA and the UVF. The republican feuds placed the
Incident Centres in the line of fire with the school girl volunteer cast as an
unwitting heroine: 'I was up in the attic when a feud broke out between
the Provisionals and the Officials. And unbeknownst to me the Movement
vacated the Incident Centres and forgot about me ... And I walked down
to have a check on something and there was no one there, it was like the
Marie Celeste. And then this man came in later on ... and I got noted for
my exemplary bravery for staying by my post. It was a joke because I didn't
have a clue what was going on'. Undoubtedly she wasn't the only one.

For its part the Northern Ireland Office reluctantly shelved their spin
doctors' idea of killing Northern Ireland with fun. It was decided to call
off a Morecambe and Wise comedy offensive given the politically brittle

atmosphere. When the Secretary of State declared the ceasefires at an end in the autumn, closing the Incident Centres and banning the UVF, the Centre on the Falls Road claimed that it had dealt with over 1,600 violations of the truce. The windows were peppered with bullet holes and around one was written: 'This is an unauthorised peep hole – please use only author-ised peep holes'. The end of the ceasefire arrangements changed little in practice as a Northern Ireland Office official pointed out: 'I used to laugh, because during their time of being de-proscribed whenever you rang from the Minister's office they would say "UVF Headquarters", which was in the Eagle Café. And then when they were prescribed, the next day it was "Eagle Café" ... Nothing changed and the business was done'. Controversy continued to rage about the nature of the business. By 1976 the British Government took the initiative to introduce the new official narrative of 'normalisation, criminalisation and Ulsterisation', in effect throwing down the gauntlet to those who saw the violence as political in nature.

Creating space for dialogue

Whatever its difficulties, the 1975 ceasefire allowed space for cross-community contact between loyalist and republican activists with a sprin-kling of community representatives. The two Joes worked to identify issues that were both practical and offered cover for networking. One such issue was job creation and the potential of cooperatives. With the help of contacts mediated through the North Belfast office cross-community and cross-border links were forged. Products from both loyalist and republican aligned co-operatives were displayed at an exhibition in Strokestown (Co. Roscommon), organised by a local priest. A Dutch organisation, 'Hulp Noord Ierland' (which initially hosted holidays for children), made available the De Haaf Centre in Bergan for study visits. Fourteen UDA members joined a party of twenty-six that visited Holland in March 1975 to discuss peaceful coexistence and co-operative development. The *Belfast Telegraph* got wind of the fact that 'Thirty delegates from Provisional Sinn Féin, Official Republican

Movement, UDA and the outlawed UVF' were meeting in Holland. The newspaper headlines provoked one DUP councillor to roundly condemn the loyalist participants, thundering that they were 'stepping on the graves of those who have been brutally murdered by the IRA'.

Two founder members from the Whiterock Co-operative were invited to attend the seminar and unbeknownst walked into a hornets' nest stirred by the media coverage. One admitted that he was scared, but weathering the controversy he had important messages to share with the loyalists – 'I was trying to sell them the idea ... that OK they had credibility in their own areas, but the credibility came from strength behind the gun type of thing. It didn't come from involvement with the people. I was selling the idea that they could strengthen their own situation and empower their own people and improve their own lot. Because they didn't have any grassroots politics they depended on the major Unionist party'. This was cooperative development with a twist to its tail, although it was undoubtedly less than helpful when Sinn Féin claimed political credit for the Andersonstown Cooperative, in *An Phoblacht* some weeks later. To add insult to injury they recommended the approach as a shining example to loyalist Springmartin.

The message delivered by the West Belfast men was not a million miles away from the conclusions being drawn by Andy Tyrie who encouraged the establishment of the Ulster Community Action Group (UCAG). The main aim of UCAG (launched in March 1976) was to address community issues. Supported by more than thirty community and tenants' groups in the Greater Belfast area, an Executive Committee was advised by a forty-member council. The vice chairperson held open the possibility that at some future point UCAG might connect across the sectarian divide. Within a month of its launch a UCAG deputation was meeting government ministers at Stormont. Although the delegation stressed the independence of the group from any paramilitary organisation, an extensive file had already been compiled by officials, marked confidential. It included a note written by a NIO official: 'As you will know UCAG has close connections with the UDA. It could be argued that this therefore makes it a sinister organisation which could be used for malevolent purposes, particularly in a political strike situation. I believe, however, that the positive aspects should not be under estimated. Anything which can turn paramilitary organisations away from violence is to be welcomed. Further, it is important that those connected with community development should be genuinely in touch with grassroots opinion. I therefore submit that we would have nothing to lose by officials seeing UCAG IN THE VERY NEAR FUTURE (sic). This as you will be aware should be very helpful politically'. In the event, the UCAG representatives complained about rent increases; argued the need for more community centres; and affirmed their commitment to combat vandalism. Leaflets circulated in loyalist areas of East and South Belfast called for local Community Action Groups to support communities to take responsibility for the good and peaceful organisation of neighbourhoods.

One UCAG delegate described the interest shown by NIO officials – Oh yes, we were in Laneside quite a lot ... I suppose most of them were MI5 or MI6 or whatever. We weren't stupid, but again we had nothing to hide; we were dealing with a political issue which was community development in the areas which we had responsibility for ... We stayed out of the hard political stuff ... Our interest was in getting them to assist, where they could, and to use their influence with the departments ... But we weren't that naïve to believe that, you know, they just wanted to talk to us ... They had their own way of making their minds up about questions they asked you that might seem perfectly innocent ..." The NIO was intrigued by the relationship between the UDA and UCAG as well as by UDA internal political discussions that Tyrie had created the deniable space for. A leading member of the UDA Inner Council was a regular guest at social functions in Laneside: 'We were invited to dinners, dos, gatherings, political talks ... We were also meeting government ministers on a regular basis, and it was a strange sort of thing because we'd be going in maybe the front door and there'd be somebody else going out the back ... We went because we thought this is great stuff, we're talking to the right sort of people. What they done they had two scribes sitting, and they continuously wrote everything we said ... The system here was really fascinating because they were continually profiling everybody here – but we didn't know this ... We took it for granted that they would be doing it to the IRA, but they wouldn't do it to the loyalists'. Flippant remarks over the post prandial drinks had to be tempered with caution.

Structuring community action

Pre-dating UCAG, a broader range of community activists met to discuss
how community action might be coordinated regionally, with consultation
resulting in the establishment of CONI – Community Organisations for
Northern Ireland. Filling the vacuum left by the demise of the Northern
Ireland Community Relations Commission, there was a belief that tenants' associations and community groups needed to cooperate to achieve
maximum impact. Tom Lovett reflected: 'There was a division, you see, a lot
of us felt if it could become a movement, like the Civil Rights Movement,
but that was one of the things that the Protestant representatives feared ...
So others wanted something less ambitious – something more like an
organisation that provided a focal point for those involved in community
action, but at the same time provided a resource and assistance – so CONI
really came from (this) ... There was a lot of debate about it ... There was
people who were very much on the left and who would have seen community development and community action as a third way, as something
that might make a major contribution ... And others whose ambitions
were very much more modest and were afraid of anything that would be
called a movement. Also I think the politics was such that they would be
a bit wary of anything that was left wing'. The divisions persisted despite a
sense of urgency about the need to build consensus around issues of shared
concern in otherwise divided communities.

   A delegate at an early conference was conscious of the difference in
emphasis: 'I think CONI was important for getting people together from
all disparate parts ... if that was the only thing it did, that was good ...
I know some people argued that it did provide a basis for Protestant and
Catholic working-class community contact, I think it did but that wasn't
why it did it'. Recognising the tensions, CONI was careful not to claim
to represent member groups. It confirmed that 'CONI will not seek to lay
down policy binding on its members; each will remain free to act as it sees
fit'. The preferred approach to UCAG was one of cordial relations. CONI
itself was committed: 'To work for community development; to promote
community harmony and be non-party and non-sectarian; to promote

the well-being of all the people of Northern Ireland without distinction; to foster facilities in the interests of social well-being, health, recreation and leisure; and very importantly to provide a central office to facilitate groups' – in short, a very full programme of work.

Delegates came together in Portrush in 1976. A delegate from the Shankill remembered: 'The two bigwigs – because I was only a young lad – were Paddy Doherty and Sammy Smyth ... And Sammy ... wanted everything tied down, he had an entirely structured approach to it ... He sat up half the night, when everyone was drinking, writing motions to put next morning. And Paddy Doherty, he got up and said "This is a great white horse ... This is a horse with no reins, just let it go" ... And I'm thinking, "Where do I stand with these two?" I think I came down on Paddy Doherty's side'. The depiction of Sammy, as seeking clarity about power and relationships was in contrast to 'Paddy Bogside', who displayed the unfettered imagination of the 'outsider'. This difference was indicative of a disparity in community-state perceptions and circumstances that haunted not only CONI, but future attempts at cross-community organising.

Two issues on which there was shared concern were the thorny issue of housing finances and the ongoing campaign against the Belfast motorway plans. A CONI Housing Action Group pressed for a root and branch review of the structuring of public expenditure for much needed social housing. A petition called for a public enquiry, but official enquiries focused instead on whether any paramilitary groups had benefitted from Housing Executive contracts. CONI also supported the Belfast Community Group Steering Committee that was campaigning for a public enquiry on the Urban Motorway plans. The Steering Group invited over an English expert, John Tyme, who made a long and eloquent submission to the Enquiry and then chained himself to a desk in protest, resulting in the hearings being adjourned. The protestors sang 'We Shall Overcome' and sent out for fish suppers to fuel a sit-in. Although the Enquiry report was scathing of the protest, lobbying delivered concessions which reprieved a number of inner city communities from demolition. The roadway that was finally constructed was often viewed as transport policy through a security lens; creating a buffer zone between the conflict-prone communities and the commercial centre of Belfast that was shattered by systematic bombing.

This proposition was presented as pragmatism by one of the policy makers – 'In the early days ... when you were looking at the impact of major road schemes and major redevelopment schemes, you were conscious of – let's make sure it's a buffer between the two sides; the gap's wide enough to stop people throwing stones across it. That's as far as it went. It was to try and make sure you weren't creating new interface problems, or if there was an interface problem to try and get something neutral at the interface; something that couldn't be contested ... It wasn't a malign thing, it was to reduce risks of conflict'. Neighbourhoods that were inconveniently located in the path of planned development paid the price of risk management.

At local level community action was proceeding apace. The Shankill Community Council launched its Fourth Annual Report in 1975, which declared community groups as an expression of the people: 'No longer willing to delegate power to others to take decisions on their behalf, without having an adequate say in the decisions being made ... A pat on the head, or a handshake from a government minister is no longer sufficient ... A constructive, meaningful role must be found'. Community participation was insufficient to save the North Belfast Alliance-Ardoyne Summer Scheme from being targeted by bombers that summer, with little explanation as to the reason why.

Preserving the heartland of the Empire

The Save the Shankill Campaign encapsulated feelings of identity that went deeper than the immediate issue of threatened redevelopment. A loyalist ex-prisoner explained: 'This is the heart of the Empire. This is what we were told when we were at our granny's knees ... Going back to the Somme (World War I), there wasn't a street in the Shankill that wasn't affected ... It was the heart of the Empire as far as we were concerned'. The implication was that the empire owed the people of the Shankill for their steadfast loyalty – particularly to the crown – just as the Shankill prized its heritage. The redevelopment of the area took little account of local sentiment causing an angry reaction to the planned pyramid-style flats, with elevated streets, that were heralded as a showcase for future living. New six-storey blocks of flats in the Lower Shankill became known as the 'Weetabix' flats given their resemblance to cereal boxes and claims that they crumbled just as easily. A local resident became the first Secretary-Organiser of the Shankill Community Council: 'Most of my job was out walking the streets, dealing with people's problems in that first year. It wasn't exactly community development in its purest sense, but it was about community action'. It was about listening to people's concerns and responding to their needs.

A meeting was organised with departmental planners to express concerns; it was to be a cathartic experience for the local worker: 'He was building all these flats, and I remember, in all my innocence, sitting saying at this meeting "You're destroying a whole way of life by doing this". And he laughed, and he said – "Sure you mean to tell me the Shankill's a natural way of life? A hundred years ago it wasn't. People get used to it – they'll get used to this". And that was the meeting over. I remember walking out seething because I was powerless. And he laughed – I'll never forget his laugh. I said "I'll never sit in a meeting like that again ..." And it was out of that meeting that in my head, certainly, that the Save the Shankill campaign came together'. Ron Weiner from the ill-fated Northern Ireland Research Centre, was an important ally, providing a theoretical framing of the conflicting interests involved. This proved invaluable in helping to clarify community objectives.

Professor Moughtin (QUB) was another external expert. Fresh from the motorway campaign, he tasked his students to redesign the Housing Executive plans, within existing constraints, so that alternate options could not be dismissed as pie in the sky. The Community Organiser takes up the story: 'We produced a version of it with houses (instead of flats) ... That was our first attempt at community planning'. With alternate plans to hand it was time to re-engage the planners: 'One Sunday night ... in the middle of winter, in Agnes Street Methodist Church, with this planner coming out with his team ... and sitting in this room surrounded by a lot of heavy looking people, and Professor Cliff Moughtin. And I remember ... (the planner) coming in and looking, and we had his plan up on the wall, but above his plan we had our plan. And he thought he was coming to talk about his plan ... and we took it off the wall and we said "You're talking about our plan". He just refused to talk about it. So we told him he wasn't leaving the hall until he started talking about it. And eventually, at about 10.00pm at night he started criticising our plan and that was the back broken. We won that and our plan got built. So Cliff Moughtin provided essential technical assistance ... we couldn't have done the stuff if he hadn't, because we would always have been poking at their plans not redrawing them'. The importance of using external expertise to develop solution-focused proposals, rather than simply being responsive, proved critical.

The next step was to build a local power base. The aftermath of the UWC strike provided fertile ground to recruit support for the Save the Shankill campaign: 'I looked around and said "Where's the power in this community?" And it lay with the paramilitaries. And I said "Look they're here for the defence of Ulster – they're here for the defence of the Shankill" ... And I went and met them ... I also thought, right, UWC, there's a lot of people about here, trade unionists, that were involved in that, and I went and saw one of the local ones, Jim Smyth, who had been in the strike, and said "Listen, we're setting this up and want you to be chair of it", because he was seen as independent – he wasn't one paramilitary (group) or the other. He also had some respectability because he worked as a trade unionist'. By the end of the year the components of the Save the Shankill Campaign were in place which included those with paramilitary connections, churches, trade unionists and some members of the Shankill Community Council. It was preparing to deliver a much more militant campaign in the face of the planned redevelopment. The Save the Shankill Campaign agendas included standing items 'Report from the UDA'; 'Report from the UVF'. The word went out 'We said "Right, no bulldozers are going in there, and the first one that goes in will be wrecked. That is it."' The threat of force to stop demolition was implicit alongside engagement with alternate planning options.

Representation on the tenants' groups and community associations that were the bedrock of the campaign reflected the diversity of the Greater Shankill area itself. In some cases street by street elections were held; in others mobilisation was around a strong personality: 'Lower Shankill ... We had two representatives from each street – elected by the street ... You had a ballot around the street'. Further up the road, in Ainsworth, it was an amalgam of elections and personalities emerged out of the locally organised defence groups. Having a trade union grounding helped: 'I was elected Secretary of the Ainsworth Community Association ... because, one, at meetings I was performing the way meetings should have happened at a trade union ... and the second thing was I had a telephone in the house'. The sense of community overcame many divisions, although there were limits: 'We used to change names, you know – Jenny's husband was Brian in the Shankill, never Brendan. Jackie Redpath's dog was not Seamus, it was Rover. Damn dog never came for me because he lived facing the Loyalist Club, and you couldn't go out shouting Seamus you know, or you'd be done'. Northern Ireland Secretary of State, Merlyn Rees may have sympathised: he had to finesse the provocative name of his dog 'Paddy' when he took up his appointment.

By February 1975, the Save the Shankill campaigners were on the march, regaled by four Orange Bands, drumming a procession down to the local Housing Executive office. A slogan was daubed on the office wall: 'No demolition beyond this point'. The financial inducements for people to resettle in other areas eventually had an impact: it was estimated that some 9,011 jobs were lost in the immediate Shankill area which also saw a population decline from 76,000 to 26,000 in just over a decade. The Lower and Mid Shankill became known in planning terms as 'a twilight zone'. The Community Organiser counted the cost: 'We were saying "No more flats, we want houses", what we didn't realise until about after three years, was we weren't going to get anything'. One neighbourhood saw 239 houses built to replace the 4,000 old houses demolished between 1973 and 1977. Demolition, together with poor conditions, created a vicious circle of depopulation that allowed planners to argue a lack of demand for local housing. Those households that remained were disproportionately older in composition.

In a highly politicised society it is perhaps inevitable that the community narrative shifted from blaming lack of official understanding to more Machiavellian scenarios. A leaflet was circulated in 1977: 'Within the past week the Save the Shankill campaign has received startling information that the Government is now deliberately attempting to wipe out the Shankill. A secret NIO report has already gone before the board of the Housing Executive which recommends the complete abandoning of plans to build any more new houses on the Shankill'. Two sources were cited alongside the leaked memo – John McMichael (a UDA leader), who suggested that there was an army plan for a Protestant East and a Catholic West (Belfast), and information provided to the SOS Campaign chairperson that he was talking to the wrong people, he should be talking to Military Intelligence. This made sense to the campaigners: 'You take the Shankill out of the equation ... and you have West and North Belfast essentially as one big bloc, because already at that point the Protestant population of the North were evacuating in droves, and you have the simple thing with the river Lagan more or less dividing the city (into Catholic and Protestant blocs) except for South Belfast which was a happy place'. For his part the Environment Minister categorically denied the conspiracy allegations. A senior civil servant also felt they were over played: 'The outsider, or political activist, is likely to see in all of this great conspiracies; it wasn't really, it was just cock-ups, you know. Our people not understanding the full consequences of what they were doing, the absence of joined up thinking'. Whatever the truth of the matter, the community narrative grew ever firmer in belief of official duplicity at work.

Living the nightmare: Flats, homes and housing

If the Shankill was galvanised in opposition to planned redevelopment, complaints about conditions in Divis Flats, in the Lower Falls, united the warring factions of nationalism and republicanism. The complex consisted of the twenty-storey Divis Tower and smaller blocks, connected by linking decks, spread over a quarter of a square mile. It was home to 1,000 families. Two community workers described conditions: 'It wasn't the flats themselves that were the problem, it was the sheer brutality of living in them where the chutes all got bunged up and rubbish was along the walkways, and you know, there was no social amenities ... The army was in the rooftop (of the Tower); the army and police were coming along all the time; there was bombs, there was people being arrested; it was quite a brutal place'. The other agreed: 'It was like one big house and nobody knew who the frig was Mammy ... and they didn't have the means to get out of it'. In 1977 the BBC broadcast 'Internment in Divis'. Local people reported more maintenance carried out the day before the filming took place than had been seen over the previous two years. One woman became active in the campaign to get the flats demolished: 'I would say by mid-70s people started seeing the faults in Divis Flats ... I didn't know what community action was, it was just like a group of people that got together and said that they were going to try and meet with the Housing Executive to talk about this'. The response from officials was not encouraging: 'We met with the Housing Executive ... (They) basically laughed; they thought it was hilarious because the flats were only up a couple of years and we wanted them down. But they didn't live there and didn't know what it was like'. With half of Belfast's housing stock – 61,600 houses – needing either repair or reconstruction, officials were less than sympathetic to the demands for demolition. A compromise offer of an improvement scheme was rejected. Women, described by the media as 'the petticoat brigade', took direct action to prevent the contractors going on site, although one reflected: 'There wasn't really a strategy or anything it was just off the top of your head you know'. The women were seen by a local political activist as born leaders – 'Very strong, articulate, able ... I think leaders do emerge and I suppose at times of great stress they just become more visible'. The campaign for demolition of the flats grew in intensity.

If Divis became a by-word for political disturbance, there were at times when it worked to the benefit of residents. On one such occasion a socially minded paramilitary unit engaged in redistributive justice for people in rent arrears: 'There was a bookies (Betting Shop) in Divis ... What happened was the guy came out of the bookies with the takings and ... they (the paramilitaries) took this guy into a flat and took his takings off him. And they basically went round everybody and said "How much do you owe? How much do you owe?" – and gave it all out. And then the rent collector came and got the shock of his life when somebody started paying; and everybody paid, and the (rent) books were all marked up. And then the rent collector came to the end, and he was taken into the flat and the money was taken off him and given back to the bookies. So nobody lost any money and everybody's rent was up to date'. By 1976, police and army patrols accompanied rent and gas collectors on their rounds, although arguably there were other things to worry about given that Divis had become known as 'the plant of the IRPs' – reference to the Irish Republican Socialist Party.

One account of an army raid reported sawn-off shotguns tossed out of a window in the Tower block. Two shotguns were discovered with the butts stuck in the waste ground below, their double barrels pointing upwards. It was claimed that the army put the word around that things were so bad in the area that the locals were now growing shotguns.

The Divis agitation was contagious, encouraging women in Turf Lodge to mount protests about sub-standard flats and deteriorating conditions resulting from poor drainage and rat infestation. Two of the protestors met with Housing Executive officials: 'And on the way down (the two of them smoked liked troopers, they bought a hundred cigarettes at a time), they bought all these cigarettes. They went to this meeting at like three o'clock, and whatever it was that they want he's not giving it to them. So the one looks at the other and says "We'll just have to stay then". And Sheila produces her handbag – just it came to her, I'll produce the cigarettes, like symbolic you know, we're prepared for this; puts the hundred cigarettes on the table and says "Well that's no problem we've enough to keep us going all night". Whatever it was (they wanted) they got it'. For her part a Housing Executive spokesperson blamed a poor type of tenant and vandalism for the environmental problems. The beleaguered Housing Executive did win unexpected plaudits from residents in the old Mill Village of Ligoniel, in North Belfast, when timber framed dwellings, fitted with adjustable windows, were constructed as pigeon lofts for four hundred birds affected by redevelopment. The local pigeon fanciers were clearly effective lobbyists.

Meeting yourself coming back ...

If threatened rent increases were a basis for cross-community action, the North & West Belfast Federation of Tenants' Associations (N&WBFTA), represented a sweep of the tenants' associations from loyalist areas across the Shankill and North Belfast, in what one leading light claimed: 'Was a brilliant group, it was superb ... One of the first things it got into was rent increases ... We had fantastic debates about how houses were financed and all that ... We used to meet on a Sunday afternoon ... I mean every Sunday afternoon, not the odd one'. Like the Save the Shankill campaign, the N&WBFTA was a completely voluntary campaigning organisation: 'Rooted in protest, direct action, opposing – they were about community action ... Politicians were awfully scared of them'. Meetings were organised throughout various estates: 'I remember touring meetings – you went from one to the other ... We were up in Ballysillan ... and then we got in a car and raced around to Glencairn. I remember going into Glencairn and Stockie (Hughie Stockman) was standing there, and the room was bunged, you know, over a hundred people in the old Community Centre ... And (he) had a podium and a mallet to keep people in order, and he was drunk. And he went "Order, order!" – and he went back and we had to push him up again ... Now some people did it by stealth ... Freddie used to call a meeting and tell them it was about grants, and he'd get hundreds in there, and then he'd get them to go on rent strike'. Trade union shop steward training transferred well to community protest.

In 1977 Housing Executive officials were confronted by a flood of complaints about 'weeping houses'. Residents were dismissive of an official explanation that the damp was caused by 'continental cement'. The Executive received some respite when the North & West Belfast Federation ran out of steam and decided to disband itself. The process took place on a summer's day: 'We sat down on the Shankill ... there was three of us – Louis West, Brian Smeaton and myself – sat out on the footpath. And Brian got a bit of chalk and we wound the organisation up. I think I proposed it, and Louis seconded it, and Brian wrote the motion up on the wall in chalk – and that was it folded'. Energy was needed to turn protest into project planning; negativity could only be spun so far.

Politics and community: A complicated tango

Although a fraught political period, the mid-1970s saw the negotiation of space and presence to allow for community-based work. Time and again community activists used their network of connections to have a quiet word, or to put a note in the system through a trusted intermediary that had links with the various political and paramilitary interests, in order to sound out an idea before taking action. This was particularly important for community development 'outsiders', with what was to become known as the 'insider-partial' proving critical during times of tension. However the danger of being tripped up by cross-wires was ever present and fears of being dubbed 'a tout' were not altogether misplaced as Brian Smeaton, found to his cost. When he was invited as a local Church of Ireland Minister, by a British Army officer to join him for morning coffee at the sanger in Cuper Street in the Shankill, he was immediately apprehensive. The possibility of even being seen in potentially compromising circumstances carried risks.

The Organiser of the Creggan Resource Centre in Derry, faced a different quandary: 'Maybe going to meetings with the army would have been a bit naughty because ... people were being shot as traitors. At the same time there was stuff going on in the area and somebody had to be talking to somebody, so it was kind of acceptable for me to go and talk to the army and police. It was certainly acceptable for me to talk to them when people were in trouble and looking for help'. But there were drawbacks: 'The army had their community liaison people, you know, and I remember, I wasn't in the job two weeks, when two Saracens pulled up outside ... and this big Major, about 6.6ft, comes walking in, swinging his SLR and armed to the teeth. He held out his hand for me to shake his hand, which of course you don't shake hands and all that, and his kind of parting words were, "Mr Heaney, we must get the men of violence off the streets", and I just laughed ... So it was difficult and you had to tread carefully'. Perceived 'do-gooder' outsiders had to be particularly careful and needed well-established credentials before engaging in any risk-taking behaviour.

Even the long established Bogside Community Association had to watch its step. The politics of who could speak to who with impunity was uncertain. At times the BCA could negotiate people out of army and police custody; arrange safe passage to England if necessary and negotiate a ceasefire for a Community Festival period; at other times they became collateral damage as when the IRA machine gunned their offices when a British Army Community Liaison Officer was attending a meeting: 'Blew the shit out of the office, then turned the sort of blame game on us, you know, we are the collaborators'. From time to time it seemed a no-win situation. For one local activist in Derry risk-taking became default mode when he maintained back-channel connections with the British. He noted how the intelligence service was talking to all kinds of people: 'Always gathering – they're harvesters, right?' His role, as he saw it, was: 'To educate the Brits ...' – a role that was to last over a prolonged period, with varying degrees of success.

The BCA was also acutely aware of the need to avoid any perception of bias in their public statements – "Press statements would only have to do with condemnations of violence against citizens ... we would not get engaged in the propaganda war within the paramilitars, between the paramilitars, and between the paramilitars and the Brits ..." This position was, however, challenged by a local Catholic priest, as the BCA Organiser recalled: 'One night at a (BCA) Council meeting, which was not so very well attended, he put forward a proposal condemning the actions of the Provos ... one-sided, Church organised, and he demanded a vote there and then at the meeting, having given no notice of it whatsoever. So we argued, not so much against what he was saying, but the way he was doing it, and eventually we won the day, that we'd call a Special Delegate meeting ... And at the meeting there were two hundred people ... and it was most amazing, a great, great debate ... He put up this whole guilt thing in saying that the blood of every innocent victim from here on in, will not just be on your hands, but on the hands of your children, and your children's children. Dreadful piece of blackmail; and he failed. But from that moment on the BCA began to disintegrate because the church began to engage in a campaign, a quiet whispering campaign against the individuals concerned'. Concern over church influence was balanced by the consternation expressed in Derry's Brandywell when an over-enthusiastic, if cross-eyed, defender shot and shattered the hand of the statue of the Virgin Mary in the local grotto. His intended target, a circling Army helicopter, escaped unscathed.

The opportunity offered by the 1975 ceasefires enabled Irish-American, Padraig O'Malley, to organise an inclusive conference in Amherst (New England) to discuss options for Northern Ireland. The participants included a broad sweep of political and paramilitary protagonists. During the course of proceedings, UDA delegates listened carefully to an articulate presentation of the case for a united, socialist Ireland by IRSP leader,

Seamus Costello, to counter their proposal for an independent Ulster. An *Andersonstown News* columnist responded somewhat more scathingly to the UDA proposal: 'I received a letter yesterday morning from the Ulster United Unionist Council. I knew what it contained before I opened it so I was not surprised when I found that I had been offered a cabinet post in the Loyalist Provisional Government. Other members of the cabinet will be Mr Andy Tyrie, Mr Glenn Barr, Mr William Craig, Mr John McKeague, and of course, Col. Edward Brush, J. P. What a line up! The post I was offered of course was the Ministry of Fenian Affairs ... It was stressed that all cabinet meetings would take place in the UDA headquarters on the Newtownards Road'. If Amherst allowed an exchange of views there was little meeting of minds as to the way forward.

A proposal floated by a number of community activists calling for a Community Convention to debate the constitutional impasse also received a lukewarm response. Encouraged by Adam Curle, Professor of Peace Studies (Bradford), a cross-community delegation met with senior officials from the Secretary of State's office. The idea was condemned by many elected representatives and withered on the political vine. Another initiative to fall on deaf political ears was the proposed Bill of Rights for Northern Ireland issued by the Shankill-based Ulster Civil Liberties Committee, whose main advocate, Sammy Smyth, had narrowly escaped an assassination attempt. Prior to the publication of the UCLC document, demands for a Bill of Rights had been the preserve of the Northern Ireland Civil Rights Association, maintained by the formidable Madge Davison. In 1976 the maverick Sammy's luck ran out when he was shot dead by republicans after appealing to paramilitaries on all sides to meet for talks. CONI issued a statement expressing its concern that people engaged in community work were being targeted. Alongside Sammy, eighty-eight people had been killed in seventy-eight days and a bombing blitz devastated town centres across the region. Grafitti in large white letters appeared on the seventeenth-century Derry city walls on the eve of Christmas: 'Shop Now while shops last'.

CHAPTER 5

When the Minister Comes Calling ...

When Prime Minister Callaghan appointed Roy Mason to replace Merlyn Rees as Secretary of State in 1975, he informed him that the relatively unknown Peter Melchett would accompany him as Minister with responsibility for the Health & Social Services and Education portfolios: 'I had never heard of the man, though of course I knew his late father when he was head of the British Steel Corporation. I felt the faintest twinge of doubt, which wasn't helped when I discovered my new junior minister hadn't even been contacted yet. Jim looked just a little embarrassed at this point. "He's sailing with his girlfriend somewhere in the Aegean and can't be reached", he explained. "But his mother's prepared to accept the job on his behalf" ... I was to discover that Lord Melchett was young, naïve and – in the environmental sense – very green, not the type I'd personally have chosen to face the terrorists'. For Maurice Hayes, on the other hand, Melchett was a welcome breath of fresh air. Without wasting time Hayes organised a series of dinners to introduce the Minister to community leaders not usually numbered amongst the official guest lists.

Melchett himself arranged frequent sorties into neighbourhoods to get a first-hand account of how things stood. His Private Secretary remembers the police escort being edgy: 'Of course we had police escorts with us, and ... at the start of the meeting the Chair of the meeting would start by asking everyone who they were, and the police escorts would always be Information Officers. So we used to have about four Information Officers on each trip'. The ministerial impressions enlivened the statistical data being collected: 'Some of the conditions that we found going around the areas with Melchett, you know – old ladies living in households that were about to be torn down and infested with rats. There was one old lady who used to catch the rats with a dish cloth and drown them in a bucket of water ...' – conditions that substantiated the complaints of many community groups.

Melchett was not the first to venture outside the confines of Stormont. The pending ceasefire of Christmas 1974 had encouraged Merlyn Rees to demand that senior civil servants should see conditions in 'problem areas' at first hand. A flurry of memos ensued, with one prickly note penned by a Permanent Secretary: '1. Many Thanks. 2. Why such a tearing hurry? After five years would Thursday 12th (rather than the 4th) not do? 3. I shall want some promise of safety and safe conduct for my staff'. The proposed areas to be visited were a mere twenty minutes from the heart of political decision-making, but were easily cast as alien territory when mediated through media images and army reports. The civil servant delegated to organise the programme admitted: 'There were areas of my own city that I'd never been in, and I would meet a young Captain from some regiment or other and realise that he knew more about a particular bit of West Belfast than I did ... There was very little identification between the Civil Service and disadvantaged areas in Belfast'. The army Chief of Staff cheerfully agreed to place armoured cars at the disposal of the civil servants on tour. There was a clear message that something needed to be done to get to grips with social need in disgruntled communities. When two researchers were recruited into the Civil Service to support policy making they found: 'No one had a clue basically what we were meant to do – we didn't have a clue ... There weren't any strong competing policies – frankly there didn't seem to be any. I think the violence was so over-whelming at that stage they sort of tried to come to grips with it. I mean in terms of normal policy making, policy options, policy alternatives ... I wasn't aware of them'. Focusing on a Belfast Areas of Special Needs initiative, Jeremy and his colleague carried out analysis of existing administrative data, supplemented by household surveys in the Shankill and the Falls. Although army search squads might know the colour of the wallpaper in local houses, this was the first time that people had been formally interviewed about local issues. The identity of one of the interviewers caused concern: 'Whenever the security forces heard that one of our interviewers was the wife of a Permanent Secretary (an English lady interested in Northern Ireland) they were extremely concerned, to the extent that they offered to have a helicopter fly over her sample addresses'. This generous offer was vetoed on the grounds that it might draw attention to the lady in question.

The report that was produced highlighted the link between the areas of worst violence and highest levels of social and economic deprivation. The employment differential between Catholics and Protestants was also noted by the authors, who concluded: 'I think it brought together a lot, and made apparent the obvious, but a lot of people, I think, had been working within their separate departmental areas ... and hadn't appreciated the multiple nature of disadvantage'. The researchers were working to an Inter-Departmental Group, but soon discovered: 'We weren't really civil servants, we didn't know the normal processes and practices. We produced our report with recommendations. One of the recommendations was the black taxis should be encouraged and legalised as a form of transportation and access; then we shunted this off to Ministers without clearing it through the civil service system, and caused apoplexy. And it had to be withdrawn and we then had to review our conclusions ... but the black taxis came out of the final report'. In this illustration of the process of policy normalisation, the 'black taxis' may have been seen by some as 'people's transport', but the official position was that they were a front for loyalist and republican terrorists.

The deftly worded final Project Report posited two syndromes (a) the West Belfast syndrome of high unemployment, low incomes and over-crowded housing; and (b) an Inner City syndrome characterised by sub-standard housing, poor physical environment, low incomes, lack of skills and concentrations of persons with various forms of personal disability, whether associated with age or health. There was little reference to the Troubles, although comparisons were drawn with levels of deprivation in other British cities. One of the researchers did venture to note: 'It was very clear the linkages between the areas of the worst violence and the highest levels of deprivation. Also at that stage the whole issue of employment differentials started coming out'. Future research was supported by material made available by the new Continuous Household Survey: 'We were able to analyse material from the survey in terms of community background, and this very starkly brought out which, you know, probably had been apparent to community workers on the ground ... It was highlighting not just disadvantage, deprivation, concentration, but it was also contrasting differences in absolute terms between the two communities ... So there was a nucleus of data and research that was coming along there that was feeding into the relatively small number of main grade civil servants of a senior level who were interested, who were open and responsive, and then, and only then, to Direct Rule Ministers'.

Ministers, it was felt, had more pressing security considerations; although tasked with chairing the Belfast Areas of Need Planning Team, Melchett had two challenges in coordinating action in deprived areas of Belfast – first, to secure local input into the planning process; and secondly, to maximise funding from both mainstream developmental budgets and additional resources. Community representatives remained sceptical with a Save the Shankill spokesperson complaining: 'It's the same old Department heads saying the same old things. Why aren't there people who actually live in the A. S. S. N. on that team?' Despite the cynicism a number of new health and education projects were announced, together with more controversial retail improvement schemes. Derry, the only other city to receive additional funding, enhanced its leisure facilities. The criticism of the Belfast Areas of Need programme by the community sector was mild compared to the annoyance expressed by DUP MP, Rev. Robert Bradford, who alleged that 92 per cent of the BAN money was spent on improving 'republican areas'. Allocation, responded a government spokesman, was based on need rather than community identity. The Alliance Party roundly condemned the allegations as a 'deliberate attempt to stir up sectarian feeling for short-term gain'.

The Minister unleashed

Roy Mason reportedly smiled at the headline in his morning newspaper – 'The Man who Brings New Hope to Ulster'. His smile faded when he realised that the reference was to Peter Melchett, a now familiar figure in community venues – often unannounced. His visit to a childcare project in the strongly republican St. James area of West Belfast caused the local organiser consternation: 'When I was looking to get a play school playgroup established I started writing to, and lobbying, Lord Melchett. Now I knew that wouldn't go down well locally, but I told everybody I was doing it. Like the thing was keeping everybody informed ... and that (it) was about our right to resources. But now Sinn Féin wouldn't have liked that at all ... it was an interaction with the state that shouldn't have been happening ... So we lobbied on and eventually got it (grant aid) ... from Melchett directly'. The Minister decided to visit the project en route to a planned event in the local comprehensive school where his reported attendance had already attracted a republican picket: 'He stopped off at the Community Centre to come in and meet us. Now how naïve is that for a British Minister? ... He arrived at the Community Centre saying "Where's XXX and where's ...?" I said "Get out, out, thank you very much, this has been controversial enough – away you go, catch yourself on", you know ... And I said, you know, "This is not helpful, this is not a good idea, I can see why you might have wanted to do it" ... I'll tell you I had an awful lot of talking down to do afterwards'. The ability to explain actions taken became an essential skill set for community activists walking the fine line between the politics of local acceptability and access to statutory resources.

Circumstances in the Greater Shankill were less fraught. Melchett became engaged with local plans, continuing to champion the area after leaving office. The Shankill Community Council Organiser was impressed – "I remember him talking to me and saying his shock that things were so protest oriented here compared to communities in England where they were more about projects. And saying to me that's the next big move. And I think that I had some notion about that as well, because by that stage ... in terms of its objectives, the Save the Shankill Campaign had a big level of success. It failed in not seeing another picture at the same time; even when you're successful you run out of steam ..." This reflected ministerial views in an interview with *Scope* magazine where he called for 'Better researched and more widely based criticism' to enable community representatives to impact policy making. In an effort to support this, the Department of Education initiated two three-year projects – a Community Education Forum and a Community Worker Research Project. Professor Hywel Griffiths was appointed as the Steering Committee chairperson.

The Community Worker Research Project funded fourteen pilot initiatives to appoint development workers, managed by local groups. The selected areas included six neighbourhood initiatives in Belfast; community development projects in Omagh, South Armagh, Fermanagh, Craigavon and outer East Belfast; and two support initiatives in co-operative development and community media. The selection struck a judicious balance between single identity Catholic and Protestant areas, as well as geographically. The centralised nature of selection annoyed the Craigavon Borough Council who refused to manage the funding allocated for the project in its area given that councillors felt: 'That they were elected representatives (and) that the people involved in the Craigavon Workers' Research Project were dangerous people, radical people ... They felt that all of the people involved in that committee were all blow-ins ... and it was the whole reds under the beds scenario'. Agreement was eventually negotiated. The Craigavon Workers' Research Project was particularly active, establishing an Independent Advice Centre, work with women and minority ethnic community outreach. The remit of the Community Education Forum that was also funded, was to encourage educational institutions to be more responsive to the training and educational needs of local groups; not overly helped by the tendency of the Forum Coordinator to describe academics as 'epidemics'. Both programmes were introduced as pilot initiatives to test practice and policy.

Community workers recruited by local groups under the Community Worker Research Project met together regularly to exchange notes. When the Omagh project worker decided to stand for election to the local Council as an independent, opinion was divided. Meanwhile Peter Melchett continued to create space for community action. Speaking at a Northern Ireland Council of Social Services conference, he drew a distinction between traditional voluntary action and the newer community groups: 'They are by nature, and perfectly correctly, suspicious of establishments among which they could class both the Council, and my departments'. Melchett continued: 'They emerged out of conflict. They may not fit in easily with the consensus model of Councils of Social Service'. Although this distinction was not altogether popular, the Minister's decision to fund a new independent charitable grant-making Trust, the Northern Ireland Voluntary

Trust (later to be renamed the Community Foundation for Northern Ireland), was greeted with general enthusiasm. David Cook, the first non-Unionist Party Lord Mayor of Belfast, was persuaded to act as Chairperson of an independent Board of Trustees. The latter included Eamonn Deane from Derry and Jackie Redpath from the Shankill, bringing community experience into the deliberately cross-community Board. Departmental funding matched private donations raised on a pound-for-pound challenge basis to establish an independent endowment for the new Trust, which was unashamedly supportive of community action.

The other policy area that featured on the ministerial agenda was that of poverty and social need. Newly established groups, such as the lone parent association, GingerBread (NI), were highlighting the fact that 9 per cent of families in the North were single parent households and some 70 per cent of these were surviving on incomes well below the official poverty level. The Falls Community Council organised a Conference on Poverty to counter suggestions that poverty was the fault of the poor themselves; and tenacious anti-poverty campaigner, University of Ulster academic, Eileen Evason, penned serial reports on the failings of the welfare system. Evason went on to direct a European Commission/Department of Health & Social Services supported Belfast Poverty Project which deployed welfare rights workers in local communities to provide direct advice and draw policy conclusions.

District Councils: Getting to grips with 'community'

Caught in the pincher movement between a hyper active minister and the demands of local communities, District Councils were at their wit's end. Belfast City Council participated with Melchett's Social Needs Planning Team, but warned against the expectations raised by short term central government initiatives. Local authorities implemented their remit for community services by establishing Community Services Departments, appointing Community Services Officers and providing grant-aid to local groups. Local elected representatives could be apprehensive, as a Belfast City Council Assistant Director of Community Services found when organising a weekend conference on community development: 'Councillors are still very nervous about it because they see their role as providing advice ... and what was happening was community groups were going and doing it and councillors weren't getting a look in, so they were feeling very much out of things. And as a result of that, they weren't terribly keen on community development, and we tended to move towards the community service type of provision of providing a community centre ... I kept trying to keep the community development strand alive'. He fielded a number of searching questions posed by the councillors such as – What is a community group? Are community associations subversive and out to replace local government? Have paramilitary bodies taken over community associations? Should councillors be on the management of community centres they are grant-aiding? Are community associations really representative?

The minute book of the Belfast City Council Community Services Committee reflected more practical challenges. In 1975 alone there was mention of an assassination attempt on one of its Unionist members; the murder of Council worker, Samuel Llewellyn; the hijacking of a pest control van engaged in a sewer rat campaign; and the intimidation of a bin lorry driver, who was coerced into tipping his load on the Springfield Road as part of local protests about housing conditions in Turf Lodge. There was still time for councillors to attend a private screening of the film 'Emanuelle' to gauge whether it was suitable for public viewing; they agreed to express their concerns 'in the strongest possible way' to the British Board of Film Censors. In 1977 *Scope* magazine published a mixed report card on how local authorities were implementing their community services responsibilities. Issues raised included complaints about levels of bureaucracy and little evidence of coherent community development policies. It was further reported that only fifteen of the twenty-six local Councils had employed Community Service Officers despite government funding being available. There were differences of opinion as to whether Councils should directly employ community service staff or delegate funding to community groups. Derry City Council opted for the latter approach.

By the late 1970s a number of Councils supported independent Community Resource Centres. In Belfast there were Centres in the four quarters of the city, with two in West Belfast, in both the Upper Springfield and the Falls. In Derry, four Community Resource Centres were supported together with Council built community centres. Operating as membership organisations, the Resource Centres provided services to community and voluntary groups in the area they served. Peter Melchett favoured this approach, arguing that community associations should be helped to employ their own Community Organisers provided they could meet a share of the cost and that the work load justified the appointment. To its astonishment, the Falls Community Council Steering Committee, in West Belfast, secured funding from Belfast City Council for an office base and a worker. The committee had been on the point of collapse, but now adopted an 'open door' policy, with the exception of church supported groups or those sponsored by political parties. Committee members chased the pigeons out of the roof space in their new, but dilapidated offices, as tasked under 'any other business'.

In Derry, the Organiser in the Creggan Resource Centre accepted his appointment with a degree of trepidation: 'I was originally from Creggan but had left it ... and coming up into a war zone. You know it was hectic in those days, and thinking to myself, you're out of your mind. What do you think you're going to do up here? I just really felt way out of my depth ... I kind of began to ... pick up the reins of guidance that were available from other people in the community ... who were familiar with what they were about ... Most of the people were coming in about one of two things – one was their (welfare) benefit and the other was about somebody who had been arrested, or a house raid, or something going on. So suddenly I found myself in the middle of slap, bang, trying to calm situations down where there was a lot of community tension; conflict between – mostly the army at that time and residents'. The Creggan, following the Bogside model, held a house to house ballot to elect the Community Association committee. Twenty-two representatives were elected to represent the area from the slate of names nominated from groupings of every two streets (forty-four streets in all). The Community Organiser had to craft a work plan from the wide range of issues that emerged from this process.

He also had to support his voluntary management committees to raise a proportion of their Centre costs, resulting in a round of door-to-door collections, bingo sessions and general fundraising, which could distract attention from community development.

Making sense of it all: Reflections on community education

Melchett's support for the Community Education Forum was in response to a pre-existing emphasis on the contribution of both adult education and community education. The trade union linked WEA (Workers' Education Association) had long been a source of community-based adult education. In addition, two university-based, but externally funded, community education programmes were piloted in Queen's University Belfast and Magee College (University of Ulster), Derry, respectively. Community activists were encouraged to flirt with the ideas of Paulo Friere, Antonio Gramsci and Ivan Illich. A crowd turned out when Illich delivered a guest lecture in Derry. This including a bus load from Springhill House in Ballymurphy, who critiqued the presentation on the way home: 'Someone asked "Well, what did you think of Illich's ideas?" Pause, then – "Well, good, but didn't we find all that out in Ballymurphy?"'. Fr. Des Wilson, who had organised the outing, was particularly scathing about academics who suggested that working-class people tended to think literally rather than conceptually. In his experience it was clear that working-class people could not only think conceptually, but up and down and around corners when necessary. Sheer survival required it, and never more so than in situations of conflict.

The Queens University Belfast based action-research project, under the direction of the outgoing Director of the Community Relations Commision, David Rowlands, employed Community Educators/Organisers in four areas across Greater Belfast – Tullycarnet Estate (Dundonald); the Bone-Clifton area in North Belfast; Rathcoole estate in Newtownabbey; and Sandy Row in South Belfast; with the Lower Falls in West Belfast included at a later date. The workers were tasked to identify adult education needs; organise learning opportunities; access available community education resources; and draw out policy recommendations. One Education Organiser, working from an old primary school building in the Lower Falls, faced more immediate concerns: 'Well you know, it was rough. Well you had to get nearly the permission of the local whatever (paramilitary) that was in charge to be there. If there was a day of action whenever they were closing everything, you had to wait until someone said you could open, or you couldn't open, you know? So you were really controlled by that kind of thing. There were a lot of soldiers around who could be very difficult on occasion ... I mean awful things would happen like we'd all be thrown up against a wall, and then somebody would look at my driving licence and they would be awfully polite to me ... It became almost like a joke, you know, just part of the whole process'. Local people attended courses and achieved formal qualifications in a 'learning environment' that was less than satisfactory: 'I mean the ceiling fell in one time. Monday night we had the sewing class and someone said "Eh the ceiling looks a bit ..." And I said "Everybody into the next room", and the whole ceiling came down. I remember two guys arriving from Social Services next day to see what happened, and they said "Oh well you'll just have to clean it up ..." And we had to clean it up literally – the gang of us cleaned it up'. Arguably this was at the limits of the standard contractual clause: 'Such other duties as may be reasonably expected'.

The Community Education Project threw up controversies and tensions when the locally based organisers identified with local issues. In North Belfast, the Project Worker was denounced as a left-wing agitator when he clashed with the Catholic Church over the siting of a proposed Education Centre. The Final Project report contained seventeen recommendations, many of them critical of existing educational provision. There is no evidence of any response by the mainstream system. The later CARE (Community Action Research Education) project was the brain child of Tom Lovett in Derry. Established in 1977, it adopted a social action model, designing an educational intervention for community activists to facilitate reflection and analysis of structural issues. In practical terms, CARE offered in-service training on community organising, labour history and theories of social change. A library of materials and equipment was provided for local communities, with the implicit intention of releasing university resources for this purpose to the horror of the traditionalist university administration in Magee College.

Working with BBC Radio Foyle, Tom crafted a series of radio discussions on community issues (including that of sectarianism) based on recordings with residents of both Catholic and Protestant single identity neighbourhoods. Community input into setting the CARE project priorities was provided for by a weekend Workshop early in the programme. The emphasis was on supporting radical social change, but with the debate becoming more ragged as the evening progressed, an intrepid *Scope* reporter identified a number of quandaries – How can people move from the stage of protest to development action? What is the role of the community activist and has s/he a right to impose his/her views on apprehensive communities? How do you develop multi-issue strategies as opposed to single focus organisations? Can you discuss community action in Northern Ireland without addressing sectarianism? Agreement of sorts was reached about the importance of understanding how institutions, structures and systems operated; the importance of economic analysis in order to understand social problems; the need to look beyond the current system rather than accepting, or simply attacking, current norms and practices; the importance of challenging sexism and sectarianism; and the need to avoid institutionalisation.

Tom Lovett, saw little divide between activism and academia, enabling CARE to sponsor conferences on Human Rights, Poverty and Domestic Violence. The Centre's involvement in the production of the New Ulster Political Research Group's document 'Beyond the Religious Divide' was, however, less planned. The policy paper that advocated an independent Ulster was duplicated on the CARE roneo-machine when the NUPRG printer let the group down the night before a public launch. UDA Chairman, Andy Tyrie, was urged to keep a low profile when he arrived at the CARE office. His suggestion to send a colleague to buy fish suppers for all concerned was vetoed on the basis of health and safety given the location of Magee in the mainly nationalist/republican city side of Derry. Prior to completion, the document had been thoroughly discussed by the various UDA brigades and companies. This particular incident undoubtedly fell somewhat outside Tom's idea of the CARE objective: 'The project

(CARE) hoped that it could offer something worthwhile, at least in terms of resources, to people who wanted no more than a chance to say their piece about local facilities or a pressing social problem'. Much of the learning from the work was channelled into Tom's subsequent venture, the Ulster People's College, in the early 1980s.

The Ulster People's College was a residential adult education centre that advocated an ethos of progressive social change. It was designed to work with community activists as well as with trade unions and other social movements. Inspired by the experience of residential education centres in the USA and Scandinavia, the interminable planning meetings ratcheted up a gear when the London-based Nuffield Foundation bought into the proposal. Lovett, who later became the College Director, met the Foundation representatives in a Belfast hotel: 'The (Nuffield) Director said "I think the best thing we can do is to give you money to buy a place" – and we nearly fell off our stools in the Wellington Park Bar'. A substantial property was purchased in South Belfast and a programme of educational work agreed. The specific commitment to anti-sectarianism was steadfastly maintained by the voluntary Management Committee, notwithstanding often convoluted discussions about how this was understood and implemented in practice.

Interest in education was not solely the prerogative of academics. Springhill House in Ballymurphy developed a thriving educational hub and the Educational Sub-Committee of the Shankill Community Council offered a parallel focus. The emphasis in Ballymurphy was on people being self-directive in the face of institutional control: 'When we started, we had nothing ... But we found it amazing that people began to come. It might have been for a very simple thing like using the telephone – there were very few telephones in those days ... Once people began to converse with each other we found that people were worried; they were worried for example about the old people ... And people said they were worried about the level of their literacy ... So English language classes started ... That developed then into people looking for history, looking for religious things, all kinds of stuff'. The need to both listen and encourage people to have a positive 'can do' attitude was recognised. Alongside classes, more creative forms of participation and expression were encouraged – open forums, public enquiries, theatre, days of quiet retreat and the relatively short-lived 'Common Grumble' – an open space for dialogue, complaint and exchange held on Sunday afternoons.

A public enquiry into education was organised in the Upper Springfield in 1978, attracting large numbers of parents, teachers, educationalists and local residents. One of the organisers explained the purpose of this three day event: 'One important purpose of this Inquiry was to make it perfectly clear that people, whoever they are, can mount a public inquiry into matters of public interest. There is a feeling that only the public authorities can mount a public inquiry. What we must do is enlarge public discussion to find out ways in which people can take over all the procedures, like public inquiries'. The verbatim report, which was presented to Lord Melchett, was published by arch loyalist and printer, John McKeague. The Department of Education remained silent.

The Shankill Education Sub-Committee lobbied for an ambitious multi-purpose education and arts hub, which was enthusiastically endorsed by Melchett. Before his departure from office the Minister passed the plans to Belfast City Council for implementation. There, however, they languished. Six years later the *Shankill Bulletin* charged the Council with (i) negligence; (ii) incompetence; (iii) slowness; and (iv) bloody-mindedness. The former Agnes Street Methodist Church that had been earmarked as the core of the Centre plan had by then been burnt down. Funding was finally conceded to allow the appointment of a Community Education Officer for the area. Although the Education Workshop that eventually emerged was smaller than envisaged, it was bubbling with ideas. There were practical projects, such as an information booklet for parents of children starting primary school; it offered a venue for WEA classes (where Queens University academic, Frank Wright, lectured on Politics and Irish History late into the night) and the Shankill Photographic Workshop, manned by photographer, Buzz Logan. There were plans for a City Farm and the *Shankill Bulletin* was launched as a regular local newspaper. The Bulletin provided commentary on topical issues, with updates on the redevelopment campaign, and acerbic cartoon reflections by 'Screw the Bap' and 'Head the Ball' – a production of Balloon Features. Regular features included the considered musings of Rubber Rat, and a Red Pepper column which offered somewhat surreal comments on local events. One edition reported on British soldiers leaping from their land rovers to take up position around the Lower Shankill post office where a delivery of cash was expected. This, it was admitted, was nothing unusual except that the soldiers had in fact surrounded the local confectionary shop with their ring of steel – rich pickings were clearly on offer.

Community news-sheets and papers were popular in many areas, fuelling communication, comment and, sometimes, controversy. Some were politically aligned, while others made a virtue of reflecting a range of views and opinions. *Community Mirror*, published in Derry, worked to a charter – (i) We aim to be a forum for all local opinion; (ii) We invite people to state their views in our pages; (iii) We seek to encourage dialogue between local people on all matters; (iv) We want to explode myths; (v) We act independently of any party, church or group; (vi) We seek ways in which local people can develop their talents and benefit the whole community; (vii) We look to community self-reliance and cooperation as the foundation of our local development; and (viii) We aim to question, to describe, to discuss and to stimulate. Activists from across the community divide in the North West met together on the editorial board. The Newry Confederation of Community Groups published 'Brass-tacks'; the Omagh Community Development Project produced 'Grassroots'; and a new community newspaper in South Armagh, initiated by the Crossmaglen Community Association, reported on cross-Border developments.

A woman's work is never done!

Women were actively involved in every aspect of the Troubles, but often in roles dictated by the demands of the time, their family and community circumstances or as a result of their politics. When a British M.P referred to republican women supporters as 'harridans in hairnets', in the early 1970s, he was undoubtedly thinking of those women who banged bin lids to warn of approaching army patrols, or who picketed army bases in protest against arrests. Loyalist women were also evident, whether active in their local communities; youth work; or, to a more limited extent, in loyalist paramilitary groups. In contrast there were women who organised as 'Women Together' in opposition to the escalating violence – a mobilisation that was repeated on a much larger scale by the Peace Women (later Peace People) in the latter half of the 1970s. The full spectrum of political sympathies and activism was reflected by women who were also to the forefront in holding family life and communities together in abnormal circumstances.

1975, International Women's Year, was marked in Belfast by the launch of the Northern Ireland Women's Rights Movement (NIWRM) and a Women's Charter. A conference was also convened in the city on domestic violence; Derry Labour Party stalwart, Cathy Harkin, raised the issue in Derry, where she also argued against the paramilitary practice of tarring and feathering. Within its Charter, the NIWRM made a series of demands, including raising the virtually unmentionable issue of women's reproductive rights. Controversy, however, remained stubbornly focused on 'the national/constitutional question'. Heated debates took place over the nature of an 'anti-imperialist' women's movement as compared to the creation of a broad alliance of women from across the community divide. There was a grumbling conundrum of what issues should be prioritised during a period of intense violence.

The cross-community aspirations of the NIWRM came face to face with women in local communities who held divergent political allegiances, while the assertion of feminist demands received mixed reaction. Local priorities could differ given personal and community circumstances. Women concerned about the prison conditions of relatives often became active in the republican Relatives Action Committees or loyalist support groups. Radical feminists objected to the fact that men could be members of the NIWRM and were increasingly drawn into other collectives. Many women preferred to commit their energies to single issue groups like the Rape Crisis Centre or Women's Aid. A Socialist Women's Group that had also been established in 1975, decided to withdraw from the NIWRM over disagreements concerning feminism and politics.

By 1980 there was such a myriad of groups and perspectives that the call went out for 'Unity Meetings'. One of those involved bore the scars:

'The unity meetings were far from unity, and it just seems to me that people had these ideas and they were really entrenched. I mean a lot of it had to do with ... whether or not there should be women only events. Some of it had to do with whether or not you supported the military (IRA) campaign, and if you didn't then you weren't anti-imperialist ... I used to say should we take guns to get nursery schools?' The emergence of the Peace People provided another point of friction depending on perspective. Although the Northern Ireland Women's Rights Movement was critical of the Peace People, it condemned the ongoing IRA bombing campaign, seeing it as dividing working-class communities and inviting reaction and repression. In contrast to Women against Imperialism, that was generally supportive of the republican struggle, the NIWRM focused on social, economic and legal issues that impacted on women from across the sectarian divide. On some few occasions, alliances formed between the various groups around a shared demand, such as the campaign to release Noreen Winchester from prison. This young Sandy Row woman had been convicted of murdering her father having been a victim of incest for many years. The campaign to secure her release was successful, supported by Lord Melchett.

The Women's Movement outside of Belfast was less divisive. There was a university link in Coleraine, where the Coleraine Women's Group lobbied for reform due to the lack of parity in divorce and related legisla-tion between Northern Ireland and Britain. Women's Groups in Newry and Craigavon were also active; in the latter women campaigned to main-tain After School provision for local children. One advocate addressed a District Council meeting: 'The first campaign we ran was about keeping the after-school club open and we were the first group ever to address the Council ... I think they were gobsmacked ... They were not used to any of the community groups to stand up and say – formally as well – we're presenting this petition; there's three points we wish to make; here's what they are; now here is what the alternatives are. You haven't examined this well enough, now we're asking you to go away and look at that and we'd like to meet you again in two weeks ... And they actually did what we asked them, which was put one pence on the rates'. This campaign was posited in opposition to an application for Council investment in the private airstrip used by one councillor's local flying club. The Women's Group invited the councillor to visit the Community Centre: 'All the kids were in the play scheme and Kate got them all to make paper helicopters and fire them at him as he came in. So this was all over the local press – "Councillor gets bombarded with paper airplanes – Battling Housewives – Militant mums" – that was us … And it was quite funny and made the point. And he was all … "I didn't know the play scheme was going to be closed down" … (And we said) "You have a real airplane, the kids only have paper ones". It was to be game, set and match to the Women's Group. The focus on childcare minimised potential political frictions that were splintering the Women's Movement in Belfast, and to a lesser extent in Derry.

The Derry Women's Collective was formed after members attended an extra-mural class on feminism. Given the Derry tendency to establish groups, and issue press statements, at the drop of the proverbial bonnet, a Derry Women's Action Group came together to focus on the needs of homeless women, lone parent families and victims of domestic violence. The members of both groups merged in Derry Women's Aid, after two activists squatted a vacant building to open a refuge. The building was owned by the Health & Social Services Board, resulting in parliamentary questions from the Co. Londonderry MP Willie Ross, demanding to know whether the squatters would be prosecuted under the Emergency Provisions legislation. A hurried phone call from Minister Melchett's office invited a representative of the Derry Group to dinner in Stormont to discuss the issue. Poverty campaigner, Eileen Evason, was selected, although there were some troubled looks when it was reported that she had lit her roll-up cigarettes off the candelabra. Whatever the etiquette, a deal was concluded. Melchett ensured that the building was transferred to the Derry Group and that the local Health & Social Services Board would consider financial support. This allowed the refuge to move from a twenty-four-hour volunteer rota to appointing a paid worker.

Problems, however, did not end there. Daily notes in the 1978 refuge record book offer insight into the pressure of maintaining a service in a dilapidated building that was heavily dependent on volunteer support. One entry mused on the question of rats (or was it large mice) and fleas: 'A flea, or not a flea, that is the question? Roswitha (a German volunteer) insists that we still have the little buggers'. On a more positive note there was also cause for celebration: 'Rowntree Trust ... may give us some money, yippee ! ! (12.50am)'. Given the location of the refuge in central Derry it was impossible to avoid the impact of the Troubles: 'Sent Thomas out to see who was ringing bell: it was the army. They took his name. Went out to enquire what was going on and they said they had seen someone with "something" long and solid in their hands. They went off but came back again and asked if we had any guns in the house. Showed them the only one we have – a small, broken, plastic rifle. They've gone again. Received copies of letters sent to XX and YY (Western Health & Social Services Board) about allegations that we're running a brothel'.

Political controversy was never far from the door as when the refuge committee advertised for a childcare worker and had to debate whether to appoint the wife of a serving British soldier to the position. There were questions about her safety; the safety of the women and children in the refuge; and the possible corrosive impact of the inevitable rumour mill within the local community. Having weathered that particular storm (and confirmed the appointment) another political crisis arose over the formal opening of the refurbished refuge by Lord Melchett. A mere twenty-four hours earlier a young republican had been found dead in a police cell. Accusations and rumours abounded resulting in protest pickets and demonstrations. Derry Women's Aid was told in no uncertain terms that no British Minister was welcome in the city. After lengthy internal debate it was decided to proceed with the opening as planned in recognition of the support that the Minister had provided. The Northern Ireland Office PR team were less than enthusiastic, however, when Melchett was photographed against the backdrop of a feminist poster: 'Women are called birds because of the worms they pick up'. Although the Minister laughed, he was not to know the controversy that his presence had given rise to and the amount of subsequent explanation that was required locally.

In its first year of operation the Derry refuge provided shelter to ninety women and over 300 children; what was unforeseen was the way in which one issue spiralled into others. Pickets were placed on the local courthouse in protest at the lack of legal remedies for women. The Housing

Executive office was also picketed given the problems getting women and their children rehoused. When meagre welfare benefits were cut, a Derry Claimants' Union was established and links made with the more developed movement in Britain. There were calls for a Community Law Centre in the North-West to supplement the provision in Belfast. The main dangers in this heady atmosphere of serial protest was the burn out of volunteers; with hyper-activism becoming unconsciously elitist, marginalising those with less time or energy to commit.

The politics of the time, in an intimate city such as Derry, resulted in often divisive discussion of the broader question of violence against women. Derry Women's Aid activists protested outside the courthouse when two British soldiers went on trial for rape, but also picketed the Irish Republican Socialist Party office after an INLA punishment attack on a local woman for alleged anti-social activities. Press statements condemned strip searching of women prisoners and the use of male warders in Armagh women's prison; and a letter was printed in *An Phoblacht/Republican News* arguing against punishment attacks on women. The rephrasing of republican icon Padraig Pearse's declamation: 'Ireland unfree shall never be at peace', emblazoned the wall of Magee College as 'Women unfree shall never be at peace' to mark International Women's Day. This particular graffiti was denounced as sacrilege by some, while the perpetrators learned the hazards of painting lengthy slogans in the face of regular army patrols.

Ideological debates filled the pages of contemporary feminist magazines, such as Spare Rib and Scarlet Women. The Belfast Women's Collective opposed British imperialism, but made cogent criticisms of the Republican movement with reference to its position on women. Women against Imperialism maintained a feminist stance but held to a more traditional republican position. Derry Women's Aid – admitting differences of opinion within its own membership – suggested that 'the struggle for women's liberation (in Northern Ireland) will at times entail confrontation with the British Army and state institutions, but it will also involve challenging the attitudes of church, political and paramilitary groups'. The wife of a republican hunger striker stated her case, as did the mother of a young man severely beaten by sewer rods in a Provisional IRA punishment attack. Apart from the Northern Ireland Women's Rights Movement, little reference was made to women in loyalist areas except the repeated mantra about the need to reach out to them. Limited contact, however, seeded the ground for misunderstanding, which a NIWRM member felt was: 'Another big issue around feminism – Protestants saw it as another strand of the Republican movement, and it was very difficult to get them in, you know, to create that cross community women's support because of that'. The question remained whether loyalist women excluded themselves from progressive politics or whether they were effectively marginalised by those that defined the nature of that politics.

Organising women within, and between, communities

At one remove from the hot house of feminist debate, three community workers organised a weekend conference on the subject of 'Women in the Community' in October 1975. The objective was: 'To give recognition to the women for the work they were already doing and to encourage them … By providing an opportunity for women from different areas to meet, we were building up a network of people who could involve others in activities appropriate to their area and their need'. For many of those involved it was a rare opportunity to travel outside their immediate neighbourhoods and to exchange views with women from other communities. NIWRM speakers contributed to a follow up meeting but it was felt that 'they were too serious'. The meetings planned tapped into the need to connect with women through their lived experience, prioritising basic issues such as childcare, poverty, isolation and lack of confidence. The approach was aptly described by a larger than life activist from Belfast as 'family feminism'. There was much sympathy for the view put forward by Joyce Macartan that no-one could feed a family by frying up a flag in a frying pan.

The importance of networking community-based Women's Groups was recognised with the establishment of the Women's Information Day Network in 1980. Thirty women from different areas of Belfast were invited to a meeting, with paid childcare and transport. One of those involved explained: 'The Day was called an Information Day, acknowledging the fact that information is a key ingredient for any individual or group in the process of gaining confidence, of getting things done or simply being heard. It is a source of power and especially so for women who are so often isolated in their homes where information is much harder to acquire'. A North Belfast Neighbourhood Worker encouraged local women to participate: 'The women I worked with there were actually very isolated as women ... They were quite marginalised ... and it was quite apparent that they needed to feel part of a wider network and they also needed issues that they were interested in as women to be taken on board. I mean it was a big thing for people like that, interested in play – particularly children – to be taken seriously ... But they needed to link up with other groups, and other women interested in the same issues'. The Women's Information Days met that need.

1980 was a particularly difficult period to initiate cross-community networking and the organisers recognised the importance of selecting an acceptable venue. Initially, priority was given to neutrality of access, but over time there was a curiosity about 'the other side': 'There was an Information Day at Hampton (NIAYC venue) and there was a newspaper – the Shankill News – and I would have loved to know what was happening on the Shankill, but I was scared to go and buy the paper, so when they weren't looking I took one ... I really wanted to know what was happening on the Shankill'. This sense of curiosity of 'other' areas resulted in an eventual agreement to alternate meetings between nationalist/republican and unionist/loyalist areas across Belfast. There needed to be ongoing sensitivity to the importance of confidence and trust building. A Catholic woman was later able to laugh at her fears when: 'I remember well we were sitting in Rathcoole, in the Youth Club in Newtownabbey ... and the windows were up high ... and they had blinds up ... And somebody passing had a thing over his shoulder – a piece of wood – but I reckon you could tell every Catholic in the room because it looked like a gunman was dandering past all the windows'. Curiosity was tempered by apprehension when safety was defined by accustomed territory and the nature of current events.

The Information Days featured invited speakers on topics previously selected by the women themselves; however the gatherings avoided an overload of 'experts'. Themes of poverty and housing rights sparked the women into protest action with planned local area follow-up and a rally at Stormont to demand a meeting with the Minister of the Environment. His refusal to meet the women without accompanying public representatives fuelled indignation. Spokeswomen were nominated to present their case on the media. Those selected had access to private telephones, but every effort was made to ensure a balance of community background. Similarly, when the Information Group selected nine representatives to travel to London to petition the Prime Minister on welfare reform the names were drawn out of a hat. It was the first time that most of the delegation had ever flown.

The fact that women were attending meetings in different single-identity areas did not escape local notice. A community worker, in Tullycarnet (Dundonald), recalled: 'At that time, you know, everything was still very volatile really. People weren't travelling much, they really weren't. Even to go down the road in East Belfast was still seen as quite a big journey ... And I felt it was important that other ideas and people came to visit the area as well'. However the introduction of difference had to be negotiated; when a local woman used the term 'Fenian' in a derogatory manner the community worker invited a Queens University history lecturer to explain the origins and implications of the term. An informal discussion ensued but leaked back to local paramilitaries: 'That also got back to the boys (UDA) who said "I hear you've got some interesting history lessons going on". And I was saying "Yes, just picking up on some of the interest, you know". And it was like "Yes, well we heard a bit about it". And I thought hmm ... It was just the way they did it; I think actually being female I probably got off with quite a lot, in many ways because I didn't appear threatening, so there was a bit of that, but there was also – and we're keeping an eye you know'. The possible interpretation and reaction to initiatives taken had to be handled with care to avoid unintended consequences.

A judicious division of labour was agreed when cross-community protests were planned by the Women's Information Day Group. Women from loyalist areas took responsibility for getting the necessary police clearance given the reservations of their republican/nationalist counter-parts. The Tullycarnet community worker described the bustle of activity – 'I mean we made the placards and so forth in the Community Centre and up we marched to Stormont ... And I remember marching up the hill ... and a number of the women were saying "God the last time we marched here it was to bring down Stormont"'. On this occasion the women were met with Direct Rule indifference. Maintaining regular monthly meetings the Women's Information Day continued to grow in numbers, refusing to be disrupted by the headline events of the time. Refusal to cancel the monthly meetings became a principle because it was impossible to know from month to month what the next catastrophe might be, a point made by one of the organisers: 'Because there were always tragedies, always catas-trophes, so you couldn't really stop'. Acknowledgement of any one atrocity would require the judgement of Solomon as to what events needed to be recognised.

The first of the Women's Centres

It was the Northern Ireland Women's Rights Movement that opened the first Women's Centre located in the relatively neutral Belfast city centre. Belfast City Council funding was secured against all apparent odds after a NIWRM committee member made a presentation to the Council, although – 'In actual fact when we did get that Women's Centre, it was kind of like you know, very hard work to keep it going ... because we were constantly looking for funding for people's wages, and people that you employed didn't agree with what you were doing or with your politics either'. The very inclusivity of feminist organising, captured in a polemic on 'The Tyranny of Structurelessness', invariably resulted in even more meetings. The Women's Centre offered services, but also spun off further campaigning.

In the North West, women activists secured small amounts of funding from charitable sources to set up a Women's Advice and Drop-In Centre.

A group member described how: 'We didn't understand fully what kind of journey we were setting out on, we just followed our nose'. The approach taken, later supported by a Derry City Council grant, was developmental: 'You don't connect with people except where they are themselves – wherever it takes people in their individual lives'. Educational courses, with related childcare provision, attracted over three hundred women each week. Discussion was encouraged on equality and creative writing, although it was primarily the 'humble courses' of basic literacy, maths and sewing that generated greatest interest. The original location in an elderly terrace house meant that the worker had to light the fire every morning and organise fundraising evenings where subscribers were provided with a glass of wine in exchange for a donation. With basic maths it was calculated that if one hundred people contributed a minimum of fifty pence each, then the rent could be paid.

Two new community based Women's Centres opened within a year of each other in the early 1980s in Belfast. The Falls Women's Centre which was based on the Falls Road adopted an ethos that reflected republicanism and feminism. Some months later the Ballybeen Women's Centre opened for business in a populous estate, in the largely loyalist eastern fringes of Belfast. This development was supported by a Neighbourhood Worker employed by Castlereagh Borough Council, who felt that the Centre was – 'Really quite innovative at that time'. A change in political party control of the Council saw a change in official attitude: 'Women's groups were just seen as radical and troublemakers and all that sort of thing and ... it was very difficult to get funding to them'. It became clear that workers also had to watch their step: 'I remember a few of us started attending the Council meetings because actually they were open but nobody ever went, so it was part of the Women's Group seeing how decisions were made in Council. And so down we traipsed and the councillors didn't know what to do with us, didn't know how to react to us ... and we'd have our tea in a china cup, and it was all very sort of nice. But then after we'd been a couple of times they really got quite worried about it; maybe felt quite threatened by it and the Chief Recreation Officer was then dispatched to speak to me about why this was happening. And I was explaining about it, you know – community education sort of angle ... I did see that they weren't that happy ... and that was then when workers ... (had) to take a back seat'. If elected councillors in Castlereagh were unsettled by female presence, Belfast City Council appointed a Women's Officer in 1983. When the incumbent resigned two years later, the idea was put on ice for some years. Derry City Council was the next local authority to appoint a Women's Officer.

The establishment of an increasing number of community-based Women's Centres raised the question as to whether facilities located within single identity communities were preferable to a 'neutral' location, accessible to all but outside local areas. In the circumstances of the early 1980s the theory of cross-community accessibility folded before both the fears and the reality of how increasingly single identity communities were organising themselves in practice. A West Belfast woman described the dynamics of local participation: 'I think a lot of it was in local areas – at that stage people just knocked on your door and said "We need you to do such and such, will you come out?" ... You know, there was a lot more word of mouth at that stage as opposed to "Oh we'll set up a commit-tee". I think people just said "This needs to be done" and natural leaders just emerged all over the place ... It was even, such and such has a car; or such and such knows how to get a minibus, or a telephone, or such and such is married on to such and such ... And because communities were so close-knit at that stage too, and people didn't tend to venture out of West Belfast because of what was going on'. The fear of moving out of one's own area was very real in often beleaguered working-class communities, whether republican or loyalist. Networking and regional support groups ameliorated some of the inwardness of single identity activities by offering opportunities to exchange experience on a broader basis. If the Women's Information Day was an example of individual net-working, the Women's Education Project (later the Women's Resource & Development Agency) was established in 1983 to provide collective support to locally based women's groups. The Women's Movement was translating itself into the Women's Sector as an infrastructure began to develop, with the Women's Centres establishing their own network – the Women's Support Network.

Testing alternatives to violence

The potential of non-violent action had been a sub-theme in political discussion since the earliest years of the Troubles. A community develop-ment worker in West Belfast noted a certain: 'Fascination about (what) non-violent action was, what are the tactics that were used in non-violent organising and what way that could be used in the situation that we're in'. The increasing levels of violence resulted in decreasing space to explore these options although individuals managed to maintain both connection and communication. A number of external theoreticians and thinkers were drawn to the teeming political milieu of Northern Ireland. John Burton was invited in by the Northern Ireland Community Relations Commission and Professor Adam Curle visted regularly, linking with the constant, if low profile, Quaker presence. A rather more exotic analyst was sociolo-gist at large, Richard Hauser, who funded a small group of community activists in loyalist and republican areas, convening them for updates at his London Embankment apartment. One was Des Wilson: 'Richard Hauser offered us financial help and this was gratefully received, thus making up an ecumenical team of Presbyterians, Catholics, Anglicans, Jews and Quakers and the rest of us working together'. Hauser's wife, Hepzibah Menuhin (sister of the celebrated musician, Yehudi) provided an element of sanity as her husband pontificated not only on Northern Ireland but also on his other enthusiasm – the Kurds. Born-again peace-espousing British Generals visited; Des scripted his next sketch for the Ballymurphy People's Theatre, and loyalist community activist, Ian Fraser, cast his eyes heavenwards at the whispered conclaves in the great man's study. There was encouragement of ideas of community-based participa-tive democracy which attracted the wrath of at least one departmental Permanent Secretary, John Oliver, who in magisterial terms dubbed the 'Astonishing new growth of community associations – some with dubi-ous connections' as 'dangerous'; holding that 'The alternative to elected representative government can only be anarchy or tyranny in the long run'. The same gentleman noted with quiet satisfaction the predominance of

'Instonian boys' (an influential Belfast Grammar school) as senior advisers to the failed Constitutional Convention of 1975/76. The sub-text of 'safe hands' was alive and flourishing.

On the streets, the atmosphere was summed up in the lyrics of local group, Stiff Little Fingers. Their new record 'Suspect Device' jumped to number nineteen in the charts, rocking to the words: 'I am a suspect device the Army can't defuse. Inflammable material is planted in my head. I am a suspect device that's left 2,000 dead'. The teenage group members hailed from Ardoyne and Ballysillan; their agent remarked: 'It would be pointless if our music didn't reflect all the carnage that is going on around us. Kids of our age have known nothing but the Troubles and there is just nothing for them in Belfast'. The band went on to sing about 'State of Emergency' and 'Alternative Ulster'.

Handbags at the Ready: The Politics of 'Safe Hands'

The 1979 British General Election swept Conservative Party leader, Margaret Thatcher, into power in a surge of blue. The new Direct Rule team had hardly settled in before the Northern Ireland Housing Executive was instructed to sell off 190,000 houses in line with Tory privatisation policies. Community statements condemned the policy as 'giant asset-stripping', while Shankill Road campaigners questioned whether there was that many houses to sell. Marking the decade-long anniversary of British soldiers on the streets of Northern Ireland, Army GOC, General Sir Timothy Creasey, paid an unannounced visit to a Sinn Féin office in Belfast that August. Such civility was blown into context by IRA bombs that killed eighteen soldiers in the North and Lord Mountbatten and his boating party in the South. In a re-energised drive against paramilitarism, Maurice Oldfield (allegedly MI6 'Top spy-catcher' and prototype for 'M' of James Bond fame) arrived in Northern Ireland as Security Coordinator. In the parallel universe of republicanism, a number of community organisations condemned the use of informers, reports of brutal interrogation of people detained for questioning and the conviction of people in Special Courts based solely on 'voluntary confessions'.

A combative Minister of the Environment, Philip Goodhart, was forthright on how government saw militant republicanism: 'As far as quite a lot of the governmental machine was concerned Sinn Féin was looked upon with the same enthusiasm as one might have looked upon a group of Nazis ... Indeed those people were regarded as semi-criminal, more criminal than political'. This narrative set the scene for the prison struggle over political status. The resulting violence impacted on local communities; in some areas it 'gelled' communities, although this could be to the serious detriment of those who adopted different political positions. If the divided communities of Northern Ireland did agree on certain social and economic grievances, James Prior, who was appointed Secretary of State, rejected their litany of complaints. In an interview with the *Shankill Bulletin* he downplayed any link between high levels of unemployment, deprivation and political conflict: 'I simply do not believe that pouring more and more money into Northern Ireland, even if that money were available which it isn't, would solve the problems. What is required is a political and security solution and until then you will not get economic prosperity. The security situation is the most important, without it you cannot get political advance'. There were, needless to say, those who begged to differ, although a simple reductionist theory that multiple deprivation equals violence was also unacceptable.

In June 1982, the Orange Order supported a march against unemployment; a number of Orange Lodges sported placards with the non-traditional demand 'Give Us Jobs', during the subsequent 12 July celebrations. The number of registered unemployed had breached the 100,000 threshold (17.6 per cent of the working population) the previous year and was still rising. Community campaigners against public spending cuts also took to the streets as Shankill Road community organiser, Jackie Redpath, called for working-class solidarity: 'The only long-term hope is the emergence of a politically conscious group with a strong base in the community who will recognise the need for wider working-class links and will be strong enough to make and maintain them'. Threats of school closures opened up a new front when Shankill mothers and grandmothers joined the Edenbrooke Parents' Action Group and engaged in direct action. Most of the primary schools listed for closure were located in inner city loyalist areas with declining enrolment numbers. Local women argued that removing a school was like 'Wrenching the heart out of the community'; re-messaged by DUP councillors serving on the Belfast Education Board as an attempt to 'de-Protestantise Belfast'. Party politics was never slow to make a political point. After a fruitless meeting with the Minister for Education, women from the Parents Action Group were also driven to make a political point, castigating the government: 'It can give thousands of pounds to supergrasses (informers) but it cannot find the money to educate our children'.

If the Minister for Education was persona non grata with angry parents, his colleague in Health & Social Services, John Patton, had an equally brittle relationship with campaigners against welfare reform proposals that effectively cut the income of claimants. The Northern Ireland Poverty Lobby was an amalgam of activists drawn from academia, trade unions and community and voluntary organisations, who condemned the stigmatisation of claimants in conditions of high unemployment. Evidence provided by Welfare Rights workers in centres across the North supported the campaign, although Conservative Government policies were not without friends in Northern Ireland, as a number of local politicians rubbished the 'poverty industry'. A Northern Ireland Consumer Council study concluded that one-third of children were living in conditions of poverty. Supported by the Belfast Community Law Centre, established in the late 1970s, door-to-door welfare benefit take-up campaigns became the order of the day. While checking that households claimed their entitlements, the real benefit of such campaigns was to raise awareness, develop a rights-based approach and contribute to collective community organising. For its part the Northern Ireland Poverty Lobby emphasised the shared nature of deprivation across local communities irrespective of their community identity.

Campaigning became the sine qua non of activist community and single issue groups. When a number of service providers decided to move against people in debt it was taken as a challenge. Chaos reigned in Derry's Rossville Flats one night when the Northern Ireland Electricity Service implemented its policy of disconnections, plunging several homes into darkness during a particularly gripping episode of the TV drama 'Dallas'. Anxious viewers, caught on the hop, rushed along the connecting balconies to watch on a neighbour's television. Indignation ran high in the Derry air. The Derry Claimants' Union protested during the Christmas lights switch-on ceremony in the Guildhall Square, then regrouped to script a street-theatre performance on the subject. Duly presented the following Saturday to a gaggle of harassed Christmas shoppers, agit-prop street theatre became a regular instrument in the tool box of protest.

When service providers decided to take a number of test cases to court in Belfast they made an unfortunate choice: '... With the onset of the Troubles everybody went on Rent and Rates strike ... Everybody broke the locks on their gas meters and the same shilling did forever and ever and ever ... I mean they came in with the Army and the police and they raided every house ... and the most they collected was a shilling out of every household ... They took so many to court and, you know, it was absolutely hilarious because one of the cases would have been a woman who would have been in her 70s, and the reason she was taken to court was like she was the matriarch of a very republican family. And they took her to court and she sat and she said to the judge – "Son, how in the name of God would I have been able to use a drill to drill a hole in my meter? Somebody has come in and done this I bet you. I bet you I was set up." And the case was dismissed and out she walked, and all the other test cases walked out behind her'. The Northern Ireland Poverty Lobby was engaged in acrimonious exchanges with Minister Patton on the very day that republican Bobby Sands died on hunger strike in the Maze Prison protest for political status.

Dealing with the fall-out of the hunger strikes

Prison protests over the withdrawal of political status had been escalating over a period of years, resulting in two republican hunger strikes in 1980/81. An unforeseen consequence was the difficulties experienced by a number of Community Resource Centres located in republican/nationalist areas. On the one hand they were in receipt of local authority funding, on the other, they served neighbourhoods that were home to the families and supporters of large numbers of politically motivated prisoners. As the prison campaign grew ever more serious a record of the Falls Community Council AGM noted: 'The question of what our position was on this critical question was discussed intensely and at great length'. A range of views skirted around the question as to when did community concern morph into politics, and vice versa? With the mounting toll of prison deaths, nightly violence and black mourning flags twisting from lamp posts, it became clear that the issue could not be avoided. The Council Organiser reflected: 'The first hunger strike – the five demands – was discussed on the margins of meetings of the Falls Council. Then, to be honest, a rather poorly attended Council meeting, if the truth be told, decided ... (everybody was being asked to put ads in the paper in support of the hunger strikers' demands) ... to put the ad in the paper to support the five demands on a humanitarian basis, or whatever – careful of the wording like. But ... Unionist councillors heard about it, raised it at the Council meetings and committee meetings ... and threatened to stop our grant; and indeed did stop our grant ... so we were without a grant for four or five months'. Reinstatement of the grant was due to the diplomacy of the City Council Director of Community Services who advised the Community Council to avoid confrontation. She person-ally investigated and reported to councillors that the Community Council meeting had been properly constituted and the controversial advertisement had not been funded out of City Council monies; on her recommendation the grant was reinstated. For the Community Council Organiser, the saga continued: 'The other interesting bit of it is that as soon as we'd worked it out that there was a possibility of complaints about this ad being in the paper we had another committee meeting. Everybody turned up at that one, you know, bit of controversy ... But the astonishing thing was that people who had doubts about the wisdom of putting the ad in the paper, nevertheless their view was, we've done it, we're sticking by it now ... and we're not going to be told. There was absolutely no question like – people in their seventies – there was no question of the Council telling them what to do. There was a determined independence ... and if they stop our grant, well, we've survived without a grant before'. In short, punitive official reac-tion to community decision-making simply served to consolidate local views on the importance of independence.

As a Community Resource Centre, the Falls Community Council was one of a number of centres that by 1979 employed 103 community workers across Northern Ireland. At least five of the fourteen groups supported under the earlier Community Worker Research Project were either Community Resource Centres or developed as such. The Omagh Community Development Project delivered initiatives around welfare rights and community arts, as well as designing the Omagh Youth & Community Workshop in response to youth unemployment, influenced by a similar model in Derry. Adopting an ethos of self-help and individ-ual empowerment, direct action was taken against the closure of rural primary schools and factories, on the basis that: 'When a community takes up an issue and campaigns, it is challenging authority and in the process more political awareness is developed about the power structures that control decision-making. The campaigns fought in this district (Omagh) have not all been successful in relation to reversing policy in favour of local needs but what cannot be undermined is the educational awareness and the heightening of political consciousness that has developed in this district as people are now starting to make links and support each other in their individual struggles'.

Each Community Resource Centre developed its own ethos and priorities. The Falls Community Council adopted an 'open door' policy, which was not without its critics, but was safeguarded by the wide variety of political allegiances and opinions represented on its committee. The Council Organiser was astute in acknowledging the importance of getting to know local residents: 'When I started the job ... the thing was to get to know who was active and I was given a list of names, and I go round knocking doors to discover that people are dead or have moved or the last thing they wanted to talk about was community action, because they had had enough of it ... So it was a bit barren at the time which seemed very difficult, but in hindsight was probably the best thing that ever happened to me'. New contacts were forthcoming from an unexpected quarter – the supervisor of street cleaning in the area: 'He became one of my best sources of new groups, because people would stop him in the street and give off about things ... And he would say "Oh yes, you have to get yourselves organised, go up and see yer man" – that's true like. And I didn't know he was doing it until three or four groups of people would arrive. He was one and the other was Paddy Brady ... He was the milkman; the same. People would stop him on his rounds and give off, and he'd say, "Away up and see Colm" ... I didn't realise it at the time, but that's how things work; that's what we now call social capital'. The Centre programme developed as a result, in addition to offering administrative services to local groups, it organised a local history project; community Sports Days; conferences on topical issues; a research facility; alongside the trademark welfare benefit take-up campaigns. Immense energy was invested in direct action over poor housing conditions: 'It just started like protests, protests every time we could get an excuse, or get a crowd together no matter what age they were, down to the Housing Executive office in College Square'. Importantly, small successes were celebrated and shared between neighbourhoods to maintain motivation.

The Organiser in the Upper Springfield Resource Centre was juggling the needs of the ninety-four local community groups in his area, but still focused on participation: 'It wasn't that they were all tripping over one another, there was different people involved in most of them, doing different things ... Now that might have been seen as being quite fragmented, but it wasn't ... There were a number of forums for people to share ideas and build up mutually supportive networks in the area ... The festival was very good for that as well'. Even with these high levels of involvement, proactive action had to be taken to ensure a well-attended AGM: 'One time we were very worried about not getting a quorum for our AGM, so we put out a rumour that there was going to be a (political) take-over attempt, and you couldn't have got in the door. It was the best AGM we ever had; it was the biggest turn out we ever had'. Tactics were important.

The wide membership base of Resource Centres often meant that workers had to manage a certain jostling for influence whether driven by personalities or politics. Political differences were particularly acute in those Centres that served diverse single identity communities, as was the situation in North Belfast. When travelling to attend an interview for the post of Director in the North Belfast Community Development Centre, the friendly local bus driver told one young woman not to bother: 'I tell you', he said, 'I come from round here – stay on the bus'. Some years later the successful appointee described her work: 'Resource Centre-type organisations took on different roles and they were very much influenced by their type of area ... You see if you wanted to you could have adopted the line of we're only a photocopying service, you know ... that's very practical ... Development work can rub all agencies up the wrong way ... Agencies didn't like that, you know. And I suppose part of the time it was always trying to explain to people what exactly community development was about'. As in other areas, the North Belfast agenda covered housing, environmental issues and poverty, but also the sensitive issue of peace lines across an area that was a patchwork of small, single identity communities, living cheek by jowl in a situation of violence.

The Centre for Neighbourhood Development (CfND): A model of neighbourhood development

Unlike the Community Resource Centres, the Centre for Neighbourhood Development worked out of an office in central Belfast, with outreach into local neighbourhoods. Its roots were in the vacuum created by the demise of the Northern Ireland Community Relations Commission, with initial planning grounded in a commitment to community self-help and a Quaker inspired social justice ethos. Its work, over the fifteen years of its existence, included investment in community skill building; a focus on neighbourhood development and participation; community action as a form of social education; and sharing its model of community development practice with key stakeholders. Six outreach neighbourhoods were selected on the basis of community identity and need (three single identity Protestant, and three Catholic) – a pattern that was to become a standing feature of demonstration projects. Attention was also paid to linking with statutory agencies, as explained by a CfND staff member: 'People working on the ground didn't really take the statutory authorities under their notice enough until like Social Services and certain Councils began to have community workers'. CfND drew together a disparate gathering of community workers at its monthly meetings, recognising that many such individuals operated in comparative isolation, with only limited peer support and even less supportive supervision.

The outreach neighbourhood initiatives were based on thinking that – 'The neighbourhood worker should be someone from that area, who knows the area ... Everybody was paid the same; everybody was involved in the committee, so the committee was the voluntary committee members and the workers who were all very involved and that created all sorts of difficulties later ... but it was a series of principles like that were stuck to'. Each of the selected neighbourhoods had a representative on the CfND management committee to ensure coordination. The neighbourhood workers were directed by management committees in their respective areas: 'They all had Tenants' or Community Associations locally whose job it was to support the worker, although the workers were employed by us. And then they set an agenda for the worker and we tried to help by bringing in other resources and expertise where it was needed, and we had regular weekly meetings with the workers ... We sent them on the part-time Youth & Community course in Jordanstown (University of Ulster), one day a week, which was more successful for some than for others'. There was also an issue as to whether the workers could meet in each other's area given prevailing fears about personal security.

The diversity of the CfND neighbourhood workers appointed was highlighted by, on the one hand, the redoubtable Danny Taggart, who struggled to work between warring intra-republican and nationalist constituencies in the Short Strand area of East Belfast, and on the other, his colleague working in the equally nationalist/republican New Lodge area of North Belfast, who went to war with officials over the building of peace walls. The latter informed local newspapers that if confidential Housing Executive documents had not been leaked, the community would never have known about a security wall planned for their area. The siting of 'peace walls' proved fertile ground for community controversy more generally given both the growing link between community identity and territoriality, alongside concerns about the suspected influence of the British Army on planning decisions. By the early 1980s peace walls were being refurbished from the original galvanised tin and razor wire barriers hastily thrown up during the early days of the Troubles. Community narratives over the subsequent decade reflected a clear alignment between barricaded space and community identity in urban areas, and the more nebulous, but no less real, dividing lines of rivers, roads and uplands in rural communities. The official history of the Housing Executive described the challenges posed by territoriality in Belfast: 'Public sector housing in the city is largely based along sectarian lines and, where both communities live side by side, walls are often required to separate them. The most daunting of these is Cupar Street in West Belfast. More reminiscent of the Berlin Wall, it separates Catholic West Belfast from the Protestant Shankill. In other locations Catholics and Protestants are only a matter of yards apart and the walls represent a constant shadow over everyday life'. What the walls in effect highlighted was a sense of place that effectively closed down inter-communal space; an example in practice was highlighted by an argument among children on a cross-community outing over which group should visit the other's area to play ball against 'their wall'. Little did they know that they lived on either side of the same wall.

The *Belfast Telegraph* reported on the one and a half million bricks purchased by the Ministry of Defence in 1981 to reinforce and heighten the wall dividing the Shankill and the Falls. A leaked letter from the Belfast Development Office reminded all agencies that the security forces had to be consulted at an early stage in the planning of proposed new buildings, road realignment and other planned infrastructure. An article in *Scope* magazine was taken up by mainstream media and Town & Country Planning journal, and while alleged security force involvement was officially denied, the Minister of Environment acknowledged that: 'We do have meetings with the security forces. It would be foolish to undertake a housing project if the people living there were to be at risk'. Community concerns, however, focused on lack of policy transparency and whether the security forces favoured community segregation as a form of conflict management.

The controversy over security influence on urban planning rumbled on in what was later described as a 'mini-Orwellian' portrayal of government policy making. Senior civil servants in the Department of the Environment echoed their Minister, but more sceptical voices suggested that the debate offered an insight into how the abnormality of a violently contested society was normalised in policy making. Street lay-out was a case in point. Broadly sweeping cul-de-sacs could either be designed to allow children to play, or to ensure that heavy army vehicles would be saved the risk of having to reverse. Whatever the policy considerations, the pervasive presence of the peace walls impressed writer, Carlo Gebler, during a visit to Belfast – 'I made the obligatory drive – first over to the Shankill … and then back to the Falls … and everywhere we seemed to run into "peace lines" … Peace line is the wrong name, but presumably deliberately chosen because anything more accurate, like "conflict inhibitor" or "social controller" would not do'. Whatever they were called, a NIO official discounted the more conspiratorial explanations: 'If there were conspiracies I wasn't aware of them and they were tactical conspiracies rather than strategic conspiracies in my opinion'. This forensic differentiation did little to assuage community speculation. For its part, the Centre for Neighbourhood Development continued working with single identity neighbourhoods, often bounded by peace walls, but drawing out inter-community synergies.

The organisation closed in 1992 when the neighbourhood worker concept was adopted in principle by Belfast City Council, although in practice job remits differed. The new workers were based in community centres across the city, with a brief to manage the buildings rather than the original CfND vision of workers being proactive. The Centre for Neighbourhood Development long outlived the two regional coordinating organisations, CONI and UCAG who both had funding withdrawn in the early 1980s. UDA Chairman, Andy Tyrie, interpreted the withdrawal of UCAG funding as politically motivated: 'The government seen it was too much of a threat and they had to say "No we can deal with you from a paramilitary point of view easier than we can deal with you in the community" ... And then there was the witch-hunt business, people who were former paramilitaries who had moved over to do work in the community, they turned round and said, "Oh no, these paramilitaries are into it." But there was nobody else to do the job; nobody else wanted to do the job'. On a more positive note a UCAG member recounted the range of work that had developed as a result of the community consciousness gleaned through the organisation. Reference was made to the networking conferences attended, although one held in the Corrymeela residential centre had unfortunate consequences for three UCAG representatives. When stopped by the British Army en route to the gathering, the names Chicken, Curry and Rice (actual names) resulted in the men being held for questioning.

CONI also lost its funding although arguably, because the organisation – rather more than UCAG – fell into the 'biting the hand that feeds you' syndrome, that was less than popular with Conservative Ministers. The disappearance of both organisations meant the loss of potential cross-community networking described by a UCAG committee member: 'We did during that time have a number of meetings and sessions with colleagues from republican and nationalist areas ... We met with some boys and girls who were extremely active, who would have been diametrically opposed politically, but that didn't come in to it. It was about how did you get that particular provision or how did you go about the other thing?'. Any such contact was now at an individual rather than an organisational level, which offered less cover or security in circumstances where allegations ran free (although in the words of one elected local representative, he saw it as his job to track down 'the alligators'!).

Juggling the armalite, politics and the community

Community action had long experience in adapting itself to changing political circumstances. In the immediate aftermath of internment a Youth Worker in Ballymurphy recognised that the average age of both the Provisional and Official IRA had dropped considerably, with a preponderance of young people in positions of paramilitary command: 'So there was a kind of general problem in the area in relation to youth work at the time – apart from the fact that you regularly had to say to older kids, "Would you mind going home and come back when you're dressed properly." In other words leave the gun at home and come back without it ... Pistols in their belts, you know ... and that created a certain amount of stress ...' – in short, not something on the curriculum of Youth Work courses. By the early 1980s the IRA had adopted the more circumspect cell structure and individuals, who had either been interned or served a prison sentence, were being released back into the community. The successful election of three hunger-strikers in 1981 also provoked a re-think within the Republican Movement about its traditional policy of boycotting parliamentary representation.

The question centre-stage at a Sinn Féin Árd Fheis was posed as: 'Who here really believes we can win the war through the ballot box? But will anyone here object if with a ballot paper in one hand and the armalite in the other, we take power in Ireland?' The initial toe in the water of electoral fortune saw Sinn Féin winning 10.1 per cent of the first preference vote and five seats (compared to 18.8 per cent of the vote and fourteen seats secured by the SDLP) in the Northern Ireland Assembly election of October 1982. The 1983 General Election returned Gerry Adams as MP for West Belfast. A republican ex-prisoner, turned community activist, explained the policy shift: 'The political struggle that went on in the jail over the hunger strike, changed a lot of mind sets and I think the political process was born during that era as well ... The hunger strike was a real learning curve in a sense that after the hunger strike you seemed to have used your utmost weapon ... But in actual fact wiser counsel within the jail was sitting, analysing ... Really what they said is "We've won the political struggle in the eyes of the world. We are political prisoners, now we set this to one side ... so what do we want? We want segregation. Well let's run a campaign to get that" ... So they broke it all down into smaller objectives. Now I think in a sort of way that mirrored then what happened in the 80s because people then said, "Look there's more to this struggle than armed struggle. Community development is a legitimate form of struggle." The interweaving of struggles reflected an evolving activism, although the process was not without its contradictions when applied to community development.

For people with an established track record of community leadership the approach adopted by Sinn Féin leaders posed a quandary. A number of youth and community workers were called to meetings with leading Sinn Féin figures; one, a party sympathiser, argued: 'What we were trying to say to Adams, you know, you don't need to do this, just support the thing from your level and it'll work like that ... There were things that we could do at a community level that ... if they touched it, it was the kiss of death'. Another community worker warned: 'He (Adams) was talking about how we are interested in doing this, and we were saying "Perfect, but be careful how you go". I mean the last thing people want is for their organisations to be taken over by anybody basically, people are doing a fine job out there'. The message was nevertheless clear that political change was in the air. A distinction was drawn by one experienced community activist between the exercise of influence and the imposition of control: 'Our impression here was that there were times in the Republican Movement (when) the idea was look at those community associations – to hell with that there going along as if they were snails, get in there and take over. Now if that opinion was uppermost at the time that's what they'd try to do. However there were times when they said "No our job is not to do that, it's to see what's being done and to help". So to us here it was a question of which opinion was in the ascendancy at any particular time'. Faced with electoral timetables political parties could find themselves at odds with process driven community development

The situation in unionist/loyalist areas was different. Here the question was where community activists positioned themselves on the loyalist-unionist spectrum; or where they were positioned by others. In the early years of both the Save the Shankill Campaign and the North & West Federation of Tenants' Associations the activist view of the preferred role of elected politicians was clear: 'Well Save the Shankill Campaign – I remember a vote at the start of it that no elected representatives would be on the committee because they would be servants of the committee and therefore they would be called on when relevant. The North & West Federation used to scare the life out of councillors and things, because it kept them in check'. A similar sentiment was shared by women campaigning for better conditions in the Springmartin estate in the 1980s: 'I mean we lived in Springmartin (and) we never seen them elected politicians ... We had no actual relationship with any elected politician in that sense (but) Hughie Smyth and people like that would have come up and seen us when we started the Blackmountain Action Group ... I can remember having a public meeting with the people of Springmartin (and) all these people, all the councillors came up and came into the meeting. I said "Before this meeting starts you folk will have to leave, you haven't been invited", and they went ballistic ... They were furious because they'd never done nothing for us, and there we were doing a plan and we'd possible money all of a sudden (and) they wanted in on it'. In the very different circumstances of the Fountain estate in Londonderry, community activists praised one particular Ulster Unionist councillor, but similarly noted the general lack of interest: 'If you're looking at the community from a distance and not living within the community you don't understand to the same extent'. The issue of elected representatives seen as being at one remove was a constant complaint in loyalist areas, although the Director of North Belfast Community Development Centre was more judicious, pointing out: 'Where a politician is genuine and do their work you can't argue with that'. There were always exceptions.

Faced with the growing alienation of unionist politicians due to the ongoing British-Irish inter-governmental talks, Prime Minister Thatcher offered reassurance, asserting that Northern Ireland was as much part of the United Kingdom as her constituency, and encouraging her Northern Ireland administration to placate local politicians by affording them public recognition. The *Shankill Bulletin*'s Red Pepper columnist was less than impressed: 'Top level moves have been made to cut out the rights of community groups and their representatives to push the cases of people they deal with, with government and statutory bodies. From Ministerial level down to the Shankill Housing Executive office, and Snugville Street "Bru", officials are refusing to listen to community representatives and have been told only to consult with councillors. Some councillors have welcomed the move and recently Councilllor XXX declared in a General Purposes & Finance Committee meeting in the City Hall that for far too long councillors and City Hall Departments had taken too much notice of community groups'. While there were complaints about moves by councillors to take control of the work traditionally done by community groups, councillors might well have retorted that community activists could not have it both ways – on the one hand complaining about lack of interest, but on the other objecting when elected representatives were active at local level. The nicety was the difference between representation and control.

If there were concerns over the politicisation of community action, there was alarm over a sudden Northern Ireland Office interest in community work. *Scope* echoed local anger when Fr. Des Wilson, then employed in the Upper Springfield Resource Centre, was arrested by the British Army and held for questioning. Sometime later, the *Shankill Bulletin* got wind of the fact that the Northern Ireland Office was circulating Belfast councillors with a questionnaire asking them to list the names of community workers in their area; provide information on their location and funding; and to give an opinion as to whether they were doing a good job. The Bulletin was sceptical of the motivations for such interest pointing out: 'It is understood shortly after these questions were asked a number of Community Centres and Housing Advice Centres, including the Shankill Education Workshop, were broken into in what appears to be a coordinated effort and a number of files were stolen, though no significant damage was done to premises'. If this was Big Brother at work the arguably chaotic administrative arrangements in many community offices might well have thwarted the mission.

Negotiating space for community action continued to be a complex minuet, with the importance of who said what, and in what circumstances, analysed to death. In strained political conditions suspicion flourished. A Resource Centre Organiser was lucky to be given 'a by-ball' after he attended a meeting in the Divis complex given that he was relatively unknown and had a Ballymena accent. A friend had to vouch for him. In short, 'the unknown' was a threat and the role of the well-connected and trusted intermediary was essential to establish what was feasible without having to approach paramilitary and/or political organisations directly. Intermediary points of communication were important at a number of levels – (a) determining the acceptability of an individual who was external to the local area; (b) explaining the rationale for a position adopted or a campaign mounted; (c) establishing what challenges could be safely made to prevailing orthodoxies; and (d) estimating the acceptability of contact with government and statutory agencies.

Ballymurphy community activist, Frank Cahill brought the role of 'insider-outsider' – or 'insider-partial' – to a fine art: 'I mean Frank was a republican ... but boy when he needed to stand up to the Republican Movement, when they would get in the way of community development, he did ... He always would have said to me "You know, community development is about the people ... But they (the IRA) belong to the people, not the other way about ..."' However, the persona and reputation of the messenger was crucial in the delivery of this message. It was not just what was sayable in a contested community, it was who said it. This situation was particularly important in challenges to paramilitary 'punishment beatings' of young people accused of 'anti-social activities'. A voluntary youth worker used his credibility as a political ex-prisoner to question these attacks, with a similar approach adopted in Divis, where the Youth Drop-In Centre used an intermediary to make representation on behalf of young people under threat.

Loyalist areas also had their intermediaries. The daughter of a well-known 'old' republican figure benefitted from UVF icon, Gusty Spence's support when she was appointed by Belfast City Council to work on the Shankill: 'It was very scary ... They (individuals associated with the UVF and the Red Hand Commando) had a Centre up at the top of the Shankill

Road; they had a brilliant project there, like above (it) was a recording studio and below was a computer suite. So Gusty wasn't long out (of prison) and he was sort of an unknown quantity a bit, certainly for me ... So I went up to meet them and I was a wreck ... Gusty says "Ah, you know there used to be a McGlade's Bar in Donegall Street" – and he was Frank McGlade as was my father. And he says "Are you related to Frank McGlade?" And I said "Yes", my frigging knees were knocking together. And he said "Frank McGlade the publican down there – the pub?" And I says "No." And he says "Oh no, not that Frank McGlade, the other Frank McGlade – Frank McGlade the republican?" And he says to me "Ah, cad ann a tá tú?" (How are you?) because "your father taught me Irish in jail" ... And he says to me "Look it's hard for you coming in, I'd find it hard, and I'll put the word out and don't worry about it, and if anything's said to you just come and speak to me." And I was fine'. Making the right connections at an early stage was important.

Intermediaries, and effective lines of communication continued to win space, and where necessary, safety for community activism. Equally, awareness of local political narrative was essential in framing issues and mobilising support; how things were said could be as important as what was said. This did not prevent tensions, competition and controversy within community organisations, but at least allowed room for them to take place. For those activists resident in single identity communities certain levels of dissent were acceptable provided it did not stray into areas where it could be exploited by 'outsiders'. When this happened the reaction was often punitive, as experienced by 'the Peace Women' in Derry, who were attacked due to their outspoken opposition to violence. The implications of mutually exclusive community narratives was recognised by a West Belfast Alliance Party councillor: 'I used often joke with people, you know, you drove up that road there (the Falls Road) and you reached a certain point, you either read things through mirrors, what was logical down there is illogical up here, and what was illogical down there is logical up here, you've got to remember that. You've got to have lateral vision once you cross over into republican West Belfast'. If community narratives helped to frame local understanding of the ongoing conflict, serving to bond them in the face of often adverse external representation, difficulties arose when single identity communities had to deal with the conflicting narratives of others.

Meanwhile the interface between community action and political influence continued, although a Sinn Féin councillor referred to the potentially contradictory positions that (a) the community had to be safeguarded at all times, and (b) the importance of community 'empowerment'. What was not open to debate was the need to keep tabs on those individuals and organisations that did business with the state. In practical terms this was experienced when women protesting over housing conditions in the Moyard area of West Belfast were invited to meet the Minister for the Environment. Their chauffeur was a community worker employed by Social Services: 'So I arranged this battered car to actually take these people up. And this guy with a beard started climbing in the back of the car – Gerry Adams ... So we arrived in a Ford Escort which had basically been stoned about twenty times, with Gerry Adams, who had been shot a few times recently, and they weren't expecting Gerry Adams ... So we were actually shown into this room which I swear almost had counter-insurgency posters on the walls ... It was in Stormont Castle ... They (the officials) must have been actually gobsmacked'. Notwithstanding the composition of the delegation, the long-running campaign over conditions in Moyard was eventually successful.

The politics of preference: Playing the ACE

By the mid 80s government policy focused on minimising contact with Sinn Féin; emphasising the normality of conditions in Northern Ireland and ensuring that community-based organisations remained free from paramilitary influence, real or perceived. With diplomatic tick-tacking between Dublin and London moving inexorably towards the Anglo-Irish Agreement (November 1985), every effort was made to keep unionism on side and to enhance the position of moderate nationalism. Although the former proved difficult, significant forces were mobilised in support of the latter. One opportunity was the allocation of resources attached to management of a new job creation scheme – Action for Community Employment

(ACE). This programme offered subsidised one year employment for the long term unemployed, delivered through community and voluntary organisations. Fears were expressed that ACE would create a pool of temporary, low paid workers and that community action would be cast as community service provision rather than development. The latter concern seemed justified when accusations flew between two church-related ACE managing agencies, working in a small rural town, about each 'stealing' the others pensioners for their respective luncheon clubs. This introduced a new form of territoriality with painting and decorating, garden maintenance, welfare rights advice and community care becoming the standard forms of ACE placements. The prizes at stake were the management fees, and core staffing costs, that were funded in line with the number of ACE places provided.

For community providers who balanced local needs with a smidgeon of imagination there were additional benefits. A North Belfast provider recalled – 'We had done a survey and amongst that age group (seventeen- to twenty-five-year-olds) there was 78 per cent unemployment in the New Lodge. So for us we used it in a very different kind of way and they (the ACE workers) wouldn't have been people involved in community action, but they became involved ... as a result of being connected ... (they) came on to the committees ... and helped out with the festivals and stuff and then got into it ... so it probably brought a load of people in'. The Crossmaglen Community Resource Centre used ACE placements to offer community transport in their dispersed rural hinterland, as well as supporting work with women and other groups. The ACE scheme offered many community groups their first source of income and paid workers/trainees, generally drawn from their immediate neighbourhood. It was not unknown for some community ACE schemes to offer cyclical employment, with individuals employed through ACE for twelve months, claiming welfare benefits the following year, and then re-employed to another ACE post. By 1986 there were some 5,600 ACE positions across the North and upwards of 700 sponsoring organisations.

Speaking in Parliament in 1985, the Northern Ireland Secretary of State expressed concerns about public funds supporting any projects linked to militant republicanism or loyalism; whether real or perceived. A number of ACE projects were caught in the cross-hairs of the political offensive launched by Mr Hurd: 'There are cases in which some community groups, or persons prominent in the direction or management of some community groups, have sufficiently close links with paramilitary organisations, to give rise to a grave risk that to give support to those groups would have the effect of improving the standing or furthering the aims of a paramilitary organisation, whether directly or indirectly. I do not consider any such government funds would be in the public interest'. What became known as the Hurd Principles, in effect, categorised community activists and initiatives as 'acceptable' and 'unacceptable' and, in a classic case of the politics of unintended consequences, mobilised a broad coalition of interests in opposition to the 'Hurd Principles'. Many others accepted the principles as a common sense government response to the unacceptable strengthening of the Sinn Féin power base.

Government departments moved smartly to strip a number of organisations of their ACE programmes on the basis of the Hurd Principles. Concerns were expressed that little or no evidence was needed before officials acted on information received or perceived. The Northern Ireland Council of Voluntary Action condemned this situation as a breach of natural justice. Others were quick to point out that the implementation was primarily directed against the republican community with a token number of projects in loyalist areas thrown in to take the bad look off things. A community programme in Glencairn was one such sacrificial lamb, falling victim to the suggestion that it had links to the UDA, despite the fact that the UDA itself was still legal at that time. An editorial in *Scope* posed the question – if there is information about individuals being involved in paramilitary organisations why does this not lead to their arrest? Lacking answers, Dove House in Derry organised a community festival to celebrate the fact that it had survived the withdrawal of ACE funding. Although funding was later restored at the urging of SDLP leader, John Hume, and the Catholic Bishop of Derry, the Project Manager was still scathing in her criticism: 'We were saying first of all that it was about social control. The government really wanted to control voluntary bodies, making decisions about who should work and who shouldn't, using money that was given for job creation to intimidate and blackmail community organisations, punishing community groups for the communities in which they operated'.

From the perspective of the Northern Ireland Office the rationale for the Hurd Principles was self-evident: 'I mean you just reach a stage when you're getting information that's showing you that you're getting your eye wiped ... So it got to a stage when a blind eye couldn't be turned anymore, something had to be done. Then it turned out that it looked as if people were being persecuted'. This sense of persecution fed the perception of a political partiality that showed preference for 'safe hands'. Needled by this, many activists supported opposition to the principles on the grounds that nobody was going to dictate what communities should do; particularly not the British Government: 'They (Sinn Féin) didn't proactively try to get on to community groups until way after the Hunger Strike ... And (then) they actually started to go on committees ... People began to say, well we've been working at this for X number of years and now you're muscling in. And then of course what happens? The State just says "No you can't have these people on your committee", you know, the Hurd thing in relation to that was absolutely crazy ... They (management committees) were just "Oh my God, you're not telling us to put people off the committee" ... So that completely backfired'. In short, the republican narrative of state control and political manipulation was strengthened.

By the late 1980s a remodelled ACE scheme placed greater emphasis on training and the rationalisation of community-based managing agencies. Church aligned ACE schemes in West Belfast were amalgamated into the appropriately named Cathedral Community Enterprises. A war of words over the role of churches as 'safe hands' for the roll out of government schemes continued, although a Presbyterian social activist pointed out that the Protestant churches involved as ACE sponsors were never 'monopoly providers'. Despite the campaign against 'political vetting' implemented through the Hurd Principles, the policy remained in force until 1995.

The out-workings of Anglo-Irishism

While moderate nationalism, represented by the SDLP, was burnishing its influence with the support of the Irish Government, media headlines described unionist reaction to the appearance of increasing numbers of

Sinn Féin councillors in Council chambers. The original Sinn Féin Belfast 'City Hall 7' were barracked as 'gangsters', 'obnoxious', 'scum', 'unacceptable', 'contaminated', and carriers of 'political AIDS'. The pained suggestion by Secretary of State Hurd, that procedures to 'out manoeuvre, out wit and out vote' would be more appropriate was drowned out by the shrilling of horns and whistles to silence the 'enemy'. Not all the newly elected republican representatives were comfortable in the Victorian confection that was Belfast City Hall: 'We went in and it was like a bastion of colonialism to me. All I can remember was the marble floors and the marble stairs and one of my major aims at that time was to beauty board it and make it feel like home ... Most of the time literally we had to fight our way in (to Council meetings)'. Council chambers remained bitterly contested spaces for a decade and more.

There were those republicans that saw the Sinn Féin embrace of electoral politics as tantamount to treachery; a stance that resulted in splits and political schisms. For his part, Adams argued for a broadening of the republican platform: 'First of all our policy is to try and fuse all the local struggles – whether its consumers, unemployed, trade unionists, women, youth – with the national question. To bring about a struggle which has a correct principled position on partition and which has a non-opportunistic and consistent position on social and economic questions'. It was this strategy that fuelled the ACE vetting controversy as the Northern Ireland Office and other political parties accused Sinn Féin of 'Taking over Tenants' Associations at gunpoint'. Fingers were also pointed at the ongoing military campaign and struggles in other arenas. A mass prison break-out of republicans from the Maze Prison in 1983 had left prison officers dead and injured, but was quickly celebrated by graffiti writers as 'A-maze-ing'.

If many officials saw the 'safe hands' policy as an exercise in simple pragmatism, one senior civil servant acknowledged: 'Well in many ways the most embarrassing thing, although I think taken with the best of intentions, was the decision to withhold funding from organisations that were regarded as penetrated by paramilitary influences, and I mean they were. You know you could look at a committee of a group and could see that you had nine members, and six of them had already served terms of imprisonment for terrorist activities and so on. And in a way I think it's quite understandable that British Ministers were saying that on the one hand we're paying a lot of soldiers to keep a lid on this thing, and at the same time we are, as it were, funding our own enemies. But I mean that was very embarrassing because whether or not you like it or not ... maybe some of it (was) undertaken with an ulterior political motive, but also activities that had the support of the local community and, you know, were necessary themselves. So there was that kind of tension'. An obvious answer was to look to organisations linked to the Catholic Church which had long condemned IRA violence. The institutional 'disciplinary' power that followed created an inevitable reaction: 'I don't think it was a takeover bid for communities. It was a takeover bid for power, and power was seen in relation to jobs and money. And of course the State put it into that kind of thing which they thought was safe, and obviously to empower the Church (Catholic) in its context'. A Catholic priest, himself a powerhouse of community activity, dismissed these claims although acknowledged statutory support for church-related initiatives: 'Of course we got attacked from all sides ... you know, lackeys of the government and all sorts of things. I didn't care what they called us, it was giving work and giving somebody a wage ... They – I mean the Church shouldn't be getting the money, it should be the community groups. But the community groups had the same opportunity; they had the same prospects as what we had, to bring themselves together, to get expertise ... But yes, it was all about control, who would control the nationalist area and all the rest of it. And I suppose a bit of jealousy too'. He argued further that the Republican Movement later imitated many of the projects established. These fractures within nationalist/republican areas went unrecognised by a loyalism that increasingly characterised such areas as 'pan-nationalist', seeing them as homogeneous in nature.

Whatever the anger within republicanism at the perceived privileging of moderate nationalism, there was all-out fury within unionism at the Anglo-Irish Agreement in 1985. Concluded just one year after an IRA bomb attack on the Conservative Party Annual Conference, the Agreement conceded the Irish Government an official voice on a range of issues concerning Northern Ireland. Street demonstrations expressed fury at the perceived creeping influence of Dublin. Unionist politicians withdrew from contact with British Ministers, including the new Secretary of State, Tom King.

The International Fund for Ireland (IFI) was set up with international aid in the aftermath of the Agreement but unionist community representatives were warned not to apply for IFI 'blood money'. The fear of being sold out was stoked and effigies of Mrs Thatcher joined those of more accustomed republican hate figures on the traditional July loyalist bonfires.

Controversy over the Anglo-Irish Agreement impacted on community work, and a number of community workers from Protestant backgrounds pointedly remarked that workers in nationalist/republican areas had often adopted political positions during the earlier Hunger Strike period. One public statement suggested that the political tension was likely to endanger cross-community work. Community Services Officers (both Protestant and Catholic) employed in some local authorities also had to deal with instructions to post up 'Ulster says No' posters in Community Centres, despite the requirement that the latter were non-sectarian and non-political spaces. One worker recalled being given a verbal warning for refusing to comply with the instruction. As the 'Ulster Says No' campaign gathered momentum, there was some local nuancing of the decree that International Fund for Ireland funding was tantamount to bribery, with UDA leader, Andy Tyrie, giving permission for community projects to apply: 'Paisley came out and shouted about blood money. XXX (working on a cross-community project) came to me and he says "What am I going to do?" ... I says "Take it." He says "What?" I says "Take it and use it for your community." He says "Will you stand by me?" I says "Certainly, I'll stand by you, you take the money because if you don't you can't help your community with it, you take it." And he finished up he took the money and I did stand by him and justified it'. The public relations opportunity of a community project in a loyalist area accepting IFI funding was obvious.

One of the major priorities of the IFI was economic development. There had been a number of community-based self-help initiatives to promote job creation in rural and urban areas across Northern Ireland. The Centre for Neighbourhood Development recruited an Economic Development Officer in the early 1980s, and 1986 saw the Northern Ireland Co-operative Development Agency established with a grant of £50,000 from government and the encouragement of the Trade Union Movement. Where community-based business ventures were able to mix and match the available government grant opportunities, commercial support and training/temporary employment subsidies they managed to survive. The important mix of business acumen and community ethos was also essential, although not easy to obtain. In Derry, Paddy Doherty, moved from setting up a Derry Youth & Community Workshop to establishing the Inner City Trust, with a view to purchasing property (often bomb damaged) and developing it for community benefit. A crucial prerequisite, according to Doherty, was to comply with 'the officialese' requirements of establishing – 'A Board of Directors with sufficient standing in the community and prestigious enough to attract major funding from government and non-government institutions'. For Paddy pragmatism was the order of the day, although preparedness to accept 'the great and the good' on management boards was not always acceptable to the more purist advocates of community self-help who continued to involve those who were rarely termed either great or good.

On at least one occasion Paddy Doherty faced the flip side of this dilemma. The Inner City Trust was nominated for an award by the Royal Institute of British Architects, to be presented by the Prince of Wales. The Prince was better known in Derry as the Colonel in Chief of the Parachute Regiment, of 'Bloody Sunday' fame. Squaring the circle of misgivings the Trust attended the Awards ceremony and accepted the prize, with Paddy attending a dinner in Highgrove Park, the home of the Prince of Wales, some months later. Paddy related how he picked up the necessary dress suit for a knock-down twenty pounds in a bomb-damage sale. Eliminating the smell of smoke from the suit necessitated two visits to the dry cleaners. In order to balance his socialising with British royalty, Paddy agreed to provide a character reference for a local woman who was standing trial in the Old Bailey in an IRA related case. Community cost-benefit decision-making was complex.

If Paddy managed to achieve a balance, the community project housed in the old Victorian Conway Mill complex off the Falls Road continued to fall foul of the Hurd Principles. Plans for this brooding structure included an education centre; a community theatre; small enterprise units, all underpinned by the sustainability of commercial space, but it was starved of government support because it rejected officially 'acceptable' names for its management committee. The children's crèche lost its ACE places and attempts by a number of agencies to support the Mill were frowned upon by government: 'The Arts Council at some stage, and the WEA, were amongst those few who broke the boycott on Conway Mill ... and it was made perfectly clear to the Arts Council that the money would be taken off them (through its departmental allocation) proportionately to what they gave (the Mill)'. Grants from independent charitable Foundations maintained arts and community education activities, as the Mill directors compared how they were treated in contrast to the Flax Street Mill in the Ardoyne, developed by an entrepreneurial priest who was acceptable in establishment circles.

With the benefit of hindsight one senior civil servant, himself a West Belfast man, argued that privileging Catholic Church supported developments was damaging to both the community processes and eventually to perceptions of the church itself. He reflected: 'I would have said the Church had a major part to play in terms of power, so much so I think that they actually damaged a lot of processes that were around ... The Church was the only conduit that was acceptable to government, so largely ... they were up there in the Castle (Stormont Castle) deciding what they wanted to do, how they wanted to do it. Nobody knew any better and that was the way it was done, and community activists were really of no consequence'. The ability of church-related initiatives to attract IFI funding was noted locally, although it was also pointed out by one of those involved: 'When we started to set up the Enterprise Parks to create a bit of local employment, we had a plethora of help from professional people who grew up in the area, still had an empathy and still had roots in the area, but weren't afraid to come back in to give their expertise ... and we found no problem forming boards and committees'. He suggested that the experience was different in working-class Protestant/Unionist/Loyalist areas where successful people tended to move out and not re-engage.

Meanwhile the political boycott of government ministers in response to the Anglo-Irish Agreement resulted in community and civil society representatives obtaining greater access. One noted: 'What happened was the unionist politicians boycotted Stormont, right? So the only avenue the Ministers had was to speak to community groups ... The only people in the loyalist community that the Ministers could actually talk to was community workers'. The invitation lists for dinner at Hillsborough Castle were amended. The political impassé was reflected in graffiti as banners proclaiming 'Ulster Says No' became increasingly bedraggled. Paraphrasing a popular TV advertisement for canned oranges, the walls proclaimed: 'Ulster Says No, but the man from Del Monte says Yes – and he's an Orangeman!'

CHAPTER 7

Civil Servants Unleashed: BATs, RATs and MBW

The alphabet soup of government initiatives was both shaken and stirred in the post Anglo-Irish Agreement period, with Dublin civil servants in situ in Belfast expressing opinions on 'northern issues'. One local civil servant was unimpressed: 'We took it very badly that they would be questioning us on what we were doing for the people of Belfast. Away and look after Ballymun (a deprived area of Dublin) ... Fix your own backyard without trying to tell us what to do'. He was involved in a new initiative, BAT (Belfast Action Teams), established in 1987, and inspired by the dual pressures of addressing inner city deprivation alongside offering career development for middle ranking civil servants. The well-honed mandarin belief in the seamless transferability of bureaucratic skill and knowledge was to be applied to the development of local areas: 'It was really about getting civil servants and public servants directly interfacing with and trying to use their talent and ability and drive to make a difference'. Nine areas of Belfast benefitted directly from the Action Teams, each controlling a small pot of funding to be allocated in a flexible and responsive manner. Seconded public servants brought individual personal background and experience to the task, with some prioritising physical regeneration and others favouring investment in local capacity and support for community initiatives. A proponent of the latter explained: 'What I really loved about that particular thing (BAT) was having an opportunity to really shape the areas ... It was moving money right to where it mattered ... and you could see so many groups, where it was happening'. Another Team member recalled: 'We were there to experiment, to try things out, particularly with community groups, different ideas and things like that. One of the Permanent Secretaries at one stage I remember him saying that if he didn't hear (about) enough failures then you're not trying ... And that was him saying if you really do what we expect you to do there'll be things going wrong'. The need to underpin this risk-taking ethos with record keeping that would keep the hovering auditors happy was often missed in the pressure of implementation. Time would show that the calibre of Action team members varied enormously.

The work of the Action Teams was to morph into what became known as the Making Belfast Work strategy. In Protestant areas the perception of the programme was described as Making West Belfast Work at a time when graffiti in West Belfast read 'Welcome to Beirut' – identification with the long running civil war in Lebanon. Whatever the conflicting community perceptions, the early years of BAT registered some local suspicion in those communities affected by the Hurd Principles. A pragmatic compromise was agreed in the Upper Springfield area, where the Resource Centre refused to accept BAT funding, but local groups showed no such qualms. Community views on the effectiveness of the BAT approach varied depending on the responsiveness of team leaders, with many commenting favourably on the support received. For its part the Shankill lobbied for the inclusion of the Greater Shankill area in the programme, although there was a sneaking recognition that it was often a challenge to develop fundable projects: 'The Belfast Action Teams, they did find it difficult to find people in the Shankill to put resources through, there were just the usual faces, you know'. One project that was already in place was the Belfast Activity Centre, known colloquially as 'Gusty enterprises', after the UVF personality. The Shankill Stress Group found a home at the back of the building: 'That was the strangest place in God's earth … They had a recording studio upstairs … The Activity Centre was very active … It was literally Gusty's idea but it wasn't under his name … He gave me permission for the portakabin … There were goats and horses and sheep at the back … It was a wee man who was just interested in animals … He used to take horse rides round with the children … And the pig was a violent bugger, and so was the goat'. Despite the impromptu nature of some of the projects supported, these smaller investments helped build essential longer term community capacity.

The question of where to draw Action Team boundaries exercised minds in a city obsessed by territoriality. Some decisions accentuated division: 'You had the Lower Shankill BAT Team but not Upper Shankill which to this day created weird divisions ... But eventually they declared the Upper Shankill, a year or two later, as a Belfast Action Team area but with a different Team leader than the Lower Shankill ... These things (the designated areas) had to be cross-community – so you couldn't have Lower Falls/Shankill. You could have had Falls/Shankill, but it was too big, so you'd Lower Falls/Lower Shankill and you'd Upper Springfield which covered Highfield ... Springmartin and over to the Springfield. So these were cross-community things which caused splits within communities if you follow me ... And the Upper Shankill Area Team came on much later'. The politics of drawing lines, attached to potential funding, influenced the remit of a number of community projects over a number of years. Fears were expressed that BAT areas might unwittingly reinforce paramilitary dominated territoriality. Much depended on the insight and connections of Action team leaders, as noted by one local activist who felt that developments in the Lower Shankill were in danger of reinforcing local paramilitary power. It was a different story in other areas.

Springmartin was part of the cross-community Upper Springfield BAT area. The BAT team leader supported the small group of women, and one man, who were working to improve the area. They were encouraged to develop a Five Year Action Plan, provided with private sector contacts, and instead of meeting in each other's houses were given use of a Housing Executive flat as a community office. Although the Five Year Plan took ten years in implementation, the importance of celebrating 'quick wins' was recognised: 'We bought paint, brown and cream paint, and we got the lads out of Farset (Youth & Community Workshop) who were on an ACE scheme, and a couple of painters, and we painted all the houses ... Everybody got their railings painted brown; round their windows brown; and cream windowsills, and within a fortnight the estate looked different and you could actually see people taking a pride in cleaning up their own front gardens. We ran a little garden competition for the best garden of the year, and you could actually see ... people who would never have bothered, buying plants and things. So you began to do very, very small things that people understood ... We had a festival every year and we invited everybody and we talked about different things'. This pace of development may have frustrated some government policy makers, but the local BAT leader understood community empowerment. A suggestion, however, that the group should interact with politicians and press was vetoed: 'Because many of the women who were on the committee their husbands were always involved in paramilitaries, so ... they had to make out at home that they were only looking to clean up the estate, they weren't looking to change the world'. Understanding local context and sensitivities was all important.

Across the peace line the value of the BAT programme was lauded by community workers in the troubled Divis flats complex: 'People had agreed that the state had turned its back on them. And the state in that sense was alien, and subsequently agencies didn't want to touch this community with a barge pole. Stigmatisation wasn't just about other communities, it was very much about the state stigmatising this area, so in that sense then support from agencies was vitally important whatever the monetary value'. The bone fides of a government programme that was seen to be operating at local level was acknowledged, although at management level the BAT programme was acutely conscious of the Hurd Principles as acknowledged by a senior civil servant: 'Well I laid down an important principle at the time, obviously the one thing we could not afford was to get involved with anybody who was associated with paramiltarism ... I mean I wasn't afraid of the Audit office, but I was sure as hell afraid of, you know, getting myself into bother because we were unknowingly involved with paramilitaries ... So I laid down this simple rule ... when we looked at a particular area we went looking for the clergymen. And it was usually on the basis of the advice that we got from the clergy that we would pick so and so, or so and so. And in some instances actually the clergy lifted the ball and ran with it'. The main complaint was that this scenario worked better in catholic/nationalist/republican areas than their counterparts in loyalist/unionist areas.

Bringing down Divis

The more responsive ethos of BAT was not always echoed by other statutory agencies. The Housing Executive, in particular, remained firmly opposed to the campaign for the demolition of the Divis Flats, which had been driven to the point of destroying empty flats to prevent their reallocation. The Executive brought the campaigners to court on charges of criminal damage, but the judge dismissed the case declaring that the Executive should be paying people to live in the flats given the conditions. By 1986 it was conceded that the campaigners had a point. Feisty Inez McCormack, a trade union official and Divis campaign supporter, reminded people that: 'The demolition of Divis is not a great mark for political parties or the churches. It is a triumph of the human spirit attested to by a people who were classified as sub-human and have proved by their struggles that they are more human than most of us'. Only a month previously, the Divis Residents' Association had to issue a press statement condemning a police raid on their office and the arrest of three of its members.

The campaign that McCormack commended had been long drawn out and bitter. Conditions in the flats complex deteriorated to such an extent that in the early 1980s a local worker described Divis as a 'separate state'. She recounted a visit by the Catholic Bishop: 'He came round terribly frail and polite, and I always remember it was dark and it was autumn time and it was cool enough, and the kids had lit a big bonfire and they had also burnt a car, and there were about three cars crashing into each other, hundreds and hundreds of kids there. And I looked at him ... and I thought ... he must think this is hell because he was horrified ... But the look on his face brought it home to me how bad times had got and how normal things had got'. Residents, for their part, still retained a sense of humour, writing in the 'Divis Bulletin': 'Heard the one about the Divis rat? According to the Housing Executive expert there aren't hordes of rats in Divis, just one or two who move round a lot and are seen by lots of people. And there aren't any cockroaches crawling up the walls either – just frustrated tenants!' The Divis Joint Development Group drew on sympathetic academics and technical experts to organise an Environmental Health Project.

Virtually burnt out by serial campaigns marked by limited success, the new Divis Joint Development Committee attended a residential think-in to agree an Action Plan. Local residents were joined by staff from voluntary organisations, individual agency workers from Social Services, the Youth Service and the Northern Ireland Probation Service (known colloquially as 'screws on wheels' – that is, peripatetic prison warders) to plan a combination of community-based services, local participation and advocacy.

A well regarded Play Project was already operating and a Youth Drop-In Centre was opened in an old store room in the complex. Even a small environmental patch was nurtured in the middle of the forbidding concrete complex, although an alternate school project for young people that had either been expelled, or truanted from, school proved more controversial. The local ACE scheme offered pensioners' services, when not completing door-to-door surveys with residents. The Divis Women's Group resorted to drama to highlight concerns. One sketch ridiculed the prescription of tranquilisers by medical practitioners – whatever the problem. The 'Dolly Mixtures' Group performed the play: 'A woman goes to the doctor and she says "Doctor I need to talk to you" –; you know, "My son is in prison and …" And the doctor would say as if it was a mantra, "Librium and valium, take one with every meal, and every day, and all your troubles will go away." And no matter what – and then another woman would come in and she would say, "The son's broken his leg and the wee girl's pregnant", and whatever. "Librium and valium" … There was at that time an awful lot of over-prescription … and certainly in Divis Flats … because of the dire nature of the place a lot of the women lived on tranquilisers'. Another favourite production ridiculed the Housing Executive's insistence that damp in the flats was really condensation, solved by keeping windows open.

The advocacy campaign was fuelled by data collection and lobbying. Regular communication with residents allayed concerns that either Committee membership or the protest action was party political: '(There) were only two members of the Committee who were involved in politics (Sinn Féin) and then we had two other people joined the Committee, who were also residents of Divis, and they were both members of the IRSP … but it was never a political committee but was really always the people … And the Committee didn't take any decisions without informing the people'. If the meetings were less than packed then a follow up door-to-door survey was carried out to ascertain people's views. The critical importance of representing people's views accurately; taking immediate steps to prevent misinformation; keeping people informed of on-going developments and maintaining engagement were all seen as essential.

A Divis Study Group was initiated by Divis resident and Belfast City Council Community Centre worker, Gerry Downes. Evidence collected highlighted the considerable quantities of asbestos used in the construction of the flats. Both this, and other design faults, featured in an exhibition mounted in the Town & Country Planning Association offices in London, in November 1985, which attracted mainstream media coverage. A member of the Joint Development Committee explained how they benefitted from the advice of British Town Planner, Brian Anson: '(Anson) started doing modelling, the different models for measuring housing conditions ... (He) had this idea that we should have an exhibition in London in the Royal Town & Country Planning Association offices which were three quarters of a mile from the Queen's residence on the same royal mile. We should all get huge blow ups of the conditions and get structural reports done ... And it was the fourth item on the ITN News that night. That was the beginning of the end'.

Alongside the exhibition, every opportunity was taken to garner publicity and support for the campaign with Inez McCormack using her trade union credentials to ensure regular contacts with Members of Parliament, including flying campaigners over to the House of Commons to brief MPs. Inez also persuaded the then Labour Party Shadow Home Secretary, Peter Archer, to visit Divis while on a fact finding trip to Belfast. Acting against the advice of his security detail, Archer agreed. A Divis campaigner takes up the story: 'We went and picked him up and brought him away on his own ... And it was really funny because I brought him to one of my neighbour's houses which was really bad; the dampness was so bad she had to paint every week over this damp on the ceiling. And when I brought him in she had all Jeffrey Archer's books sitting out for him to sign. And it was the wrong one'. If Peter Archer was less colourful than the Conservative Party ex-MP and author that some of the residents expected, the same could not be said about Queens University microbiologist, Geof Sirockin: 'I looked out the window and I seen this character wandering round Divis Flats, and he had pink trousers on him and red braces ... He was like the nutty professor like, but he knew his stuff ... When you think of it now you couldn't have paid for people ... They done that all free, all to be involved in the campaign'. His technical expertise formed the basis for a report on 'Housing and Health in West Belfast', published in 1987.

Those statutory sector workers supportive of the campaign often found themselves in the institutional firing-line, periodically being denounced as 'communists' and 'agitators'. However, once the official decision had been taken to acquiesce to the demolition demand, the mezzo level struggle for credit commenced. It soon became clear that the local campaigners were to be virtually side-lined. One member of the Development Committee, who was also active in the Laity Committee of the local Catholic church, was particularly bitter when the church hierarchy claimed that it was its influence that had swung the decision: 'I never went back to Mass for a long, long time after it ... For years and years we tried to get them (the Church) involved and they just didn't want to know'. The struggle for attribution was to continue, with Gerry Adams emphasising Sinn Féin involvement in this and other community campaigns in an interview with the *Irish News*.

Meanwhile life continued in the parallel universe of conflicting versions of normality. The unemployment rate in the area was consistently between 65–70 per cent, but residents contributed food and money to ensure a decent wake when people were murdered. When the Director of a local NGO finished a talk on the hazards of glue-sniffing – an endemic problem with young people at that time – he found the wheels of his car missing; they were returned sharpish on instructions of a local matriarch. Gatherings that verged on the political when held in the local City Council Community Centre were registered as fishing club meetings: 'The code for a political gathering ... was a fishing club. Everyone had fishing clubs. Divis – where's the nearest bloody pond when you couldn't get in and out of the area? And if you'd seen the people going to the fishing club ... angling for something but not for fish'. The nuancing adopted prevented unnecessary confrontation with the Council.

Demolition and redevelopment were duly implemented. The retention of a tower block, that hosted a British Army base on its roof, meant continued amusement for local children: 'The helicopters used to deliver (to the base) that was incredible. I look back on that now, a helicopter a couple of hundred feet above a residential area, a densely populated area; and the noise of it ... What happened a couple of times was that the soldiers would have had their stuff hung up (to dry) ... The kids would be running about with these big green army uniform trunks and vests, they all got blown over if they hadn't got it all tied down'. This neighbourhood worker was also aware that community participation was decreasing as streets of houses replaced the condemned flats, given that attention now focused on the novelty of garden gnomes, trellises and newly painted front doors.

Life beyond the motorways

Community action in urban areas was undoubtedly the loudest and most visible, although the inclusion of both the Crossmaglen Community Association (South Armagh) and the Knockninny Community Resource Centre (Co. Fermanagh) in the early Community Worker Research Programme highlighted the challenges of working in rural areas. The Northern Ireland Voluntary Trust launched a Rural Awards Scheme in 1983 to maintain this focus; followed by the Rural Action Project (NI), supported under the European Commission Second Anti-Poverty Programme (1985–1989). The Anti-Poverty Programme also sponsored work with the unemployed in Belfast and Derry.

Having managed to negotiate a rare example of statutory cost sharing to finance a multi-functional Community Centre, the enterprising Crossmaglen Community Association became involved in the redevelopment of the town centre, but ran up against the politics of the area when awarded the Christopher Ewart-Biggs Award by the Northern Ireland Voluntary Trust for its local community newspaper. It was told in no uncertain terms by the local 'boys' that it would be unwise to accept the award, given that Ambassador Ewart-Biggs had been assassinated by the IRA. The scenic Ardboe community, on the shores of Lough Neagh, faced rather different challenges. There, a Lignite Action Group was formed to oppose open cast mining. One ingenious tactic adopted involved the parcelling of the land into pocket-sized segments that were sold to globally disbursed buyers to frustrate efforts by the mining companies to acquire it. This was one of the many projects supported under the Northern Ireland Voluntary Trust Rural Awards Scheme.

Awareness of the importance of pacing development was essential for success in rural areas. The Creggan Community Association, working in Carrickmore, Co. Tyrone, was a case in point where local agreement over the need for a second Gaelic football team highlighted the need for new sporting facilities. This was followed by plans for a Community Centre and social housing. Evidence was gathered through community research to support advocacy. The Community Association itself amassed a land bank of two acres for a playing field and Community Centre site. The Centre, when built, offered a community focus, hosting socials, classes, a drama group and a small ACE scheme. An evening course on rural community development raised the issue of project sustainability which encouraged the local group to develop tourist facilities in an attempt to maximise income.

A watershed research report, in 1980, argued the urgency of addressing issues in 'rural problem areas'. These were mapped across some two-thirds of rural areas, and 15 per cent of the population, of Northern Ireland. The pattern of deprivation was characterised by high levels of unemployment; low educational attainment; poor household amenities and low farming incomes. 'Pluriactivity', dependence on household income drawn from a range of employment and welfare benefit sources, was highlighted. The emphasis of the report was on the need to enhance local self-confidence and assist rural communities to increase their living standards without inducing dependency. Reference was made to the Crossmaglen and Knockninny examples, but also other rural areas, with Draperstown, in Co. Derry adopting an early social enterprise model. The application of rural community development to the 'problem areas' identified, inspired the collaboration between the Northern Ireland Voluntary Trust, the Northern Ireland Council for Voluntary Action, the Northern Ireland Rural Association and Strabane Citizens' Advice Bureau to establish the Rural Action Project (NI). RAP (NI) worked in four rural areas: South Armagh and West Fermanagh along the Border, the Sperrins hinterland of West Ulster and the Glens of Antrim in the North-East. Area Development Workers were employed to support local groups to plan, and take forward, a series of interventions. Work with local women in South Armagh and West Fermanagh sparked a whole new meaning to the community action principle of starting where people are at, as the women who arranged the altar flowers in the local church were recruited to make up numbers in a Women's Discussion Class to warrant a funded tutor. In West Fermanagh, books on family planning were placed at the bottom of the mobile book box, camouflaged by recipe books and guides to patchwork; less controversial issues included ideas about how women could maximise their income from farm management and diversification.

The focus on increasing household income proved central to community concerns, whether this was de-stigmatising the uptake of welfare benefits in the Glens of Antrim or exploring the potential of agri-tourism and farm diversification. Supported by the International Fund for Ireland, thirteen different farm diversification ventures were actively pursued. These ranged from snail farming to organic vegetables and from rearing angora goats to deer farming. Even in these areas the impact of the Troubles was felt. During a public meeting on deer farming in South Armagh an expert from the Scottish Highlands described the high fencing needed to manage the deer. A local farmer responded by shouting up from the back of the packed hall: 'Brits!' The Scottish visitor looked confused: 'Yes?' he queried. 'Brits cut fences', was the taciturn reply, accompanied by a general nodding of heads. When patrolling locally, camouflaged British Army patrols cut through fences as they crawled through the countryside. The ironic suggestion that 'Brit flaps' might be negotiated was dismissed. Concern was also expressed about low flying army helicopters panicking the livestock.

South Armagh hosted a European Commission delegation from Brussels keen to see farm diversification in practice. As the mandatory tea and scones were served, be-suited officials from both Belfast and Brussels struggled into their wellies to survey some particularly bedraggled angora goats, shivering in the sweeping rain. Little did they know that these specimens were luckier than their fellows who had fallen victim to the adjacent Belfast-Dublin railway track. The delegation was rapidly moved on to a pilot initiative in snail farming, established as a substitute for Eastern European snail supplies adversely affected by contamination from the Chernobyl Nuclear Station meltdown. Notwithstanding the potential rewards of niche marketing, the product itself proved elusive due to the camouflage of the surrounding undergrowth. A visit to an organic vegetable project proved equally frustrating when it transpired that the vegetables had yet to be planted. However, at least on this occasion local events intervened when an IRA mortar exploded into the nearby Army base in Crossmaglen, providing some local colour. A final visit was hastily arranged to a local mushroom farm – where the produce was static and could be photographed. The officials returned to their respective offices with baskets of fresh mushrooms and stories from the frontline. Despite the local difficulties, the ripple effect of bridging social and agricultural interests, supported by EC attention, served to nudge open the door of the steadfastly traditionalist Department of Agriculture (NI).

A District Council Community Services Officer reflected on the differences between community action in an urban and rural context: 'Totally different ... apathy, negativity, cynicism, no effort, lack of cohesiveness, lack of roots – people put together in a (urban) estate ... In the countryside, people born and bred; knew each other – knew what they had for breakfast, the whole lot. So when there was a call for movement to get a community venue (or whatever) ... that togetherness was already there. It was a matter of marshalling it'. Another Development Worker described community mobilisation in the mountainous Sperrins area, where local history groups, sporting events and Women's Groups each played their part. He even referred to the contribution of cross-community sheep dog trials, noting that the cross-community aspect referred to the owners not the dogs. On a less positive note, the very connectiveness of rural communities could also be problematic. An accepted hierarchy of authority figures could exclude more marginalised groups unless inclusion was carefully planned and negotiated; whilst local tenacity of memory meant fear of failure. People had to be supported in taking risks by appropriate information, models of practice from other areas and proactive strategies to ensure broader participation.

Funding made available for the regeneration of rural towns and villages by the International Fund for Ireland could run up against local circles of influence. A rather cynical Community Service Officer was less than impressed: 'It was a gravy train led machine, the IFI ... (attracted) a more well-heeled type of person who could identify with enterprise centres and business units ... No problem that, that was its agenda and that's what it attracted, and the whole ethos of the IFI, you had to form a company, not a Community Association, but a company with Directors ... It was business lines, business led ... It was community development at a middle-class level ... When the money was gone a lot of those groups disappeared'. While the individuals involved were described as 'decent people', there were occasions when communities split over initiative ownership and resource allocation. Divisions appeared along class lines, but also between those who were viewed as political moderates and political 'undesirables'. In addition, the often politely unspoken tensions between Catholic and Protestant community identities, served to complicate matters further. There were few that were not acutely aware in a rural area as to 'what foot the other kicked with'. Community divisions in towns and villages might be unspoken in 'mixed' company, but they ran deep and persistent, marked out by patterns of land ownership, school attendance and what shops were frequented by whom.

At a strategic level the Rural Action Project (NI) contributed to a debate about where future rural policy should reside. An initial impulse to argue for an Inter-Departmental response was warned off by a sympathetic senior civil servant who pointed out that inter-departmental mechanisms meant that no one would take responsibility or be held accountable. He argued that the Department of Agriculture should not be let off the policy hook. A subsequent departmental review saw the Department of Agriculture (NI) renamed as the Department of Agriculture and Rural Development (mirroring the direction of the European debate), and agreement to set up a Rural Development Council, alongside a community-led, membership based Rural Community Network (NI). The latter supported relationship building between community activists and groups in rural areas, developing Sub Regional Networks to promote community action and support cross-community collaboration. The Rural Development Council placed an increasing emphasis on the more quantifiable results of economic development designed to address income and employability issues. Practice was soon to be picked over and deconstructed, with project development counter-posed to community development, and the latter reimagined as 'capacity-building'. As the Council and the Rural Community Network parted ways, the Department of Agriculture & Rural Development (DARD) was driving forward a raft of new strategies linked to European funding. Mirroring the BATS in Belfast, RATs – Rural Action Teams – were deployed in disadvantaged rural areas.

Making Belfast Work: The politics of perception

The causal relationship between socio-economic deprivation and political violence remained a subject of debate, with the political calculus of poverty and community differentials providing an added twist. As the late 1980s peeped into the new decade, wall slogans spat defiance: 'Semtex kills more germs than Vortex!' This was a world away from Downing Street where Margaret Thatcher smiled that 'We are quietly pleased' to be returned to power in June 1987. The carnage caused by the IRA bomb at the Co. Fermanagh Remembrance Day ceremonies that same year saw her enquiring about the possibility of redrawing the Border. Secretary of State, Tom King, was forced to explain that any such exercise would be difficult given the territorial complexities of single-identity communities. He demonstrated his case by reference to the colour coded military maps then in use – areas designated in orange, green and yellow.

Although a direct connection between poverty and violence remained unproven, the sense of alienation and political marginalisation experienced in many communities was regularly reported on by the more prescient of BAT team leaders. If they were feet on the ground the perspectives of their more distant civil service colleagues shocked an Irish official based in the British-Irish Secretariat at Maryfield: 'One civil servant who was in charge of economic development saying "The only time I ever saw West Belfast was from a helicopter." And sort of said it as a joke ... but then civil servants were legitimate targets. I mean Bloomfield got the bomb in the house, so the Provos (Provisional IRA) are not without blame'. Political apprehension could easily reinforce class and professional stereotyping, as described by a statutory health worker working in West Belfast: 'At departmental level – absolutely no appreciation that it would be different in North and West Belfast than any part of North Down ... The first time

I drove to Andersonstown ... even just seeing the amount of soldiers around with weapons was very scary for me ... Seeing a soldier crouching down just beside the garden wall and the wee child playing just up – you know ... And we all became inured to it; but there was no appreciation I felt from the Department about any of that'. The suspicion of deliberate disengagement was also felt within loyalist communities: 'I think there was a class thing in it too, to be quite honest with you ... People from Campbell and Methody and Inst. (leading schools) I've had them say to me ... let them kill all around them, you know, there's that sort of attitude ... It's not articulated but it's there'. In contrast, however, there was a number of policy makers convinced of the need for radical action. The series of events that followed the shooting dead of three IRA volunteers in Gibraltar in 1988 infused their position with a sense of urgency.

Television coverage of both loyalist, Michael Stone's, attack on mourners at the funerals of the IRA members, as well as the subsequent killing of two British Army corporals at the funerals of those killed by Stone, was graphic. One woman who attended the second set of funerals with her two small children, became caught up in the horror: 'I have to be honest, what I felt that day in the first hour or two, I learnt in a split second what makes people kill is hate and fear – absolute fear ... it's fear for your own children will make you do anything'. A priest from the nearby Clonard Monastery who gave the last rites to the two plain clothes soldiers was deeply affected – 'It was terrible ... As I anointed one of the soldiers a local woman came up, took her coat off and put it over the dead man's head. "He was someone's son", she said'. Reactions in West Belfast ran the full gamut as four days later Belfast city centre came to a standstill when an estimated 12,000 people protested against the killings.

This litany of death shocked the official system and crystallised fears within government that Northern Ireland was in grave danger of tipping beyond 'an acceptable level of violence'. Brian Mawhinney, a Direct Rule Minister, agreed: 'In my view Northern Ireland was very close to the edge of serious and bloody breakdown ... (It) called into question what we thought we had achieved by way of political progress'. A civil servant who was party to discussions at the time believed: 'They had this awful scare that here was a society that ... was going away completely and nothing you were doing was having any impact on it and you really needed to address it quickly. And you know, it was torn between the hawks who said "Let's put the boot in – raze the place to the ground" – that's not quite apt, but that sort of hard line ... and (those) who put in (a submission) saying "Look you've got to do something now, you can't let it go on any longer, now is the time"'. Tellingly, the submission advocating the more reasoned line was passed to the Secretary of State without first going through the regular channels of the system.

The work of the Belfast Action Teams continued but they were soon working alongside the Making Belfast Work initiative which was launched to stimulate greater economic activity and local enterprise; improve the local environment; equip people in the most disadvantaged communities to compete successfully; and to harness community goodwill and enthusiasm. In an atmosphere where something had to be seen to be done, MBW was tasked with bringing in the heavy hitters at government level, skewing departmental budgets in the process. The new approach was not uniformly popular, resulting in what has been described as 'a competition of egos' between senior civil servants who championed the BATs and MBW respectively. One was dismissive of MBW: 'I'm not sure that Making Belfast Work ever amounted to all that much ... I think there was a group of people sitting in Stormont Castle pontificating about things ... MBW was very top down and everything that I had done (relating to BATs) was bottom up, so there was a world of difference'. However a proponent of MBW argued: 'It wasn't done for security reasons, it was done because there was an obvious, obvious need and there was a realisation that in tackling these issues we were proving to people that the social and economic problems could be caught, or cured, or attacked or reduced in a way without having to resort to violence. In many ways the violence made things worse ... There was recognition that this was going to be a long term process; that we had to experiment with a whole lot of things in the hope that some of them would work and become mainstream'. The proposition benefitted from the support of the then Permanent Secretary of the Department of Finance, George Quigley.

The weakness at the heart of the MBW strategy was the limited commitment among government departments to mainstreaming successful initiatives and a fear that MBW risk-taking might result in a climate of blame if innovative approaches failed to work out as planned. A swingeing report by the Public Accounts Committee in the early 1990s confirmed the 'worst fear' scenario and: 'Absolutely barbequed the whole MBW approach ... How can you be certain that you're not giving money to the IRA? You know, that kind of thing. It led to a culture of caution and to major changes in procedures'. The result was a watering down of the original concept that had been launched, perhaps somewhat inauspiciously, in the Ulster Museum. At community level there was a continued welcome for government interventions that made available additional resources for community projects; particularly in the context of the political hiatus that remained within local authorities. Many people also valued the greater access to senior civil servants and policy makers, although those of a more Machiavellian turn of mind queried where information went in the system. Appreciation was expressed when MBW officers demonstrated imagination and were prepared to bend the rules to circumnavigate obstacles; although there were still those who questioned whether the enhanced engagement was with the socially concerned state or the political state.

Perceptions were important, particularly in circumstances of prolonged conflict where it has been argued that selective collective memories often acquire symbolic importance, given that interpretation of experience is shaped by a communal narrative that 'makes sense' of current realities. The interface between external and internal perceptions forced a response in West Belfast in the aftermath of the media frenzy following the killings of the two British Army corporals: 'We were the terrorist community; we were just a pack of animals, we were this, that and the other and all the rest of it. And as that all started to spin out over those weeks, months, after it, you know, just this unmitigated terrorist community – burn them, hang them, shoot them thing, you know, you could almost sense a "Is that how low we've stooped? Is that what happened to us?" But you'd also at the same time have to say, but what drives people to that? ... And I think there was a sense of us having to basically find ourselves in terms of a number of things ... well we're not that ... I remember being in loads of discussions round this ... There are reasons for people, you know, doing what they do ... It's not what we are, it's not who we are, it shouldn't be what defines us'.

One response was the launch of the West Belfast Féile (Festival) in 1988, with the intention of creating a more positive self-image. This built on an earlier West Belfast Festival, organised in the 1970s as diversion from the anti-Internment bonfires and related rioting that marked the first week in August.

The reinvigorated West Belfast Féile became an important signifier of self-identity: 'The West Belfast Festival was really started in our offices (Falls Community Council), and you know that was (Gerry) Adams own idea or somebody selected ... and if they wanted it to happen, boy, did it happen ... People were just fed up with twenty years of war, and they needed something brighter in their lives'. The later line-up of international speakers and performers developed from what had originally been a collection of home-made floats on the back of coal lorries, with children dressed up in black bin liners. In staunchly independent Ballymurphy, the week-long festival was more spontaneous in nature, with events such as Costa del Ballymurphy, complete with giant paddling pools swamping local clubs. Perhaps not surprisingly, the Ballymurphy organisers were not faced with the quandary confronting the Féile Committee when MBW funding became available: 'It took us a long time to decide whether to take the money or not ... Went back to the Festival Committee and it was ... "Does that mean we have to water down who we are and we wouldn't have political discussions and all the rest of it?" So we debated that for quite some time and we decided we would take the money. We would have the posts but we wouldn't water down the message. And we never have done'. Small gestures – even when in apparent contradiction to official positions – could serve to challenge set perceptions. A number of MBW actions built on this, so that by 1989 there was some acknowledgement of a shift in policy: 'We were the terrorist community, basically, who normally people didn't want to touch with a barge pole ... It must have been '88–'89, there was a bit of a shift ... You know, when they demolished Mackies factory (a complex in West Belfast), Richard Needham (Minister of State) then said we must consult the community – that was unheard of'.

Perceptions were running amok in unionist/loyalist communities as well. One consistent complaint was the perceived successful positioning of the Catholic community as the underdog: 'Another thing that went on to the detriment of the Protestant community was that the Catholic community was always seen as the most oppressed, so (when) there was international support and international funding, it tended to focus towards the Catholic community'. Post the Anglo-Irish Agreement there was a view that the combined forces of Dublin/Irish-America effectively privileged nationalism and the Catholic Church, supported by a less than trust-worthy British Government focused on battling resurgent republicanism by taking particular note of needs in single identity Catholic communities. Fingers were pointed at the investment in enterprise parks across West Belfast (some of which straddled the 'peace line') and at their ability to attract government grants. This perception was challenged by a community activist from the New Lodge (North Belfast): 'I mean there's been the idea on the loyalist side ... that we've got everything, and somehow that we were handed money. And then when they get involved they realise how difficult it is, you know, nobody's arriving with barrel loads of money ... we went through applications. We talk to groups about that and they says, "Oh we didn't realise that, we thought that someone just gave it to you" ... But there was that sort of perception, and I definitely think that there is a historical thing there where people in loyalist areas thought the state would look after them. And it's their state, it's a Protestant state for a Protestant people; or a Protestant government for a Protestant people, and that's been perpetrated by some politicians'. There was, however, the influence of the Catholic Church (and allegedly its related Knights of Columbanus), that had established a Catholic Caring Fund to seed fund initiatives that then attracted large government grants. One clerical figure explained the rationale: 'I think they (the British Government) had written off places like West Belfast as hopeless cases, you know, the same as you'd write off people as hopeless, which is a terrible policy', arguing that it was a social duty to provide people with employment that would hopefully divert them from paramilitarism. He dismissed the 'social type work' that attracted small BAT grants, which others might describe as community capacity-building.

What often went unrecognised in Protestant communities was the internal fragmentation between republicans critical of the apparent privileging of moderate nationalism and nationalists that viewed church-related initiatives as a bulwark against militant republicanism. It was not unknown for MBW officials to get caught up in the antagonisms of the time: 'The difficulty with the Church was a personality thing – it was a question of power ... Give us the money – we know what to do with it. Just give us the money ... And there was a lot of the system at that time saying "Look this is a safe route". And I also think there was a political dimension to undermine Sinn Féin. I am sure that was part of the thing'. Another civil servant described the importance of informal networking: 'I think what emerged then, and subsequently, was that the interpretation of what was actively happening at community level tended to be based on a narrow core of people ... If you were at some of the NIO (Northern Ireland Office) or Central Secretariat dinners it was the same people who turned up all the time. Certainly initially you were getting a fairly middle of the road SDLP, Catholic Church perspective. And a lot of the projects that were funded at that stage were very much of that ilk. And it was only post about '91, '92, that you got a widening out and a tension emerging between the political influence of the Church and the SDLP and the emerging influence of Sinn Féin'. Dining for influence continued to be important around the well-dressed table at Hillsborough Castle, although the forthright request by an elected SDLP representative that all MBW projects in West Belfast should be run by him first was firmly faced down: 'The awful thing was that (the Secretary of State) turned around and said "Would that be alright?" And I said "No, it wouldn't." I said you can't do that ... that's giving power of veto to a local politician ... I said I'm quite happy to tell him on a monthly basis what we're doing but can't cede power to do that'. Drawing the lines between consultation, influence and control became another art form.

Perception was also influenced by the lens of class, profession and communal identity. A Further Education worker operating out of a community-based centre described the official cold shoulder, remembering how a senior colleague: 'Was afraid to acknowledge her knowledge of me in that senior team ... I was just "Mrs Green", and I mean an awful lot of people would have had that attitude to you'. A worker in the health sector felt the impact of normalising judgements: 'Well traditionally then you had a service that is dominated by professional values, which is that we do know better, because that's what our professional training has been all about ... And on top of that you had ... often some kind of political analysis ... around the people that were causing the problems – rioting on the street and all the rest of it ... sort of feeling, sure it's them out there ... what do you expect?'. The situation was aggravated by an agency perspective that failed to take account of the impact of the conflict in adherence to the official mantra of normalisation. Those workers who advocated a community approach often spoke of the need for the protection of agency champions or to work below the radar.

Within the under-growth of local communities, perception and rumour could often be reinforcing. Support for cross-community activities could be interpreted as a signifier of uncertain loyalty as experienced by a long-term activist in the Fountain estate in Londonderry: 'At that time the UDA was only a name ... People didn't know how strong they were, or to what lengths they were going to go, so there would have been a reticence about making decisions that normally would have been made without a thought. People were beginning to look over their shoulder ... This very prominent UVF man informed me that one time I was to be whacked (shot) ... They seen me as a Fenian lover, that is to put it bluntly ... They didn't know where my loyalties were ... The mind ticks over when they cannot assess you, cannot put you into a box, they start thinking the worst'. Another community activist received a phone call just before Christmas warning her not to bother buying a turkey because she wouldn't be around to eat it: 'I said "That's alright, I don't like turkey anyway."' The alignment of perception and power (particularly if the latter was felt to be challenged) could be a lethal combination.

'Up the hoods'

The so-called 'hoods', young people engaged in 'anti-social behaviour' such as 'joyriding' (stealing and driving cars), ignored all power structures, whether security forces or paramilitaries. In circumstances where policing was either contested or unacceptable the role of paramilitaries as 'guardians' of 'their' community often became accepted, if not acceptable, with irate community residents demanding action when by-standers were injured or killed as a result of out of control cars screeching through built-up areas. In later years the term 'joyriding' was replaced with 'death riders' to underline the point. The response was punishment shootings and beatings in both republican and loyalist areas, which commenced in the early 1970s and continued over the years. One notorious piece of waste ground to the rear of a Falls Road public house became known as 'wounded knee' given the regular use for punishment shootings – often by appointment. The surgeons in the Royal Victoria Hospital were known for their orthopaedic expertise in treating the victims.

A Youth Worker in Divis worked with the neighbourhood hoods – 'They were almost like moles, you wouldn't have seen them during the day ... There was one of them killed, shot dead, ... And he was king of the joyriders ... and that night 300 cars were stolen in West Belfast. This was their response ... as a tribute to him ... It was an anti-authority thing'. A number of diversionary schemes, such as stock-car racing, were pioneered. Conferences were organised to discuss alternatives to punishment shootings, and at least one Probation Officer breached the official anathema against contact with Sinn Féin to make his case: 'I just got fed up with paramilitary shootings and I wrote an article for our union newsletter about it, and it was picked up by the front page of *The Guardian* ... and then Sinn Féin got concerned about me ... I went up and met them with my senior management ... I said "Look I've made my point, I'm not going to do anything else."' He then had to arrange meetings with other political parties to emphasise political neutrality. In addition to official contacts, it was the informal contact role of community insiders that was most effective in brokering alternatives to planned punishment beatings. Reports that the police were bartering immunity from prosecution for known joyriders in return for information posed additional difficulties – allegations that were denied although without convincing those that saw internal community fragmentation as a deliberate tactic.

A number of political ex-prisoners took a position on the issue: 'Your gut instinct was these young people were marginalised ... If we exclude them then we're going to exclude them further, and they're going to be self-perpetuating. So we started off a Youth Club ... on a Monday night it was called "Hoods' Night" ... for anyone that was barred from all the Youth Clubs in the area, they would come into this ... We'd no real idea of how to run a Youth Club or anything ... So we formed a committee, and I always remember ... we said we'll need to do finance ... so we made the biggest thief in the group and put him in charge of finance. So we went, we can watch him, whereas if we'd put anybody else in charge he would have been trying to steal the money ... It's like really when you talk about empowering, that's what that was'. Agreement was negotiated with local paramilitaries that the young people involved in the project would not be beaten or shot. Another important initiative developed due to the demonisation of the families of the hoods saw a number of Parent Youth Support Groups, coordinated by the West Belfast Parent Youth Group, established. This received funding from both BAT and the Probation Board.

In 1989, concerns about punishment beatings brought together youth and community workers from West Belfast and the Greater Shankill. The Farset Youth & Community Development Group and the Shankill Development Agency agreed to set up Steering Groups to take the work forward: a Youth Strategy Group; a group to reactivate community movement in the Greater Shankill; and a programme for regenerating cross-community action in Greater West Belfast. MBW supported aspects of the plan, although the times seemed less than auspicious for effective cross-community work. Contact was arguably maintained on the basis of tenacious personal relationships built up over many years, as much as it was about shared concerns.

Councils in a continuing 'state of chassis'

By 1991 the MBW budget was set at £27.5 million, although there were fears expressed that the programme favoured larger community infrastructural organisations: 'I do think that it left a lot of the smaller groups out in the cold and at the end of the day some of these groups will be the mainstay of community work'. As BAT morphed into MBW the latter was positioned as government intervention on a larger scale, with increased emphasis on the big impact, albeit accompanied by greater rigidity in procedures and processes given audit and accountability pressures. District Councils faced different dilemmas with many still mired in the fall-out from unionist protests against imposition of the Anglo-Irish Agreement. The campaign of disruption within local authorities saw grant-aid withheld from a wide range of Community Resource Centres, Advice Centres and other projects. A Steering Group of the organisations affected met under the auspices of the Centre for Neighbourhood Development. Some funding finally trickled through when a government appointed commissioner authorised payments in those local authority districts affected.

Abuse at Council meetings continued to dominate the order of business in response to the increasing presence of Sinn Féin. One unionist councillor, who was active in the community, shuddered at his memories of council meetings in Belfast: 'It was like a bear pit when I went in, it was very, very difficult ... Nobody spoke to each other – and that was just the unionists ... I have a natural propensity to say hello to people and tell them, you know, that they are doing well, and sometimes that didn't go down so well' Another councillor described the atmosphere as though there had been barbed wire thrown through the middle of the chamber. Community Service staff were not immune from the default mode of calculation as to whether they sided with 'them' or 'us': 'I remember when I was Principal Neighbourhood Worker there with responsibility for right across Belfast, going to Committee to speak ... There would have been all that, you know, blowing whistles and banging ... I mean if they had been doing it when one of the Sinn Féin councillors was speaking it would have been one thing, but they also did it blatantly when I spoke. It didn't cost them a thought ... I mean some of the people within Community Services worked very hard to issue a policy on this and a policy on that and it would have been laughed at and thrown there'. A number of workers took refuge in least said, soonest mended, with work reports being fashioned accordingly. Tactical calculation also played a part as when a Community Service officer timed consideration of certain grant applications when particular councillors were on holiday.

Externally local authority officers could be caught in the politicisation of community issues, both centrally and locally. One such contretemps arose over the official openings of new Council Centres, with Ardoyne Community Centre being a case in point. A Sinn Féin inspired 'Peoples' Opening', complete with unofficial plaque and the Irish tricolour flag, resulted in the centre being closed until these were removed. On another occasion, gun in hand, loyalist Councillor, George Seawright (later assassinated) was seen scrambling over the roof of the Whiterock Centre, in West Belfast, to remove the Irish flag. Antagonism could also arise when individual councillors were nominated to act as local authority representatives on Community Centre committees located in 'opposing' single identity areas. Community groups often argued that their non-political constitutional standing made the imposition of political appointees unacceptable. The debate rumbled on, opposing the right of local authority representation on funded organisations to suspected deliberate political interference for sectarian reasons.

The system adopted by Belfast City Council ran into difficulties where local management committees were dominated by a specific political and/ or paramilitary faction. While this was known to happen on both sides of the community divide, a Community Services Officer sent to investigate guns discovered stashed in a Centre in a loyalist area had good reason to feel uncomfortable: 'Of course word got out that I was coming up to do this because I had to inform the staff and the union that this was something that had to happen ... And that's how much access the UDA had to the Centre at the time, they had the keys and everything ... Going up and seeing my name, date of birth and where I lived and my car registration ... painted on the side of the Community Centre ... They were there for six months, never removed. It was incredible'. Equally, however, community centres were important facilities in areas where external access could be difficult; they acted as important local hubs, regularly used for wedding receptions and socials as well as offering services. It had been known for women to ensure that community centres remained free of paramilitary control as noted by a Community Service Officer: 'What I did then when I got the women who were there (in the Centre) from the Pre-School Playgroup ... I said we can't run a pre-school because we are not in control of the building ...

and they chased the boys (paramilitaries) out'. However much depended on local relationships and the extent to which community residents had a sense of ownership of the local centre.

In comparison to the political hot house of Belfast, which was to change over the years, very different approaches were adopted by the other twenty-five local authorities, which lacked any detailed strategic direction from central government. The latter seemed focused on programmes delivered through the variety of BATs, RATs and MBW; although community scepticism was alive and well, as evidenced by the title of a 1990 conference – Is West Belfast Working?

CHAPTER 8

Community Action: Relations in Practice?

In the early 1990s it was not uncommon for 'cross-community' work to be implemented in 'very cross communities'. The perceived dangers of venturing across entrenched community boundaries were formidable. In the opinion of a republican: 'The only thing you heard about the Shankill was the Shankill Butchers (paramilitaries who carried out brutal sectarian murders), I mean that was it ... You still had a view of Protestants and the Shankill as sort of being a colonial demon that terrorises our community in support of the British Army'. In response, the loyalists stereotyped a 'Pan Nationalist Front' of Catholicism/republicanism/terrorism: 'I never went beyond the Falls Road and the Royal (Victoria) Hospital ... but when I got older and actually went into what was known as West Belfast, I thought, My God this is it. You know I couldn't believe it and I would have been in my twenties'. In rural areas the divide was less physically marked but still ran deep in the psyche with fields dubbed catholic or protestant and a mental mind map of the safest – most communally aligned – routes to drive or walk home even when it added miles to the journey. There was an unpredictability about 'the other' that invited fear, all too easily stirred to fever pitch during times of tension when 'the word' went out along community networks.

The daily diet of sectarian attacks fed simmering anxieties, while reports of talks between SDLP leader, John Hume, and Sinn Féin President, Gerry Adams, fuelled the loyalist narrative of a Pan Nationalist Front and republican fears of being 'sold out'. Despite the inauspicious political climate there were still personal and organisational links bridging the community divide. Voluntary sector organisations operated across diverse communities by focusing on specific needs and issues; with the Northern Ireland Council for Voluntary Action espousing a determined and conscious cross-community ethos for the sector. Development interventions at local community level initiated by voluntary organisations routinely prioritised work in equal numbers of single identity republican and loyalist areas to maximise the potential of combining community development and community relations in 'demonstration projects'. The downside was the limited funding available that resulted in much of this work being short-term in nature, staccato in output, and consequently of limited impact.

There was also those organisations whose raison d'étre was community relations. The Corrymeela Community, which pre-dated the Troubles, had long recognised the sectarian fault lines of Northern Ireland and was committed to addressing them on an inter-faith basis. Grounded in a commitment to reconciliation and mutual understanding, Corrymeela facilitated many early cross-community linkages: 'I think there was a lot more crossing of the lines, there were a lot of subterranean linkages, just people could be called on … I think conflict resolution per se wasn't a term used. I think there was a number of attempts at people trying to meet one another to discuss how to deal with dilemmas … I suppose looking back there was a lot more across class and across difference, and there wasn't the sharp distinctions that there are now'. In the early years of the Troubles, the Jewish Centre in North Belfast became another source of 'neutral' space; while the Quaker houses often facilitated quiet, back-channel communication. Efforts to address issues of community division in a more public manner remained fraught due to the increasing politicisation of community relations. By the early 1990s, there were two key groups of people that were least likely to be engaged in what was termed as cross-community work – those living in areas most affected by the conflict, more often talked about than talked to; and those living a reasonably comfortable middle-class existence removed from the violence, but still voting along sectarian lines. In contrast, much progress had been made in moving a number of institutions (such as the Trade Union Movement) from a declared position of being 'non-sectarian' to a more determined commitment to being 'anti-sectarian' in policy and practice.

The politics of community relations

The demise of the NI Community Relations Commission in 1974 saw community relations policy relegated to a desk in the Department of Education (NI) – where it was maintained by 'Mr Community Relations', Donald

Davison. In 1987 the Central Community Relations Unit (CCRU) was set up, heralding a new approach. Reporting to the Head of the Northern Ireland Civil Service, the Unit was given the green light to review and challenge policy across government, with the aim of 'Bringing the two sides of the community towards greater understanding'. The then civil service supremo, Ken Bloomfield, explained the rationale: 'You remember community relations was brigaded with education ... I've always felt that when hardy comes to hardy and departments are under pressure with the crucial discussions every year about allocating public expenditure, they will always favour their core functions over the sort of add on bits ... When CCRU came in ... I was in the luxurious position of being able to say to colleagues "Well look I'm telling you the Secretary of State wants this done" ... You see the whole idea of having a Ministry of Community Relations was, I think, misconceived, because there's a risk if you do that that everybody else will say "Well community relations is their matter." And it should be everybody's responsibility – there should be a community relations dimension to everything that's done ... What you needed to do was sort of say that community relations was a sort of golden thread running through the activities of all other departments and agencies'. In more formal terms the role of CCRU was to (i) ensure that policy decisions within government be informed by evaluation of their effect on community relations; (ii) review periodically the most important policies and programmes to assess their impact on community relations; and (iii) develop new ideas about improving community relations and supporting those working to improve relations and reduce prejudice. The persona of the Minister of State with responsibility for community relations was always important. On at least one occasion a ministerial colleague, upon hearing that the current incumbent had alighted from a helicopter, was heard to mutter: 'The ego has landed'.

Two reports commissioned in 1986 highlighted very different approaches to community relations. The Department of Education (NI) focused on contact between children from different communities, whereas the Standing Advisory Commission on Human Rights (SACHR) report argued for a coherent government policy and the creation of an independent community relations agency. The authors (Mari FitzDuff and Hugh Frazer, 1987) recommended that the new agency act as a focal point for organisations already active in the field, as well as promoting research and training, and providing policy advice to government. They noted the interface between community development and community relations. Within a period of three years two of the core recommendations were realised – the establishment of the Central Community Relations Unit and the creation of the Northern Ireland Community Relations Council. The suggested creation of an independent Community Development agency, also recommended, was ignored.

The design of the new Community Relations Council was influenced by an ad hoc group of individuals from civil society brought together by CCRU officials. This included a range of interests and approaches – inter-community contact programmes; appreciation of different cultural traditions; Mutual Understanding in education; community development experience; and a sectoral focus on reconciliation and anti-sectarianism. Any new community relations agency had to take account of the expanding legal and regulatory framework in the area of Fair Employment and Equality, a subject of discussion. An analysis of community relations typologies, prepared by FitzDuff in 1989, helped frame the parameters of the new agency. There was less agreement as to whether it should be a funding body or focus on advice, support and policy critique, although the civil service favoured the former. One of the officials pointed out: 'Well there were two things – there was the community relations bit and the community development bit. (The latter) as I understood it to be understood by government was if we were giving money to community organisations we were doing community development. That was the understanding of community development – there was no notion of trying to sort of interrogate, or get a feeling for, or direct or get involved so that you could get a better feel of where resources should be deployed. The community relations debate, on the other hand, was this big debate as to whether you should have a policy which pushed more and more towards integration and towards people doing things together'. The outcome of discussion eventually settled on three approaches – community relations in terms of cultural traditions (respect for diverse traditions); equality and equity between communities; and improved relations between communities as they were encouraged to work together.

The Northern Ireland Community Relations Council was launched in 1990 as an independent agency; it was government funded and had one-third of its Council members appointed by government. An early Strategic Plan outlined its role: 'To assist in the creation of just and sustainable solutions to the many issues that divide communities in Northern Ireland' (1991). This encompassed the ambition: 'To increase understanding and cooperation between the political, cultural and religious communities in Northern Ireland'. Although many regarded this objective as being self-evidently praiseworthy and uncontroversial, the framing of the Council itself was viewed in other community narratives as either being part of a state conspiracy to downplay the British colonial dimension of the Troubles, or a liberal sleight of hand to minimise the republican/terrorist threat. In between these extremes were those who shrugged their shoulders and agreed that the problem was that 'the communities' understood each other all too well and simply chose not to relate to each other for well versed reasons.

On the conspiracy side of the axis was the argument that sectarianism was integral to the existence of the Northern Ireland state. Priority given to inter-communal relations was roundly condemned as a distraction from both structural inequalities and the role of the British state. Concerns were also expressed that an over emphasis on the internal (endogenous) explanation that sectarian tensions were the cause of the Troubles simply served to cast the British Army in a benign role as impartial referee rather than as a security tool of the state. From the unionist perspective there was a fear that any analysis of poor community relations cast aspersions on the validity and credibility of the Northern Ireland state and the need to pursue an ever more vigorous war against terrorism. Over and above these positions was the inevitable accusation that the Community Relations Council was simply another government funded quango to rehearse the concerns of 'the chattering classes'. The popularity, or otherwise, of the Council could, in part, be measured by who joined, or resigned, from the board over time and a close monitoring of which groups/communities benefitted from its grant-making. For its part the Community Relations Council adopted a more focused community relations approach than the earlier Community Relations Commission, working with over 1,000 groups during its first four years, to address the 'softer' issues of understanding and communication, as well as some of the 'harder' issues of rights, equality and political differences.

With the CRC up and running, the Central Community Relations Unit had local government in its sights, inviting Councils to submit proposals for community relations programmes with the objectives of (a) developing cross-community contact and cooperation; (b) promoting greater mutual understanding; and (c) increasing respect for different cultural traditions. The rub was that programmes had to be agreed on a cross-party basis, a particularly challenging requirement given the prickly relationships between elected representatives. Despite the difficulties, all but one of the twenty-six Councils had community relations programmes in place by 1993, albeit of various degrees of ambition. The refusnik was North Down Council on the Northern Ireland 'Gold coast'.

Over and above the emphasis on 'good relations', legislation to address equality of opportunity and equity of treatment remained controversial, as fair employment became a cause celebré for Irish-America, amongst others. The Fair Employment (NI) Act was introduced in 1989, the year that local parent power pressured the delivery of an Education Reform Order to make provision for integrated schools. The demand for equality, and equal treatment, became a frame for mobilisation that was often posited in opposition to, or at least trumping, the emphasis on community relations. Cynicism about winning 'hearts and minds' demanded instead a bracing dose of strong legislation, although, arguably, communities in the shadow of 'peacewalls' required both.

Who's the poorest of us all? The politics of poverty

Even at the height of loyalist/unionist indignation over the Anglo Irish Agreement, the *Shankill Bulletin* reported a cross-community protest: 'In an unprecedented display of solidarity black taxi drivers from the Falls and the Shankill, unions and Home Helps blocked their roads off in protest at cuts in the social services'. (December 1986). If community organisers were to deliver cross-community action then it was essential to be able to draw on strong local credibility: 'I was certainly consciously, and others were, (of) making a statement that joint working-class politics were part of the ... solution at that time. But you could only do that if you had a good strong base in your own community, otherwise it was an irrelevance'. In short, cross-community action had to be grounded and practical. The NIVT (Northern Ireland Voluntary Trust) collated evidence from its grantee partners across the divide and joined the fray, berating government policies that failed to address poverty. Subsequent commissioned research into multiple deprivation, argued the importance of multi-agency strategies; the involvement of local people in decision-making and more effective targeting of resources. Once again there was reference to community development as an essential element in securing local participation.

At community level the debate around equality and equity was increasingly framed around the perceived differential impact of social and economic disadvantage as between single identity communities. Calculators were at the ready to establish who was the poorest. Obair – the campaign for employment in West Belfast – was launched in 1987. The following year, a Charter of Employment Rights was publicly endorsed, with supportive academics helping to make the argument: 'It was very clear where the discrimination was coming from – the levels of discrimination, the levels of poverty and deprivation, and it was getting that information to use ... You basically had to have sophisticated arguments even though people would have come back and said, "Oh well, you're a terrorist community, we're not dealing with you." You still had to have the bare facts to come back and say – "These are the arguments, this is the human rights base that you should be working on." ... But there were a lot of sympathetic academics, or people who would have been socially minded even if they wouldn't have agreed politically with people in the local community, they would have still seen the argument in terms of human rights and equality and about poverty and deprivation. And they were key to a lot of information that was generated and a lot of good work that was done on the back of it'. The statistics helped to broaden discussion from being corralled by the narrower base of the 'national question': 'It got you out of the straight-up republican narrative and actually gave you a social analysis rather than propaganda ... And it created space for alliances of different people who did actually see the point of mobilising outside of the remit of the party

(Sinn Féin), and understood the importance of doing that and bringing in different people, and the two weren't synonymous'. The subsequent campaign to win support for the Obair Charter was internationalised, with particular focus on the USA, where the chronic levels of unemployment in Catholic areas were explained as (i) a history of neglect by successive unionist and British administrations; and (ii) continued discrimination in the allocation of funding, the location of industry and development of economic infrastructure. High rates of unemployment, it was argued, were not accidental, but due to a system of ingrained structural discrimination with the community differential in employment statistics across both public and private sectors adding grist to this mill. This analysis became linked to the McBride Principles which demanded US disinvestment to achieve legislative change in the North; a campaign which divided the jobs hungry Trade Union Movement.

Richard Needham, Minister for Economic Development, rubbished Sinn Féin agitation about unemployment, arguing that the ongoing IRA bombing campaign was the major disincentive for economic investment. Unionist politicians were less than impressed, continuing to condemn government policies as designed to offer economic and social inducements to republicans. This view was reflected by a Protestant Church Minister – 'I think in the early days it would have been seen as, you know, we have completely different ways of developing, and as we saw it, the more monolithic republican, Catholic, nationalist – they were together on this, and that they'd been running a state within a state anyway, and that they were geared up and tooled up. Whereas over here we're really needing to build capacity for all our little pockets of stuff that were going on, and that there was a totally different starting point for these communities in beginning to get restitution ... In fact there would be a perception that the government are actually buying the peace on the republican side, that there's much more investment of money going in there in order to get stability ... whereas over here we're not as crucially involved'. The often unconscious reading, and misreading, of the reality of the circumstances of 'the other' was not uncommon.

Meanwhile, Needham's colleague, Direct Rule Industry Minister, Rhodes Boyson, faced the difficult task of convincing an audience of under-whelmed English industrialists that the streets of Belfast were safer than anywhere else in the United Kingdom. This official message of 'normalisation' flew in the face of daily life where people were searched going into city and town centres, as well as when entering any shop. Although this routine was second nature to the beleaguered citizens of the North, it may have seemed bizarre to visiting industrialists. The security industry, as well as glaziers and the construction industry, benefitted from demands for bomb damage repair work, but inward investment remained a challenge. It may have been a slip of the tongue when Needham referred to: 'The little known story of economic and social war against violence and those who waged it on all sides'. Needham was part of a Direct Rule administration that added the third priority of 'Targeting Social Need' to the existing objectives of 'Defeating Terrorism' and 'Strengthening the Northern Ireland Economy' in public spending estimates.

The Targeting Social Need objective was plagued by a certain ambiguity over interpretation as to whether it was about addressing deprivation or the issue of community division, with possible knock-on impacts in terms of community relations. The discomfort within government was reflected by one policy maker: 'I think subconsciously people weren't willing to accept the depth of division and it was watered down – it's hard to believe this but healing community divisions was watered down into targeting social need … There was a philosophical argument that you should be concentrating your resources in the areas of greatest need … but our original analysis was that the problem of community divisions, part of the division was due to the difference in socio-economic conditions experienced in different parts of the community, but the core of the issue was community division. So the third public expenditure priority should have been healing community divisions, and when you say Targeting Social Need it does subtly change; maybe more than subtly'. This analysis was supported by a colleague who acknowledged that the policy challenge was initially framed in terms of addressing community differentials but this proved unacceptable to both Ministers and a number of senior officials. On probing the point further he explained: 'I suspect, one, is an admission that something might have been done, that they had responsibilities for, that might have been producing community differentials and not wanting particularly to highlight that.

Secondly, I think a concern with the majority population's view, and always a concern that the dominant Unionist position would react and respond very negatively to programmes for Catholics. So as I say I think … there was considerable concern not to exacerbate worse than this'. Concern about exacerbating the post Anglo-Irish Agreement unionist alienation was acute, although the focus on social need was also politically sensitive.

There was still a consciousness amongst officials in the Central Community Relations Unit that there was: 'Always a big file in Stormont called sort of West Belfast. What the fuck do you do about it? … Part of the NIO believed in a sort of economic war, you know, you needed to be battling on a number of fronts, both the military front and the economic front, to sort of draw people away from, as it was then in a sense, from violence and into the political. Although the political at that stage would have been into the SDLP as opposed to into Sinn Féin … And the statistics had been around for some time … the existence of this core of statistics that clearly showed that there were large slices of Catholic society that were disadvantaged … across a whole range of policy indicators. But nobody had ever pulled them together and said "Let's do something about it". Those with the ability to collate and interpret the statistics, oiled with the insider knowledge to use information for policy change, played an important role in feeding the evidence into the evolving Making Belfast Work (MBW) initiative, despite the cynical nomenclatures of 'Making Belfast Worse' or 'Making West Belfast Work'!

The Targeting Social Need (TSN) policy was not without challenges, pithily summarised in an external evaluation of the strategy, which concluded that TSN was 'a principle awaiting definition … shrouded in confusion'. In an attempt to create a common baseline, Manchester University was commissioned to produce an index of relative deprivation. The Robson Index was published in 1994, but was already subject to much community speculation as to the league table. It was even reported that on one occasion a special meeting was called by Strabane District Council when it was found that the Council area no longer topped the list of areas of highest unemployment in the United Kingdom. Fame was relative.

Maintaining the edge, the West Belfast Economic Forum was established to monitor local economic statistics and developments in West

Belfast. Simmering community concerns over the impact of disadvantage resulted in localised research in a number of other areas. Two inner city Belfast communities, geographically adjacent but divided in communal identity, were examples. The Bridge Community Trust worked in the Lower Ravenhill area of East Belfast, seeded by the concerns of members of the local Baptist Church about the area. 'The Bridge' initiative was set up with active volunteer support and benefitted from the purchase of a building by the Urban Mission Trust. An ACE scheme allowed subsidised staffing to be sourced for the provision of services – welfare rights advice; a Parent and Toddler group; a Women's Group; a community transport scheme; a youth project; and a café among others. The closure of the café at noon during its early years elicited a less than favourable response from residents who hung a sign on the steel shutters saying: 'This is an Irish café, it closes for lunch!'

It took repeated door knocking, household surveys, public meetings and the circulation of a newsletter, 'The Ravenhill Reach' to encourage local participation. The latter was organised into the Lower Ravenhill Community Association (LRCA) in June 1990. The faith-linked motivation, allied to practical project development, attracted statutory funding from both LEDU (Local Enterprise Development Unit) and the Belfast Action Team (the Riverside Action Team); followed by Making Belfast Work. As with Catholic Church in West Belfast, seed investment by the church levered additional statutory resourcing of local assets to add to the limited income generated by a second-hand shop that The Bridge ran. What was noteworthy in this initiative was the work dedicated to generate both participation and community ownership.

Less than a kilometre away the nationalist/republican Lower Ormeau held a Peoples' Planning Festival in 1988, organised by the Lower Ormeau Residents' Action Group (LORAG) and supported by Community Technical Aid – a NGO offering planning and technical expertise to community groups. It was concluded that as little notice was being taken of the community voice, there was a need to undertake local research to identify an anti-poverty strategy. Described in terms of the gaelic aphorism: 'Ag duine féin is fear a fhios cá luionn an bhróg' ('The wearer knows best where the shoe pinches') – local people were trained to carry out household surveys.

The information gathered was complemented by focus group discussions and statistical data. The initiative was funded by the Joseph Rowntree Charitable Trust, the Belfast City Council and the NIVT (Northern Ireland Voluntary Trust). A sympathetic academic from Queens University Belfast analysed the findings and edited the subsequent report: 'Unlocking the Lower Ormeau'. With unemployment rates in the area standing at over 40 per cent, the report identified social and economic recommendations, although reference was also made to the impact of the Troubles. Forty residents had been killed in this single identity community, which was a by-word for riots during the annually contested Loyal Orders' parades. As was the case in West Belfast, community activists saw structural deprivation framed by political preference and inequity of treatment, contributing to a growing narrative whose central theme was the demand for equality.

Across the city, the North Belfast Community Development Centre was attempting to balance acutely sensitive community perceptions alongside a concern that the residents in small Protestant areas were feeling increasingly isolated. One such area was Torrens, a dwindling community adjacent to the expanding nationalist/republican hinterland of Ardoyne/Oldpark and Cliftonville. The Belfast Action Team supported a four year neighbourhood development programme, supplemented by a jigsaw of independent funders. Working principles were established – (a) local issues affecting people's lives must be tackled as a matter of priority; (b) residents should be supported and encouraged to take action on these issues; (c) policies and administrative systems should be judged by their effect on people's quality of life; (d) investment in community awareness and participation was essential; and (e) the community worker appointed must work alongside people rather than on their behalf, to emphasise local decision-making: in short, standard community development practice. The Project Report detailed the seven steps adopted in this neighbourhood approach, which ran from project initiation; the building of relationships; clarifying goals and priorities; developing and strengthening local groups; and helping establish links, partnership working and networking. Again, the accepted stuff of community development, although in an era marked by the proliferation of special programmes, staffed by seconded civil servants, a useful aide memoire.

The political and community tensions always at play in North Belfast affected the Community Development Centre itself: 'I (the Director) had to, all the time, make it clear that I had no (political) line … If I had at any stage given any political allegiance I would have been out the window. I had to really work tremendously hard just to gain people's trust and people's confidence … It was tough working in North Belfast, very, very tough … very, very scary … I think on both sides there was the feeling "Oh, we're worse off – definitely worse off than they are." But what they didn't seem to realise was that they were on exactly the same benefits; exactly the same sort of housing … but it was trying to get people to be receptive to that'. The Community Development Centre was forced to move office after a bomb attack. It mounted the scorched front door of its old office as an art feature in its new premises on the post-genteel Cliftonville Road. If the government was Targeting Social Need, community development could also find itself targeted.

Framing community development

There remained the issue of how to frame and message community development as a process of value in itself, but also as potentially complementary to community relations. Practitioners were disturbed by the government cuts of up to 15 per cent in grant aid to local authority community services as well as about the apparent contradictions in statutory approaches – 'I think previous communities more or less shaped where they wanted to go and then looked for funding. I think more recent government has been shaping the funding stream and communities have to fit … and that's not always a good fit, and it's not always delivering what's good for the community. Because I think also the nature of government is to ensure that there is a competitiveness amongst organisations going after the funding. But then when you're going after it they want you to cooperate, so it's like you're crying, you're getting slapped for crying, but then they're going to give you a bottle'. Community development principles were getting lost in the subsequent confusion. By the late 1980s a number of community workers set up the Community Development Review Group to develop a framework for community development. Meeting on a voluntary basis, they planned a conference: 'The Lost Horizons, New Horizons' – which brought together the usual list of suspects and some fellow travellers. The debates were wide ranging and self-critical. Eamonn Deane, Director of the Derry-based Holywell Trust, argued that the often used phrase 'where people are at', had lost any meaningful impact on practice and that community workers could sometimes shy away from challenging exclusionary economic and social structures. The conference facilitator, David Donnison, warned that community work could silence the very people that workers thought they were giving voice to. The relationship between community development and community relations was debated, as was relationship with the women's sector and anti-poverty work. Local Council workers in attendance heard one of their fellows describing their situation as 'walking a tightrope of razor blades'.

The Community Development Review Group met for a further three years, organising a series of commissioned studies, conferences and focus groups. Three inter-related reports defined community development in Northern Ireland as a process which embraces community action, community work, community services and other community endeavour, whether geographical or issue based, but with an emphasis on working with the disadvantaged, impoverished and powerless to achieve societal change. Specific reference was made to the nature of community development as challenging prejudice and sectarianism. Recommendations considered the implementation of this committee-drafted definition addressing funding, education and training support. There was a call for government to make a clear commitment to community development on an inter-departmental basis and to establish a long-term Community Development Fund in place of sporadic, short-term programmes. In addition, it was suggested that the relationship between the voluntary sector and the community sector should be clarified and an annual Community Development Consultative Conference held to facilitate ongoing reflection, consultation and participation. By 1993, central government responded with a 'Strategy for the Support of the Voluntary Sector and for Community Development in

Northern Ireland', setting up a Voluntary Activity Unit to take the lead. One of the main aims of the VAU was to promote and enhance the effectiveness and efficiency of governmental commitment to community development.

In a related, if separate trajectory, community workers from a Protestant/Unionist/Loyalist perspective came together in 1991, in the Community Development in Protestant Areas Steering Group. Their view was that the experience of community development was not unidimensional across Northern Ireland, raising questions as to whether the approach was effective in communities that feared to be seen as anti-state; and were ambiguous about change. The power held, and lost, by unionism was acknowledged by long-time Shankill activist, Jackie Redpath, who argued that community development provided Protestants with the space to dissent, irrespective of perceived political loss. Specific issues raised included difficulties with resident engagement and mobilisation; concerns about attempts by elected representatives to control local activism; the chill factor spread by paramilitary influence; and the central importance of cultural identity. The proposition that community work was by necessity anti-sectarian in nature was also interrogated. While the importance of cross-community work was recognised, it was held that this was only feasible where there was local community support and confidence to engage with those holding different perspectives.

A number of seminars were held to examine Protestant/Unionist/ Loyalist identity – or identities – as well as the experience of community action in Protestant areas, described as being more individualistic than their Catholic neighbours, and tending to 'moan and complain rather than act'. Commissioned reports took up the issue of comparative disadvantage. It was held that government programmes could respond more easily to deprivation across large swathes of territory, such as the mainly nationalist/republican West Bank of Derry or West Belfast, whereas the pockets of poverty that often afflicted Protestant communities, tended to go unnoticed. A 'Poverty amidst Plenty' report threw out the challenge to Making Belfast Work to redefine its geographical focus. A Steering Group member concluded: 'Well if anything it brought it all on the radar screen of government ... I remember, I think it was Making Belfast Work ... and (they) said it changed the way they looked (at areas) ... It also raised issues among the churches and politicians ... I think it showed for the first time some of the problems in Protestant areas, but also some of the radical thinking – some of the new thinking as well'. A Catholic worker employed in the Shankill was more sceptical, suggesting that community development was no different in Protestant areas, but that the areas themselves were slower to adopt a self-help community action approach. There was a tendency, instead, to rely on elected local councillors; with councillors keen to maintain a dependency relationship.

The views of the Community Development in Protestant Areas Steering Group informed the work of the Community Development Review Group. The expansive definition of community development adopted by the latter teetered between the specificity of the issues raised by the PUL group and the criticism by those – mainly republicans – that it failed to address the particular circumstances within Northern Ireland, except for the commitment to challenge prejudice and sectarianism. The importance of community development practice being rooted in an explicit value base was welcomed by the Northern Ireland Voluntary Trust and the Northern Ireland Council for Voluntary Action (NICVA). In later years it was to strengthen the hand of Jimmy Kearney, who was appointed to head up the Voluntary Activity Unit within the Department of Health & Social Services, and his ebullient aide-de-camp, Joe Wright.

Partnership working: Getting with the buzz

A whole new vocabulary was waiting in the wings: 'scaling up', 'community capacity-building', 'consultation', and the prima donna of them all 'partnership'. The European Commission actively argued the virtues of partnership working and designed its Third Anti-Poverty Programme (known as the Community Action Programme to Foster the Economic and Social Integration of the Less Privileged Groups because Prime Minister Thatcher dismissed the term 'poverty') around the concept. Working in the Brownlow area of Craigavon, six eurospeak principles framed a five-year (1989–1994) programme – inter-agency strategies; the multi-dimensional nature of poverty; economic and social integration; additionality of resources; community participation; and partnership working. Local tenants and community associations had taken the lead in producing a 'Greater Brownlow Review' which called for an agreed strategy for the area to be developed through community-statutory coordination. The Southern Health & Social Services Board was an enthusiastic supporter of the initiative and the Brownlow Community Development Association was formed to structure a key role for local residents. Initial consultations prioritised five approaches – community enterprise; community work involving women, families and children; youth provision; community arts; and community work around health issues. By 1989 these plans secured European funding and the Brownlow Community Trust was born.

Even with a fair wind behind them partnership working was not without its tensions. Community activists expressed disappointment that the 'culture' of meetings favoured the more formal statutory ethos, and that the 'real power' within the Community Trust management board remained in the hands of the statutory representatives. There was also a concern that there was little evidence of partnership working at other levels of statutory agencies. Despite this, the recorded history of the Trust argues that access to decision-makers improved and was better than that experienced across other areas of Northern Ireland. The impressive range of practical initiatives seeded ranged from development work with minority ethnic women, to a Lay Health project and adult education with Traveller families. The Chrysalis Women's Centre grew out of the vision of the Brownlow Women's Forum and the focus on play provision resulted in Craigavon Borough Council adopting a new play policy. One unfortunate point of controversy was a visit by Irish President Mary Robinson; disapproval was expressed by a number of Unionist politicians, including a Board member of the Community Trust.

This experience of partnership informed MBW thinking in Belfast, underpinned when the Director of the Brownlow Community Trust joined MBW as an adviser on partnership working. Practical trial and error was also to hand in the Greater Shankill where activists recognised the need for longer-term development strategies: 'It was building up from '93, it

started out as a Strategy Group for the Greater Shankill, which was good ...
It was based on saying we'd been all project led since Peter Melchett's time ...
What we need is a long term strategy. So this community for the first
time sat down and thought twenty years ahead – or tried. It was the first
community, I believe, trying to do that. And that's '93/'94, we came up
with the strategy, and then the question was who's going to implement it?
Where do we get the money? And who's going to be the guardian of it? ...
It was a partnership model but not incorporated, and then (later) became
incorporated'. This community process hung in the balance when an IRA
bomb shattered lives on a busy Saturday afternoon on the Shankill Road
in October 1993.

Killing ten people and injuring another fifty-seven, the premature
explosion represented the greatest loss of life in a single incident over the
previous six years. It set in train a spiral of retaliatory attacks, but on the
Shankill itself there was a sense of stunned disbelief and collective trauma.
The Manager of a Youth Training Workshop questioned his commitment to cross-community activities: 'It nearly pushed me over the edge ...
I remember standing in the Shankill and I said "What the hell am
I going to do?" Because we had Catholic and Protestant kids working
together ... was I right in bringing Catholics and Protestants together?'
He spoke of the comfort drawn from a visit by a nationalist SDLP politician and his wife who came to express sympathy. A number of community
projects, particularly those employing Catholic workers, closed down for
a couple of weeks to allow the dust to settle. Prior to re-opening, there
was often quiet checking with individuals close to paramilitary thinking
to assure safety.

The sense of crisis in the Shankill was not helped when in November
1993 the *Observer* newspaper reported on British Government secret back
channel communication with Sinn Féin and the IRA over previous years;
although vigorously denied there were few who were slow to make the
connection between fire and smoke. A response to community initiatives
helped to maintain stability, with a senior MBW policymaker acknowl-
edging: 'The idea of partnerships came from the Shankill ... (They had)
started toying with this notion of setting up a partnership, partially to hold
on to that level of independence, but also partially to try and deal with

the internecine stuff that was going on in the Shankill, trying to put everybody together into some sort of overarching partnership in the name of the Shankill. And I'd gone to several meetings about this ... and the more I listened, the more I thought this isn't actually a bad idea'. Reference to 'internecine strife' was not unique to the Greater Shankill, but continued to plague the strategic planning approach. A MBW Team Leader in the area shuddered when describing a residential workshop to progress the idea of a Shankill Strategy: 'I remember I took forty-five people away ... for a residential to get some kind of coherent working together ... and I had to stand in the door to stop half of them walking out at lunchtime on the first day ... The predominant emotion was anger – anger at each other; anger at the world; and they got really angry at the facilitator who had never handled anything like this before ... I said "Billy (a participant), some of these issues are going to blow up and we're going to completely lose this. I want you to get up and say 'Stop', and let me take it from there." So that's what he did and I said, "What do you want? You've got a flipchart so you can come up here and do what do you want?" ... And that did become constructive'. Another Workshop participant felt it was like being involved in 'the Third World War'; agreement finally settled on a 'Shankill '94' project to tap into community fears and hopes.

Discussions over identity were central to 'Shankill '94' which featured a landmark conference, in October 1994: 'Beyond Fife and Drum' – to bring together a wide range of political and community participants. Community engagement was reinforced by the happy coincidence of a visit by Prince Charles to the Shankill where he enthusiastically supported community planning approaches: 'Prince Charles was visiting the Shankill ... which everyone thought was the greatest thing since sliced bread; finally the Shankill had been recognised. And we (MBW) had to work very hard to make that happen ... But when he was there you see, he mentioned this thing about community planning. He'd seen this thing done in Scotland or somewhere, and he thought this was great and we should do it and so forth. And he mentioned this guy ... his favourite architect ... and I felt I needed to follow this up because at some point he'd probably drop a note to the Secretary of State or something ... So I arranged a lunch for him (the architect) and the Shankill ones ... He explained to them what it was all about, so they thought this was brilliant, and eventually over a period of time we arranged the Shankill Community Planning Weekend, which actually was fabulous'. Reports on the weekend were carried in the local press, with an estimated 600 people plus contributing to the visioning exercise. Sixty-two community based groups, forty-five statutory agencies and five political parties were represented.

Discussion was underpinned by statistical stocktaking which in itself was depressing – 85 per cent of local people had no educational qualifications and over a third of men were unemployed. 'The People's Plan for the Shankill' was produced, facilitated by an English team that were described as a force to be reckoned with: 'It was amazing ... I mean those sixteen people arrived and they worked shifts, when eight of them were sleeping, eight of them were working – twenty-four hours. And they actually produced a written report on the Monday night on the way forward for the Shankill, and out of it six actions – we were going to work on health; we were going to work on education; we were going to work on employment; we were going to work on young people – you know, all of those things, housing. And each one of these points was going to be addressed. The strategy was brilliant, and the Greater Shankill Strategy was brilliant, out of that then flowed this idea of forming a partnership, and I'm not sure whether that's where it went wrong'. The optimism was tinged with endemic low expectations.

The new sense of energy was also seen in the Shankill Women's Forum – 'The Women's Forum was brilliant, absolutely brilliant – well it started off brilliant, it took a bit of a downhill turn ... I mean I remember going to the Women's Forum meetings and you couldn't get into the room; we literally were squashed, we were all three sitting on top of each other ... There was something in terms of information sharing ... I think where it went wrong was it kept an open approach, so there was a meeting and everybody knew about it and anybody could come in and out ... To me it really was not structured and ... there is something about structure here that helps things to work'. If the 'tyranny of structurelessness' syndrome haunted the Forum, complaints about the partnership approach was that it was structured to the point of exclusion. The Shankill Community Council expressed reservations: 'We had our problems with the Partnership Board, basically and simply we didn't like the way it was structured, how it was structured, how people were appointed; we kicked up hell for years'. One Board member attributed the tension to competing personalities, but another reflected: 'I think I've come to the conclusion that you need to build partnerships among mutual interests, and they last for a period of time around things that are mutually beneficial, but trying to build partnerships for the sake of building partnerships in a conceptual sort of way is hard going'. Another criticism was that Partnership Boards invariably became an arm of government, becoming distant from local residents: 'It was like being a shop steward in a factory, it was easier to talk to one person than to talk to 400 ... I think in setting up the partnership, I think the system ... thought well here we'll only have to talk to half a dozen people here and they'll be responsible and they'll do this and they'll do that'. Meanwhile a beleaguered MBW Team Leader was left to juggle complaints, finding himself in the uncomfortable position of having to draft the reply to a letter that demanded his removal, sent by an elected representative to the Secretary of State: 'But being a civil servant when it came down (from the Secretary of State's office) I had to write a reply. I mean I never experienced anything like that'.

The Greater Shankill Partnership Board pre-dated four other partnerships across Belfast that became a feature of MBW strategy. A 'Handbook on Partnership Working' laid down a number of principles, including: 'The simple principle that there had to be representation of the different sectors ... There was a huge argument with Belfast City Council ... We'd say "You cannot appoint people to these partnerships just on a whim. You're going to have to put the people that represent these areas on it and that means in some areas you're going to have to put Sinn Féin on it" ... And that was the big politics at that stage to sort of say "You're going to have to accept these people" ... And then the community side also had to accept that it had to have some sort of transparency and democracy ... because you certainly had to revisit what was the basis of representation at community level'. Designing a process that could handle these tensions in a situation where suspicion was second nature, needed diplomacy and imagination that: 'Would have defied the Boundary Commission' (the body that drew the border in Ireland in the 1920s).

Of the five Partnership Boards that finally emerged in South, West, East, North Belfast and the Greater Shankill, North Belfast proved the most difficult to negotiate: 'I mean there was always a question mark that over hung the Partnership, whether there should have been two partnerships with an under-arching partnership that brought them together, and it's always that debate in North – do you do two and find a structure that brings them together or do you insist on doing one, and you're always damned if you do one and damned if you do the other, because ... unless you can get everybody actually wanting to be on board each have the capacity to destroy the other'. MBW decided on a single entity. There was less tension around establishing the South Belfast Partnership Board. East Belfast worked out a collaborative arrangement between the East Belfast Community Development Agency and the new structure, with similar relationships being crafted in West Belfast to take account of existing organisations such as the Falls Community Council and Upper Springfield organisation. In both areas overlapping personality and political interests and relationships were brought into play; the new West Belfast Partnership Board was chaired by Sinn Féin Councillor, Alex Maskey. The importance of legitimation was recognised from an early stage, as reflected by a MBW policy maker: 'If partnerships are to be effective instruments of social policy and practice in regenerating disadvantaged communities we need to ensure there is a structured and coordinated mechanism for relating to the centre, otherwise we run the risk of contributing further to the ghettoisation of poverty'. She described community-based partnerships as being like arranged marriages, working as long as there is a dowry and divorce clause.

The Londonderry Initiative adopted partnership-lite, but again came up against geo-politics challenges. The tiny Protestant Fountain estate became part of the TRIAX partnership which represented a predominantly Catholic area: 'We were part of the Bogside, Brandywell and Creggan, but when you take the total catchment area of 13,000 and there's only 300 people in the Fountain, with different traditions and different culture and different outlooks, it's not working'. There were also the standard concerns over allocation of funding; the accountability of workers; and potential statutory control. Up the hill in the Creggan estate, fears were expressed about blunting the radical edge of community action: 'What the partnerships did they got everyone round the table, but you definitely lost your campaigning edge'. For some, however, the partnership model was as good as it got, as a veteran of the turbulent Greater Shankill Partnership believed: 'Had it not been for the Partnership I think it would have been a lot worse ... because at least there was some sort of structure in place for that tension to be channelled through. Now if that hadn't been there I dread to think what would have happened'. In short, while not necessarily ideal, the partnership approach provided a framing of sorts for local decision-making.

Creating space for cross-community confidence

Achieving acceptable structures to frame statutory-community relations paled into insignificance compared to the edginess of the quiet conversations about alternatives to political violence. Dr Roy Magee, a Shankill Road born Presbyterian Minister, took the initiative to meet loyalist leaders: 'My role was really only nudging the loyalist paramilitary leadership with one elbow and the Irish and British governments with the other'. His was one of a number of civil society overtures. Individuals in Derry had long established contacts with the IRA leadership; in West Belfast, Clonard Monastery hosted tentative talks between a number of protagonists in the conflict. There was, according to Fr. Alex Reid, a: 'Moral obligation to get involved'. As early as March 1989, Gerry Adams signalled that Sinn Féin had an interest in a 'non-armed political movement to work for self-determination' in Ireland. Secretary of State, Peter Brooke, responded, conceding the difficulty of defeating the IRA militarily, and suggesting that talks with Sinn Féin would not be ruled out in the event of a ceasefire. He further specified that Britain had no 'selfish economic or strategic interest' in Northern Ireland. The IRA declared its first Christmas ceasefire in fifteen years, although a New Year bombing campaign saw traditional Winter Sales being merged with that of fire damaged stock. One weary back channel negotiator accepted: 'The importance of doing things and keeping things going and not despairing, and the small things that you didn't think were very important on the day become sometimes very important, right? I think also the learning of the analysis is a very important thing, and you need to know what the hell's going on; and it's not just about, you know, going out and throwing holy water or giving hugs or whatever it might be, it's about good interpretation'. Interpretation and perception on all levels were critical.

For the general public, and particularly the residents of interface areas, this was a period of tit-for-tat violence which caused some to question the effectiveness of cross-community work, specifically 'ghettoaway days'. With twelve separate flashpoint areas identified along the length of the Springfield peacewall in West Belfast, activists from both sides of the wall put their heads together to develop a strategy to encompass both community development and conflict resolution. This, it was agreed, would involve incremental steps, working within single identity communities as well as between them; but only the latter when there was a clear rationale. A Standing Conference was established in lieu of a management committee, and the Springfield Inter Community Development Project (SICDP) was launched to work from three different locations – the Ainworth Community Centre (Upper Shankill); the Upper Springfield Resource Centre (West Belfast) and Farset Enterprise Park (on the Springfield interface). This multi-location approach helped ensure the safety of staff and participants, as well as underlining the single identity dimension of the work. The International Fund for Ireland funded the post of SICDP Director in 1990; development workers appointed over a period included both IRA and UVF political ex-prisoners. A Community Leadership Coordinator was supported by the Ulster People's College to deliver leadership training.

The UVF prisoner was originally approached to become involved during his 'working-out' day release from the Maze Prison: 'Jackie Hewitt, Jim McCorry, Joe Camplisson all approached me, and Louis West, and said "Will you do this piece of work because what we're trying to do is to pull together this cross-community stuff, and the difficulty round the cross-community stuff is that people are being killed every day and people don't necessarily see the benefit of it, but what we need to do is to get people to start to think about the whole economic and social conditions." You know we started on these pieces of land, found out who owned them, what they were going to do with them, because if they were not going to do anything with them, could we convince the Department of the Environment ... could they actually take them off people and say this is going to be for community use? ... So all our community action was all around planning'. When employed by SICDP after his release from prison, he described how: 'We had designed this notion of Standing Conferences, so people had the right to come and say what they wanted at Standing Conferences. We would administer and do it for them – bring people together, but they had to choose the topic and also had to choose the speakers ... I think we probably had about four of them in two years ... It gave people in the community the urge to do this sort of thing and it was about challenging government as well ... It would have been done to include everybody (cross-community) ... (But) in terms of the work we never used the terms of cross-community, we always talked about inter and intra ... So we tried to get people together, you know, from the same social and economic background, forget about the religious stuff, if people wanted to walk and talk about that then we had other strands in the project that could actually do that'. The continuum between community development, community relations and conflict resolution was recognised, but activities were nuanced to the pace of local confidence.

The SICDP made its position clear – (a) belief in inclusive dialogue; (b) recognition of the role of political parties and government in decision-making about interface areas; (c) the importance of economic investment in community initiatives; (d) both inter-community cultural initiatives and single identity projects; and (e) work to reduce sectarianism through issues of community concern. It saw single identity work as mobilising inter-community engagement over time. It also acknowledged the importance of 'insider-partial' individuals – in this case political ex-prisoners – who could open and maintain channels of communication. Respected Sinn Féin Councillor and ex-Hunger Striker Pat McGeown was publicly involved in SICDP, and the UVF staff member provided street credibility with loyalism, alongside building the confidence of the UVF about parallel political discussions: 'Alex Reid and Gerry Reynolds (Clonard Monastery) were both doing sort of go betweens between the Provos and the UVF at that particular time, so they were saying what I was doing; so what I was reporting back was exactly what they were dealing with ... We were using the same terminology and everything, and I think that gave people confidence in what I was doing ... They were quite happy to have somebody like me, you know, talking, because they could actually wash their hands of it and say "nothing to do with us".

Despite this the process was not without difficulties. Periodically SICDP workers had to argue down critics on their 'own side' to create space for each other; their respective status as ex-political prisoners helped. Similarly, some of the public discussions between interface residents were hot and heavy; these fears and aspirations were recorded and shared in a pamphlet: 'Life on the Interface'.

Two broader civil society initiatives were designed to open space for inclusive dialogue on options for Northern Ireland. The prevailing government media ban prevented interviews with individuals deemed to have links with paramilitary groups. The 'Beyond Hate' conference, organised in Derry by the Hollywell Trust, and the Opsahl Inquiry, were both launched in 1992. The 'Beyond Hate' event invited an international audience to address the issue of 'living with our deepest differences', throwing open the platform to any participant who wished to contribute. Sinn Féin representatives were amongst those who accepted the invitation. The Opsahl Citizens' Enquiry was a more ambitious venture, involving over three thousand people and organisations in making submissions to a seven person panel, under the chairpersonship of Norwegian Professor Torkel Opsahl. Both republicans and loyalists made submissions. An impressive report captured suggestions, contradictions and options from all quarters in an inclusive manner. Both approaches accepted the importance of creating space for inclusive exchange, although in the tenor of the times, the motivations of those designing the projects were carefully scrutinised by all concerned.

Inclusion, according to some, still had to know its place. Northern nationalism was as outraged as unionism in 1992 when Irish President, Mary Robinson, travelled to West Belfast to meet activists and representatives under the auspices of the Falls Community Council. The visit had been signed off by the Irish Government to open political space: 'The Robinson visit was very important psychologically ... It was important for a variety of reasons; it helped to define the Irish presence, that it had a degree of independence ... Also it helped to end demonisation, and you can't really have a peace process with demonisation'. The carefully choreographed event included President Robinson meeting, and shaking hands, with Gerry Adams. The community cover was denounced: 'The editorial in the *Irish News* was actually addressed to us – me and Eileen Howell ... saying that we had sullied the Irish President and dirtied her hands ... and calling on us that day that we still had time to withdraw this invitation ... But that was the attitude, who were we to drag the President into the mud, to bring her to West Belfast ... But just so vociferous were they against her doing this because they knew that once she'd shook his (Adams) hand, somebody had to deal with him. Other people had to meet him ... people had to deal with us'. An adult education organiser had advance notice of the proposed visit; she contacted her senior managers: '"Confidential, Mary Robinson – Whiterock buildings – afternoon, and I've been told to say anybody's welcome who wishes to come." Not a bloody one of them (came) – they were scared'. Norms of acceptability remained rigid in circumstances where people still experienced violence and prospects of peace seemed remote. Those civil servants drafting the Northern Ireland Structural Funds Plan (1994–1999) for European funding might have picked up straws in the wind when a Community Relations sub-programme was proposed for the first time, although framed in terms of reducing support for terrorism. The official narrative still held notwithstanding the political developments stirring in the weeds of back channel contacts and communication. Meanwhile, as far as many of the public were aware the loyalist slogan of '6 into 26 (counties) won't go' was still mathematically valid as compared to the republican claim that '26 + 6 = 1'!

CHAPTER 9

Peace, Imperfect Peace ...

The school holidays were ending on 31 August 1994 just as P. O'Neill issued an IRA statement declaring the complete cessation of military activities in recognition of 'the potential of the current situation and in order to enhance the democratic process'. It was not the most rousing prose penned by the nom de plume IRA spokesperson, but it was in clear response to Gerry Adams's analysis that conditions were in place for moving the peace process forward. The *Belfast Telegraph* headline trumpeted: 'It's Over'. above a photograph of weeping women. A cavalcade of cars, draped in Irish tricolours, drove triumphantly through West Belfast with horns blaring. DUP leader, Rev. Ian Paisley, warned of impending Civil War and the Ulster Unionist Party leader described the situation as 'de-stabilising'. As the British Government agonised over the lack of the word 'permanent' in the ceasefire statement, staff in a West Belfast Community College were less conditional in celebrating: 'We were enrolling students and the ceasefire is announced, and I mean, Oh my God this is just absolutely amazing. So I sent someone off to the Off-Licence to buy a few bottles of champagne so we can really celebrate. So we were in the common room, I got the glasses and the champagne, and this guy comes up to me and he says – this is a teacher from the central organisation – "Do you always do this at enrolment?" I said "A ceasefire has just been announced!" "Oh", he says. No impact at all. And this place is singing, you know, people are running up and down, waving flags out of cars ...' – another case of the mutual incomprehensibility of competing narratives.

With impressive rapidity the European Union offered a Peace & Reconciliation programme just weeks after the ceasefire statement; while across the Atlantic a group of influential Irish-Americans lobbied for the engagement of US President Bill Clinton. Some members of this group attended the Combined Loyalist Military Command (CLMC) declaration of a loyalist paramilitary ceasefire on 13 October. Veteran UVF leader, Gusty Spence, noted that the ceasefire was conditional on a continued IRA commitment to peace and offered 'abject and true remorse' to 'innocent' victims of loyalist violence. The US administration issued visas for both republican and loyalist representatives to visit America. Promises of increased financial support were made; a conference to promote trade and investment; and the appointment of a Special Economic Advisor to Northern Ireland – former US Senate Majority Leader, George Mitchell. If the international community was positive, political storm clouds gathered closer to home when British Prime Minister, John Major – successor to Margaret Thatcher – made IRA arms decommissioning a pre-condition for Sinn Féin inclusion in peace talks. Adams argued for 'parity of esteem' for his party to little avail. Initiatives on the socio-economic front promulgated a different message as a Community Work Programme offered 500 places for unemployed people in West Belfast, and 250 in both Strabane and Fermanagh. The DUP denounced this as 'appeasement' of Sinn Féin. Freshly painted graffiti on the Shankill proclaimed acceptance of the unconditional surrender of the IRA; just as new wall murals in West Belfast were unveiled in honour of dead IRA volunteers. The message was clear, even if politics was shifting, there was an imperative to assuage the sacrifices of the past, and particularly the families of combatants who had died in the struggle.

Civil society response to the ceasefires all but shattered the official narrative of 'normalisation'. The Northern Ireland CBI (Confederation of British Industries) released a document which argued that the peace process would help spur economic growth. It also agreed to participate in the Group of 7 (G7), which brought together the Institute of Directors (IOD); the Northern Ireland Chamber of Commerce; the Ulster Farmers' Union; the Northern Ireland Agricultural Producers' Association (NIAPA); the Northern Ireland Committee of the Irish Congress of Trade Unions (NIC-ICTU); and NICVA (the representative body of the community and voluntary sectors), to argue for 'peace, progress and prosperity'. In effect the G7 assumed the role of cheer leader for peace.

Moving rapidly, the Northern Ireland Voluntary Trust (later renamed the Community Foundation for Northern Ireland) circulated a survey on what community and voluntary groups saw as the hopes, fears and opportunities in the post ceasefire context. The main priorities clustered as – (a) Political/Civil Liberties/Human Rights issues; (b) Economic growth and job creation; (c) Social development in areas of multiple deprivation and disadvantaged rural areas; and (d) Greater investment in community development. Participative democracy was identified as important given the pressing need to: 'Devise local and national political structures that empower all people'. There was also acknowledgement of the needs of individuals, groups and communities that were experiencing 'hurt, anger and resentment' as a result of the impact of the conflict. Responses exuded a sense of early optimism that community activists could contribute to the design of new societal structures and relationships.

Spring 1995 was marked by mixed messages. The Irish and British Governments worked to agree a Framework Document to format the peace process and British Army daytime patrols in Belfast were withdrawn. There was still uncertainty about how quickly political inclusion would be deemed acceptable. Panic ensued when Gerry Adams attempted to shake hands with Direct Rule Minister, Malcolm Moss, during his visit to West Belfast. Adams was told that 'It was not appropriate'. He, in turn, replied that 'It was disgraceful that he (the Minister) could come here and accept the hospitality of the local people and then behave in such a boorish way'. A Northern Ireland Office official explained: 'Me and mine were the official hand shakers. We had to get out at all ministerial (visits) and get in the way, if there was a hand coming out we had to grab it. That was – in trying to bring all sides along, and unionism had its demands – you can't fall over these people ... It was more to do with the need to preserve the integrity of the British Government at a time when we were trying to get political'. The public narrative of the non-handshake in an area where Adams was the M.P. might have played well with unionism but allowed Sinn Féin to extract political kudos from British rigidity. For its part, the establishment decried Sinn Féin as being just 'at it'.

All off to Washington DC

When interviewed the day after the IRA ceasefire, a community activist
from the Greater Shankill hadn't the heart to tell the animated interviewer
that she had been involved in cross-community work for years. She did
distinguish, however between engaging in joint work rather than cross community contact for the sake of it. She also described the pressures within
her community: 'As in the Roman Catholic communities community
politics are intense ... We have at least four or five different traditions of
unionism within the same community and there is an internal debate in
this small area as to who represents us and what is the best way forward.
This has always been a cause of major concern to community workers as
we must be careful not to tread on anyone's toes. One of the tricks a good
community worker has to learn is to praise everyone and then get on with
the job! We take the view that politics are too important to be left to the
politicians'. Her co-respondent from West Belfast was more guarded –
'I think we (the community sector) have played a crucial role in alleviating the worst effects of the violence while maintaining a sense of hope and
vision for the future'. Government funding supported two area-based initiatives to take forward that vision – the Foundry Regeneration Trust on the
Catholic side of the West Belfast interface and the Forthriver Regeneration
Trust on the Protestant side. Although in regular contact, and with good
working relationships, there was still a mezzo-level wariness as evidenced
by the West Belfast Economic Forum complaints about 'the apparently
politically motivated necessity to ensure that expenditure in Catholic areas
is matched by expenditure in Protestant areas'. This approach was viewed
as particularly annoying given that statistics suggested higher levels of
deprivation in many nationalist/republican wards.

On a day-to-day basis a Foundry Trust worker found the cross-community dimension of the programme exciting: 'You had this access to people
from the Shankill who were a different country to me ... I mean I remember
for the first time meeting Billy Hutchinson, and really staring and looking,
and he put his hand out for me to shake, and I thought "Oh, you've crossed
the Rubicon now" ... I just took an instant liking to them I have to say ...
you get to know them and you're listening to them and they're talking

about their community needs, and you can just see how genuine they are ... I'm not saying you warm up to the whole thing overnight, but you've an opportunity to meet and to talk about these things, and quite apart from an agenda that you'd set up for a meeting there are the conversations that you'd have besides that'. The design allowed both Regeneration Trusts to work independently in terms of local area priorities as well as to meet jointly on a monthly basis. Common approaches were agreed in terms of dealing with the government. Among the ambitious proposals developed was the construction of a University of Ulster outreach campus on the interface; a promise that faded over the years. A civil servant who was privy to discussions about the Springvale proposal was aghast: 'You wouldn't believe the opposition there was to Springvale, I mean it was bitter. And it was "Why would you put something in there for those people?" It was awful ... Although there was a high level of integrity in one sense, there was still (the attitude) we will absolutely not do anything which either threatens the union, or on the other hand, looks as if it's rewarding people for violence. And a lot of them (civil servants) believed that a lot of money was going into those areas over that period of time, and was ill deserved'. There were dark, if unsubstantiated, mutterings that economic appraisals could be tweaked to damn any unacceptable initiative; whatever the truth, the imaginative interface campus was doomed.

Even in the context of cross-community working, tensions remained. When an American businessman suggested locating his enterprise in a Business Park on the Shankill side of the peace line, a Foundry Trust worker admitted: 'I'm quite ashamed of it now ... I sent him an email saying "Come on, you need to move into West Belfast, we've had ... umpteen years of discrimination, etc., etc." So you know it didn't all happen overnight'. Less sensitive about how their advocacy for West Belfast might be seen in other communities, the Clár Nua (New Programme) network produced a policy framework for 'the reconstruction of nationalist West Belfast'. The single identity community consultation that informed it was remembered fondly by a local activist: 'That was a magic period – I thought that was one of the best community involved processes that I had ever been in ... (We) were asked were we interested in creating this new agenda ... Yes, absolutely. And then we just set up a whole number of groups and we had a big conference meeting, and the report was published and off we went with it to America'.

In reality the judgement call was between investment with a single identity focus rather than prioritising cross-community partnership working.

The arrival of political influencers from the United States and the European Union required locals to display a modicum of openness to 'the other side'. The Foundry Regeneration Trust took the initiative: 'I remember writing to Jean Kennedy Smith (then US Ambassador in Dublin) and inviting her up. And she got in touch with us and said, "Look, technically I am the Irish Ambassador, and I'm not supposed to come up but I will." And she came up, and then she would have given you different contacts. And then, I think at that stage we got a name (as being) people to contact ... (Contacts from the United States) came over to me and we went through all our issues. They talked to Jackie (Redpath), went through all his issues (on the Shankill). Then George Mitchell – first day in Belfast – we were the first people he met. We did the West Belfast thing, and then he went and did the thing with the Shankill ... At the White House conference on Trade and Investment, the following May (1995), Jackie Redpath and I both spoke from the same platform (calling) for investment in Northern Ireland'. Internationally, evidence of hands across the divide, played well.

Joint approaches seemed blessed with political acceptability when Sinn Féin organised a Tus Nua (New Beginning) conference in Conway Mill in March 1995. Loyalist, Billy Hutchinson was a speaker, as was Dr Martin Mansergh, representing the Irish Fianna Fáil party, who called for an end to political vetting and marginalisation. However outside tight political circles, there was still uncertainty as to who had the authority to engage with 'the other' and on what basis. One local activist had her knuckles rapped: 'People didn't know what the hell was happening ... There was an uncertainty of well you won't sit with the government ... There was no "Well it's OK" ... and some people got away with stuff and some people got their knuckles rapped ... There was a vacuum where people didn't know what was acceptable'. The prevailing vacuum meant that a step too far could draw accusations of 'selling out'. The power to decide what was acceptable, and by who, continued to perplex.

Tension was reflected amongst the community activists who were funded to attend the prestigious White House Conference held in Washington DC, in May 1995. Those business leaders who attended the conference to forge trade links may have been somewhat bemused at the lobby game of who was meeting and talking to who, that the community sector understood all too well. A meeting choreographed between Sinn Féin leader, Gerry Adams, and Secretary of State, Paddy Mayhew, attracted close attention; while the PUP (Progressive Unionist Party) and UDP (Ulster Democratic Party) representatives mocked the isolationist stance of Democratic Unionist politicians. The community contingent itself kept close watch on each other convening in often abrasive caucuses. A previously unknown Northern Ireland Community Forum, hastily pulled together by major social entrepreneurs, was soon put in its place; and a certain coolness amongst West Belfast activists was apparent. Disagreement over who had the right to speak for 'the community' was spiced with allegations that some individuals were being deliberately positioned as the unelected community voice. There was also controversy over the political efficacy of presenting a common message with the Shankill. A supporter of a joint approach explained: 'I thought the most powerful thing was that if we say this together we will be respected for saying it together – it will be much more powerful than saying two separate things ... Looking at the needs of both our communities who had lived through a conflict ... But I have to say, if I was being very honest about it, I came in for a lot of criticism for all that locally ... Some people felt that we should really just be focusing on West Belfast alone ... That there was absolutely no need to worry about the Shankill, let them worry about themselves'. US political advisors, like Department of Commerce, Chuck Meissner, argued that investment decisions went beyond narrow single identity interests, but the implications of this message remained challenging in the set territoriality of Northern Ireland.

Community infrastructure: A fundable concept?

While politics played its course in local communities, 'mainstreaming' was the order of the day as government departments moved the community development deck chairs. The new Voluntary Activity Unit (VAU) coordinated an Inter Departmental Group on Voluntary Activity and Community Development which engaged in: 'Meetings about meetings basically ... They only came to the meeting before we met to discuss whether we were meeting ... It was like "Yes Minister", only worse in than that this was the real world we were talking about'. As ever, money made available under two measures of the EU Structural Funds (1994–1999) – a Community Infrastructure Measure and a Targeting Social Need Measure – focused the mind. Joe Wright, the VAU wheeler-dealer recognised an opportunity: 'The European funding, Community Infrastructure, was absolutely vital, and we were lucky because we could get projects up and running. The voluntary sector certainly came in and delivered quickly. I didn't want a project that you could talk about for the next six months, I wanted the money spent that year because, you know ... well slippage at the end of the year ... The boys in Community Relations, Education. I would say "You can't, what, (spend)? Give it to me, get that money round" ... I picked up a lot of money'. While the community and voluntary sectors celebrated, the increasingly powerful Audit Office looked askance at developments.

The framing of the community infrastructure concept was the brain-child of NICVA who spun the more accustomed physical infrastructure terminology that Brussels was comfortable with to the benefit of the community and voluntary sectors. NICVA had well established European links to draw from. The VAU also benefitted from the credibility of the Northern Ireland Voluntary Trust in funding delivery. Delegation of more modest grant-making under the Community Infrastructure measure allowed the Trust to design a Regional Community Support Programme which funded community projects in areas of need outside of Belfast. With maximum grants of £20,000 p.a., for periods of up to three years, the Support Programme targeted (i) the participation of local communities in identifying need; (ii) ensuring that disadvantaged groups were involved in the design and management of activities; (iii) supporting activities to promote the confidence, ability and effectiveness of locally based community action; and (iv) enabling local communities to contribute to policy discussion and decision-making. Belfast had a parallel Belfast Community Support Programme which prioritised community education, employability and development opportunities in partnership with MBW. For the Northern Ireland Voluntary Trust, as an independent funder, this opened a new, uncertain era of managing EU funding programmes.

The work supported was multi-faceted in nature although an attempt was made to identify indicators to capture the notion of 'community infrastructure'. These noted the number of local groups; the range of activities; their representativeness; whether there was increased community cohesiveness; the effectiveness of community resource organisations; and evidence of networking and advocacy on community issues. While small development grants were still seen as important, larger grants supported salaried development posts. The continuum between social and economic development was often apparent as when the Loughgiel Community Association in Co. Antrim secured resources to build a new community centre and a business park, thereby equipping itself to provide support services for older people; a community transport scheme; and accredited training in literacy, numeracy and IT. In Fermanagh, a Community Development Officer worked in Garrison to support a Women's Group, as well as a new 'Shared Frontiers' initiative for people affected by mental illness, in partnership with the Mental Health Unit of the Area Health and Social Care Trust. The programme recognised the often organic nature of development within communities with one issue or initiative sparking another.

The demand for funding to employ salaried workers, under the Belfast Community Support Programme, raised concerns that increased reliance on paid workers would be a disincentive to volunteer community activism. There were also questions about the sustainability of the salaried posts, although groups were encouraged to lever longer-term resources from statutory agencies. The Upper Andersonstown Community Forum in West Belfast was successful in this regard: 'The NIVT (Northern Ireland Voluntary Trust) provided the first grant to the UACF to employ a community development worker. This enabled the committee and users to identify the provision needed locally ... in turn a funding strategy was developed and implemented. NIVT was the "anchor funding" agency which enabled the entire Forum's development'. The Community Forum attracted substantial funding for its work from a range of sources, although its success was in large part due to the inventiveness of the Development

Worker who retrieved an dilapidated building from use as a shebeen: 'We ended up getting part ... of the building to start work. Meanwhile back at the ranch we had a number of advice workers ... At that time we had heard about DLA (Disability Living Allowance) ... We investigated that and then set up a surgery in the shebeen, and filled in all their (the customers') DLA forms – showed them what to do'. The agreement was that for every successful DLA claim the Community Forum would receive another section of the floor space – bit by bit. Eventually the whole building was reclaimed to be developed as a children's centre and community hub. In the post-ceasefire optimism, the first grants for self-help reintegration centres for political ex-prisoners were awarded under the Belfast Community Support Programme (Tar Anall in West Belfast and EPIC in the Shankill), a harbinger of the ongoing peace process.

Conscious that there were disadvantaged areas that had not benefitted from effective community action, the Northern Ireland Voluntary Trust established an outreach programme working in areas of 'weak community infrastructure'. These were defined as areas 'where social need and disadvantage sit alongside the absence of locally organised, locally managed, accountable and participative community development activity'. An initiative was needed that would be flexible and could offer development support without requiring local groups to make application. Eight areas were identified for action-research investment – four in Greater Belfast and four regional. For comparative research purposes the areas comprised the standard mix of rural/urban and Protestant and Catholic communal identity. Using peripatetic project workers to stimulate development a number of learning points emerged: 'It is not helpful to throw money at areas, as part of the process involves local people understanding their needs and developing local solutions. Often this requires very little financial investment. It is more important to access support and guidance alongside small, flexible amounts of money'. The calibre and commitment of the project workers was also important, given the need to facilitate community networking and linkages with other agencies. The barriers to developing effective community infrastructure were named as (i) an absence of previous development or the disempowering experience of ineffective development initiatives; (ii) lack of accessible community venues; (iii) geographical isolation; (iv) where an area was in the development shadow of an adjacent support agency but had limited engagement with it; (v) political or paramilitary dominance in the area resulting in competitive power blocs; (vi) cultural barriers, such as reluctance to take state money or fear of appearing 'disloyal' by making demands on the state; and (vii) funding related barriers, such as lack of confidence in managing grant aid. The centrality of trust, confidence and community motivation, linked to patient capital, were seen as being essential for community self-organisation. The learning from the Demonstration Programme was looped back into the Inter Departmental Group on Voluntary Activity and Community Development where, notwithstanding the best efforts of the VAU, it languished. The Northern Ireland Voluntary Trust proceeded to negotiate resources to support a subsequent initiative, entitled Communities in Transition, from the International Fund for Ireland and the Atlantic Philanthropies (formerly the obsessively anonymous Tara Consultants). The identification of appropriate impact indicators to monitor community infrastructure continued, although this task seemed of more interest to funders and government departments rather than to community organisations themselves that were invariably immersed in general busyness.

Supporting peace and reconciliation

European Union President, Jacques Delors, wasted no time in getting sign off on the Special Support Programme for Peace and Reconciliation (1995–1999) with the declared intention of consolidating the peace process. This ambitious initiative had two strategic objectives – to promote the social inclusion of people on the margins of social and economic life; and to address the needs arising from the peace process in order to boost economic growth and advance social and economic regeneration. Designed to ensure that it would be additional to mainstream government funding, a novel feature was the appointment of a number of Intermediary Funding Bodies (IFBs) drawn from the voluntary sector to act as funding

delivery mechanisms. Another important innovation was the establishment of District Partnership Boards, comprising an inter-sectoral mix of
representatives (a third from the community and voluntary bloc; elected
representatives; and the Employer, Trade Union and local statutory bloc).
The appointment of the 182 community and voluntary representatives
to the twenty-six District Partnerships – coinciding geographically with
local authority areas – was managed through NICVA, who described it
as 'a mammoth exercise', but saw it as an enormous boost for participative
democracy and inter-sectoral working.

The generous funding package supported projects across Northern
Ireland and the six southern Border counties in the Republic. It rapidly
became known as the 'Delors' package'; 'the peace money'; or even just
'P & R'. Despite the lack of a snappy title (it was said that Delors had suggested N. I. Pax, which was vetoed given its Latin, and potentially Vatican,
connotations), and a logo displaying a particularly militant dove (with
boots and the European flag in its beak), the programme was participative and flexible, and therefore popular. It took at least three years before
either the Audit Teams caught up with it or creeping bureaucracy spun
out red tape. Its genius was that it was a 'Special Programme' rather than
subject to the heavy audit and reporting requirements of mainstream EU
Structural Funds.

The Northern Ireland Voluntary Trust was the IFB with responsibility for Programme Measures on community capacity and the inclusion of women (Measure 4.1.); the inclusion of 'vulnerable groups', which
encompassed victims and survivors of violence and political ex-prisoners
(Measure 4.4), as well as working in partnership with the Combat Poverty
Agency and ADM (Area Development Management) in southern Ireland
on Measure 3.4 (Cross Border Reconciliation). Work was hectic, as over
4,200 applications were received, and some 2,432 grants awarded, over a
four year period. Some memorable applications displayed a surreal view
of 'peace and reconciliation' and cross-border reconciliation, with at least
one Programme Officer adopting a three pile appraisal process – fundable,
possible and 'mad'. An application from a fishing club for running costs on
the basis that the fish swam across the border fell into the last category, as
did an application for a camper van to facilitate travel across said border.

While the Northern Ireland Voluntary Trust awarded grants ranging from £100 to a maximum of £100,000, it argued with the EU authorities that the money available should be spent more sparingly, over a longer period of time. This was ignored given the prevailing mantra that money had to be seen to be hitting the ground to create a feel good context for peace. Spending targets became the dominant narrative with an inevitable drive towards larger projects that could absorb more money. The value of the small and local was still evident as illustrated by the £2,500 awarded to the Short Strand/Ravenhill Family Group to pay for residential workshops to enable women to meet together across a troubled sectarian interface in Inner East Belfast.

The specific naming of the inclusion of women as a Programme priority allowed support for Women's Centres and Networks. The Chairperson of the Omagh Women's Area Network recalled: 'Looking back ... my strongest memories are of the camaraderie, the struggle for our Network to retain its autonomy, the disappointment of failed funding, exhilaration of successful funding, and on a personal level, the experience of having to breastfeed my six-week-old son, Freddie, and chair a meeting at the same time'. The Women's Support Network received £100,000 to provide an accredited training programme for women activists on a cross-Border and cross-community basis; whilst more controversially, the Conway Education Centre, working from the beleaguered Conway Mill, was funded to employ an Adult Education Officer. All applicants were asked to explain how their work would further peace and reconciliation. The answers were varied. The Northern Ireland Community Relations Council sought to add meat to the bones of what was becoming an increasingly contested and politicised concept.

The Rural Community Network was another designated IFB, delivering grants for community-based actions under the rural regeneration measures of the PEACE Programme. It placed a strategic emphasis on investing in an infrastructure of Sub Regional Rural Networks, with the aim of ensuring coverage across rural Northern Ireland. These Networks supported community development; facilitated the sharing of information; and ensured the inclusion of both main community identities to promote cross-community work and peacebuilding. With nine

Sub-Regional Networks established – Regeneration of Mournes Area Ltd; East Down Community Network; North Antrim Community Network; Oakleaf Community Network; Omagh Forum for Rural Associations; Strabane Community Network; Fermanagh Rural Community Network; Regeneration of South Armagh; and Cookstown & Western Shores Network – an impressive level of coverage was achieved. The RCN was assiduous in interrogating itself, and those that it worked with, as to how reconciliation could be effected in practice.

Although the 'Peace money' gave a major boost to the community and voluntary sectors in terms of funding opportunities, there were also dangers. The set time frame adopted encouraged a competitive scramble for money without allowing adequate time for participative planning and paced development. The fears already expressed by the NIVT about increased dependency on relatively short-term paid workers in place of community self-help also came to pass, although one community activist argued: 'Small neighbourhoods have not been able to access funds. Some neighbourhoods are not organised. There has been little investment in resources to motivate local groups who feel "What's the point?" Volunteers and community activists need the support back up from fulltime workers'. Other dangers included a justifiable fear that there was limited central government commitment to mainstream any of the community development work initiated under the European funds. All this in the overall context of a less than helpful sectarian political pound count of the comparative allocation of money rather than any perceivable interest in the nature of the work supported.

A more generous interpretation of party political interest could be attributed to the fact that community development was now clocked on the political radar given the increased level of resources available and local lobbying undertaken by unsuccessful applicants. This came to a head in an informal exchange between one IFB and an elected SDLP member. When the latter queried as to why an application put forward by a community group in his constituency had not been funded, the reasons were explained but he was also informed that he was too late, as a Unionist representative had already been in touch to make the same enquiry. 'The bastards', he spluttered. 'You were quite right not to fund them!' However even as the 'Peace funds' continued to flow, the peace process that had given rise to them seemed to be driving towards the rocks.

'Shove your doves': Graffiti on the Shankill

Whether this graffiti referred to the dove bedecked Peace and Reconciliation programme is unclear, but a confrontational stand-off over Loyal Order traditional parades was a harbinger of things to come as early as July 1995. The following March, IRA unhappiness with the stumbling peace process was marked by explosions in London's Canary Wharf signalling the breakdown of its ceasefire. There were those who shook their heads knowingly, but the new situation presented unforeseen consequences for the unfortunate staff in Foyle (previously the less politically correct Derry) Women's Aid. Having agreed to deliver domestic violence training to the police in the optimistic climate of the previous autumn, they were now tipped off that they ran the risk of being accused of 'collaboration'.

Tensions and violence also played out along community interfaces. The jury was out on whether this was an unintended consequence or deliberately manipulated in order to convey covert messages. New interface peace-walls and gates were still being built to the dismay of at least one woman living in the shadow of a wall: 'In actual fact the day the IRA announced their ceasefire was the very first day that the first foundation went in for the new wall ... I was furious because the money that was put into that wall. They closed down all the youth clubs, all that kind of thing, and they put a permanent twenty-four-hour police guard on the road. What it cost to deploy those cops would have kept four youth clubs running with extra – but that was the way it was'. In 1995 the Belfast Interface Project came out of the experience of work to alleviate interface conflict. The new organisation's remit focused on major issues of concern to interface communities in Belfast, taking action around gathering and disseminating information; influencing statutory decision-making; and facilitating local groups to address inter-community relations around a number of contentious interfaces. The tendency for communities to consider violence from 'their side' of the interface as defensive and justifiable, as compared to seeing violence from the 'other side' as aggressive, was noted. But so too were the very real fears of interface residents concerned about threatened attacks. Research showed that many of those involved in interface confrontation very often lived outside of the immediate area.

Events likely to provoke violence were listed – parades/marches; football and Gaelic matches; bonfires (particularly on 11 July Orange festival); and Halloween (due to availability of fireworks). The aggravating effects of alcohol abuse; the 'night time economy', that is, the location of fast food outlets and off-sales premises; and the flying of paramilitary and/or national flags was also referenced. In one rather bizarre tit-for-tat development, the flying of the Palestinian flag in republican/nationalist areas resulted in Israeli flags on display in neighbouring loyalist/unionist areas to the bemusement of anti-Semitic English National Front supporters over in solidarity with loyalism. Tensions within the ongoing political negotiations fanned the increased street conflict, with many politicians happily reverting to justification of actions by 'their side', while decrying the aggression of the 'other side'.

It was the Catholic community in the Garvaghy area of Portadown that found itself in the eye of the storm in May 1995 when the Garvaghy Road Residents' Group opposed the return of a traditional Orange Order parade from the picturesque Drumcree Church to the town centre, through their estate. In the test of wills that followed, violence spread across Northern Ireland as roads were blocked by loyalists in a systematic programme of protest. When the parade was eventually allowed to proceed through the contested area it saw a battered Garvaghy community as sullen audience to an unusual unionist coalition of interests which resulted in Queens University law lecturer, David Trimble, becoming leader of the Ulster Unionist Party. Over following years Drumcree became both a symbol of defiance for the Orange Order, as well as a focus of mobilisation for republican 'concerned residents' in contentious interface areas. The renamed Garvaghy Road Residents' Coalition laid in supplies; hosted international observers and parade monitors; and prepared for confrontation. Radio

Equality, an illegal station staffed by volunteers, was launched to share information, but later extended its programming with interviews, agony aunts, a phone in and music. This was not enough to offset the tension of living in a frontline area: 'Many women I have spoken to have contacted their doctors for sedatives ... My own sister who never took a tablet in her life has got a prescription for Roche 5s. Once she gave the doctor her address – Garvaghy Road – these drugs were dished out like sweets! Many mothers are laying in Calpol to help the children sleep through any trouble!' The stand-off and violence of the mid-1990s resulted in a government commissioned review of parading. In 1997 a Parades Commission was established to adjudicate on future events. This was not enough to prevent a local newspaper headline in early July: 'Will the Last Person leaving Northern Ireland please turn off the Light' – as summer holidays were planned to escape the mayhem.

Portadown threw the spotlight on a new loyalist paramilitary group that rejected the ceasefires – the LVF (Loyalist Volunteer Force). In June 1996 the Northern Ireland Council for Voluntary Action moved quickly to condemn LVF death threats against Catholic cross-community workers in mid-Ulster. The Community Relations Youth Workers' Network offered support to those under threat and decried 'the apparent silence from those in statutory agencies who also have workers involved in community and youth work'. The threats were eventually lifted, although community relations were not helped by the repeated glossing of community development as largely nationalist/republican in nature. This depiction may have been both a perception and a lobby for a greater allocation of European and statutory funding to be awarded to single identity Protestant areas, but the subtlety often escaped those who saw EU peace money, like community development, as essentially designed to buy-in republicanism.

The politics of perception also affected the North Belfast Community Development Centre which faced the fall-out from the violence following a 'Tour of the North' Loyal Order parade in its combustible hinterland. Nationalist spokespersons condemned the planned event as triumphalist in nature, attracting unwelcome policing; unionists argued that the vociferous objections were deliberately engineered by a Sinn

Féin inspired campaign; and those caught in between would have gone on holidays if they could have afforded to. The serious inter-communal rioting resulted in eighty-seven families losing their homes. The Director of the Community Development Centre and her staff moved quickly to take stock of the situation having physically observed the violence by driving through local communities. The Centre became the heart of a community support response which involved accessing temporary accommodation; arranging financial support for the displaced families; offering emergency refuge; and negotiating with the relevant statutory authorities. In the face of a woefully inadequate statutory response a Families in Crisis group was established. Despite its proactive role the Community Development Centre was caught in the local firing line for either not doing enough, doing nothing or doing too much. The Director was exasperated: 'Some of our most outspoken critics were people who had not been active during the summer and others who refused to recognise the sensitivities of dealing with such situations when you are accountable to the very communities that are engaging in violence'. The Centre Committee commissioned an independent inquiry undertaken by a panel of four external, but well-informed, individuals. The interview process offered people an opportunity to give their version of events so that these could be shared with others; to consider statutory and other agency responses to the crisis; to identify how the community sector could improve communication and dialogue within the area; and to propose recommendations for more effective handling of periods of civil unrest. The report presented different perceptions of what had happened rather than making any judgements between competing accounts. The urgent need for dialogue both within each community, and between the two main community identities, was flagged up, as was the fact that when people felt excluded from decision-making (as was the case in the Protestant community) suspicion and fears were exacerbated, resulting in a sense of heightened insecurity.

What was not captured was the toll that the crisis had on the Community Development Centre staff. One recalled: 'It was horrendous ... I can remember standing out the back of CDC and the smoke coming across when they were petrol bombing those flats in Cliftonpark

Avenue. Not knowing whether I'd get home that night ... I think I did have a nervous breakdown. I was sitting with babies (in the centre) and we were sending Brendan out to the local chemist to try to get baby food for babies. We were trying to get people accommodation in South Belfast'. The acute pressure continued over a number of days. One pragmatic initiative designed to alleviate matters was the establishment of a Mobile Phone Network in an attempt to sort out facts from rumour should violence threaten to erupt again. The objectives were to allow communication between districts within a single identity community; communicate across the interface with other communities; communicate with local political leaders; contact the police – should a group chose to do so; and contact statutory agencies. An Interagency Working Group for Displaced Families was set up by the statutory sector to develop procedures for future emergencies. Community activists lobbied for and were offered a place on the Working Group.

At the macro level, the Northern Ireland Community Relations Council sought to identify principles and good practice for effecting community development in segregated spaces. It was concluded that spatial segregation was one of the most enduring aspects of the conflict but that feelings of personal security were a necessary prerequisite to community development. The importance of a local community being sufficiently self-confident in its own identity was an important pre-cursor of cross-community outreach; however, cross-community initiatives could also be a positive factor for area development. While processes underpinning the continuum that moved single identity work to cross-community understanding were examined, fears were expressed that when single-identity work became a comfort zone, it had the potential to simply reinforce prejudice and fears, resulting in rejection of the all-important cross-community dimension. Certainly the political mood music of the time was less than conducive to hands-across the divide thinking. Even faced with political stand-off a certain wry wit was demonstrated across the Lower Ormeau/Donegall Pass interface in South Belfast, where a cheeky artist used orange paint to print footprints down the centre of the Ormeau Road in response to republican graffiti 'No Orange feet on our road'.

Say goodbye to dinosaurs!

Grasping the opportunity of the cleverly crafted electoral procedures (designed to ensure that small loyalist parties would be represented at the peace talks) women came together to launch a political party. The slogan on their committee-designed election poster was 'Say Goodbye to Dinosaurs', emblazoned in green, white and purple suffrage colours, against the backdrop of a cartoon dinosaur. Male politicians were not amused, and one was overheard at the election count: 'Say Goodbye to dinosaurs and Hello to dragons'! The under-representation of women in Northern Irish politics had long been an issue and had been highlighted in a position paper that women's groups had prepared for the 1995 Beijing UN Conference on Women. The members of the delegation that travelled to China brought with them a patchwork quilt made up of individual patches sewn by the various community-based Women's Groups to express their priorities. The absence of political voice and presence was a constant issue. Contact had been made with the cross-party Women's Political Association in Dublin; and republican women pondered the question through a Clár na mBan (Agenda of Women) consultative exercise. In 1995, University of Ulster academic, Monica McWilliams, organised a conference on 'Women, Politics and Ways Forward', where a diversity of views were expressed. These ranged from support for existing parties to proposals for a cross-political party pressure group, like the Women's Political Association, although others felt that there was a political gap that women should fill for themselves.

When the Northern Ireland (Entry to Negotiations, etc.) Act made provision for the election of regional representatives (two representatives for each of ten parties with the largest cumulative vote across Northern Ireland) to the forthcoming peace talks, a number of women did the sums and concluded that there was room for a women's party to stand. The decision was in part prompted by the constant lament of the established parties about the difficulties of finding women who were prepared to stand for election. The Northern Ireland Office had named the parties who would contest the election; a phone call to suggest that a women's party might stand was met by stunned silence and the promise of a return call. This came some thirty minutes later – what was the name of this new party? Silence! – and the promise of further conversation. Frantic tick-tacking came up with the name the Northern Ireland Women's Coalition (NIWC) to hold open the space. With only six weeks to the election two meetings were called in the Ulster People's College to debate the proposition. Despite differences of opinion, there was sufficient consensus to proceed. The point was made, however, that this was not just about getting women to the peace talks, but about participative democracy in practice and the essential cross-community dimensions of a new politics. The nomenclature of Coalition instead of Party was deliberate, emphasising that the NIWC welcomed women from different backgrounds and political allegiances. What was required was commitment to three guiding principles – inclusion, human rights and equality. A co-leadership arrangement was agreed; one from the Protestant community and the other from the Catholic community – Pearl Sagar and Monica McWilliams respectively. An advertisement was placed in local newspapers inviting potential women candidates who supported the three principles to make contact. In the event, ninety-eight women stood as candidates to garner the regional collective vote that returned the Northern Ireland Women's Coalition as the ninth party on the ten party list. Two representatives were at the table of the peace talks chaired by US Senator George Mitchell. They were supported by many others through policy and negotiating teams that ran with rather more enthusiasm than political experience, although a necessary process of accelerated learning put the commitment to demystify politics into practice.

The successful election campaign drew on what women had learned through community and trade union organising, as well as memories of civil rights activism. The nascent Coalition had no office, no funds and one of its leaders had been nominated to the position during her absence in Australia. Another stalwart volunteered for the position as Treasurer on the basis that she was likely to end up in prison for debt but she needed the rest. Two major turning points were gifts of £10,000 and $10,000 respectively from the Joseph Rowntree Memorial Fund and the Global Fund for Women, and voter analysis offered by Queen's University political scientist, Sydney Elliot, which resulted in the slogan '100 votes for 100 women', making the project manageable. Derry NIWC candidate, Helena Schlindwein, exclaimed: 'D'you know we can do this. We can run a kitchen table election campaign!' The finer points of campaigning were even discussed by two Coalition supporters in a local shop. Sharing notes about how to protect election posters from the rain, one confided that she had used cling film. The Fermanagh based team were even more audacious, borrowing a loud hailer from the local police station on the basis of some spurious excuse. They judiciously forgot to mention that the loud hailer was for electioneering purposes – but they did return it as promised.

The reaction of the established political parties ranged from patronising to downright hostile, with female members being mobilised to condemn the venture as superfluous. DUP Deputy Leader, Peter Robinson, was particularly dismissive: '(These women) haven't been at the forefront of the battle when shots were being fired and when the constitution of Northern Ireland was in peril'. The West Belfast Women's Network published an Open Letter complaining that: 'Proper consultation with women's organisations should have been undertaken before any decision to contest this election was taken. This would have allowed these issues (reform of the RUC; political prisoners; decommissioning; and the exclusion of Sinn Féin from the talks) and others, such as your accountability to have been fully aired'. Replying on behalf of the Coalition, Monica McWilliams pointed out that six of the ten signatory groups to the letter had been invited to the decision-making meetings, but had failed to attend. The day following the election a newspaper graphic of ten male silhouettes around the talks table had to be hastily corrected in their evening edition, with one of the silhouettes being identified as a woman – tieless. The headline 'Hen Party Leaves the Nest in Style' may have been a sub-editorial compliment, but it was the soul of politeness compared to some of the comments made about the NIWC by some elected members of the Forum of Dialogue and Understanding, which met alongside the peace talks. McWilliams commented that the title was a misnomer, describing the elected assembly as the Forum of Abuse and Misunderstanding.

Small 'p' politics in action

As the Northern Ireland Women's Coalition faced up to large 'p' politics, so-called 'small 'p' politics' remained alive and well within communities. The shared challenges facing women in deprived communities were still poverty, violence and political exclusion/neglect. A new 'Women in Politics' project attracted EU Peace funding, but carefully crafted relationships with the full spectrum of political parties given that women had varied political allegiances, alongside the unspoken fear that an overly close identification with the Women's Coalition might alienate other politicians, and even put statutory funding at risk. For community-based Women's Centres there was also the constant need to keep an eye on the political sensitivities of their local areas. The impressive Windsor Women's Centre, a model of participative planning, was targeted in two devastating arson attacks when it played host to Irish President, Mary Robinson, in 1996. Located in a loyalist area of South Belfast, rumours circulated that the bouquet presented to the President was green, white and yellow; more to the point, permission had been neither sought nor given by local gatekeepers. The smell of scorched art work underlined the message to the Centre management, stay in line or else. Similar sensitivities were discussed in the Shankill Women's Centre when a worker attended an event with Mary Robinson. It was a case of – 'I remember going into work on the Monday and it was like "What have you done?" You know? And the committee knew – they knew this was coming up – they knew that I was going. I think it was kinda then that I started thinking we need to be careful what we do here'. Heightened insecurities were most evident in Protestant areas, where Women's Centres had been courageous in questioning accepted certainties and practices. The Shankill Women's Centre offered Irish language and history classes, while women in Greenway Women's Centre, in East Belfast, published their poetry and creative writing to challenge stereotypes; it was Centres in these areas that had really pushed the boat out.

Women's Centres across the Greater Belfast area came together to rally support for the Falls Women's Centre after the Belfast City Council threatened to withdraw funding on the grounds that it was sympathetic to republicanism. The resulting alliance was formalised into a Women's Support Network in 1989. A full-time Coordinator was later appointed and a joint programme of work agreed, although for a period there was still a certain diffidence in dealing with community differences, irrespective of the shared narrative of mutual support. Much had moved on, however, from the brittle stand offs that the earlier Women's Movement had experienced. The Women's Resource & Development Agency continued to play an important role in networking women's groups through its services and feminist advocacy. Sharing the WRDA office in South Belfast, the Women's Information Day worked coordinating meetings across Belfast. Its approach was informed by word of mouth communication as explained by the organiser: 'Five groups of ten women and those women are selected because they are in positions to pass the knowledge on … We select women in organisations that can pass the information on but also gather information'. The theory of change was the power of information. Even the International Fund for Ireland was getting in on the act when it signed off its Communities in Action Programme in 1995, which prioritised community-based support for families, young children and marginalised young people. A number of the thirty projects, funded under the unfortunately named CIA, developed innovative practice which proved to be sustainable, either as individual projects or as part of broader community infrastructure.

The increased funding available over the 1990s consolidated the shift from a Women's Movement to a Women's Sector, without much reflection on the implications. For those working at community level the emphasis was on activities. Women in the Ballybeen Women's Centre in East Belfast were learning IT; women in Magherafelt were reaching out to their sisters in the rural hinterland; women in Derry opened an impressive new Women's Centre; and feminist writer, Cynthia Cockburn, celebrated the 'transversal politics' of the women involved in the Women's Support Network – a phenomenon whereby women could remain true to their own identity while simultaneously being open to respect those from different identities. No such terminology was needed in Derry where: 'It was very healthy because a lot of discussion did take place. When you've built up friendships with women from different groups it was fairly easy because you could do it over a cup of tea or a cup of coffee, but there were certain times when it was far better that it was done in a controlled situation … there'd be someone there to facilitate ... A couple of meetings were organised to talk about women and the church, and that raised issues for women who just accepted that they were Catholic or Protestant or whatever ... And I think the other thing that was lovely about the Women's Centre was, we said OK sometimes we are not going to agree, and what was also interesting about that was it wasn't necessarily unionist/nationalist women that weren't agreeing, it was internal, because I would have had a lot of problems with some of the republican women, and I'm from a nationalist tradition'. The challenge was how to conduct difficult conversations without fracturing the group or alienating individuals who might find themselves in a minority in terms of community identity and/or views.

Operating in the hot house of Castle Buildings (Stormont), difficult conversations became par for the course for the Women's Coalition. The first ever female Secretary of State, Mo Mowlam, proved an important ally, organising impromptu meetings in the ladies' bathroom when her officials tried to veto meetings due to the perceived marginal status of the Coalition. If this inside track was important, it was not strong enough to circumvent the time honoured political system that both the established parties and the local media seemed wedded to. The latter could not get their head around the idea of having a dual leadership, although they paid attention when one of the two, Pearl Sagar, offered a chorus of 'Stand by your Man', in response to a DUP heckle that the women should go home to 'breed for Ulster'. A young Coalition member was also quick off the mark when she retorted that she would knit a balaclava for a young UVF supporter when he told her that women's feet were smaller than men's so they could stand closer to the kitchen sink. The balaclava was the traditional face covering of paramilitaries, who were also referred to as 'the woolly faces'.

Community development post-ceasefires

Calculating the nature and extent of change within communities in the post ceasefire period remained an art rather than a science. An activist in fractious North Belfast referred to feelings of increased security but warned that this could be turned on or off depending on the political dynamics of the time: 'There was also a sense, certainly within nationalist areas ... that with the IRA ceasefire things had changed for the better ... and within the unionist community, conversely, there was a real feeling of fear and loss, and God, what was coming down the line now?' She described how, in apparent contradiction of their apprehensions, residents from a small Protestant estate approached the Community Resource Centre for support notwithstanding the fact that: 'Well within nationalism, a huge sense of hope, and within unionism I think there was a huge sense of "Oh my God if they're happy, we must be (in a) bad (way)"'. The see-saw inter-communal balance between optimism and pessimism was still a zero-sum game.

The work of various networks supporting local community effort through Resource Centres and other infrastructural organisations was celebrated in a report on 'Resourcing Local Community Development', which, in turn, was followed up by a Community Participation Working Group in the Greater Belfast area, which included the new Community Arts Forum. The diversity of the sector was seen as positive, although its limited influence on policy making was deplored. The Northern Ireland Community Relations Council threw down the gauntlet of community relations to the Working Group: 'Fundamentally we feel that the definition of problems and opportunities for local communities is artificially narrow. Our work ... shows the real fears and anxieties that communities face in responding to the consequences of ethnic differences and how it affects their quality of life, life chances and even life itself. An essential prerequisite for the development of effective participation structures is the need for a more embracive consideration of the issues that affect communities'. Use of the term 'ethnic differences' became more marked in community relations vocabulary, although it was not without its critics. The Northern Ireland Council for Ethnic Minorities (NICEM) was established in the mid-1990s, with EU Peace funding, to raise the issue of minority ethnic communities outside the two dominant communal identities, a small, but often silenced group.

With the building blocks of community development and community infrastructure analysed to within an inch of their terminological life, the government Voluntary Activity Unit beavered away to promote greater understanding at inter-departmental level, although it was questionable as to whether anybody was listening. The results of a mapping of the community and voluntary sectors by NICVA (Northern Ireland Council for Voluntary Action) in 1997 did grab attention when it was estimated that over 5,000 groups were engaged in a diverse range of activities, employing over 30,000 paid workers and involving some 65,000 volunteers. The collective asset base was calculated as over £250 million, with an annual turnover amounting to some £400 million. Government grants accounted for 42 per cent of income. The 'State of the Sector' report became a regular feature, although voluntary sector data was more readily available than information from the more amorphous community sector. Hard on the heels of this data collection, the Voluntary Activity Unit sponsored the first Compact between government and the community and voluntary sector (sic) in Northern Ireland in 1998. The Compact laid out the shared values underpinning the relationship between government and the sector, alongside respective roles, commitments and principles. It also offered definitions of both community development and community infrastructure. NICVA became the voluntary sector guardian of the Compact, during the launch of which Secretary of State, Mo Mowlam, welcomed the community and voluntary sector as an official social partner.

The other set of statistics that generated comment was research into the 'cost of the Troubles', once again linking deprivation and violence, while raising questions about the allocation of 'the peace dividend'. There were still questions as to what was peace and whether reconciliation was now acceptable. A Women's Centre worker was uncertain: 'All that cross-community stuff that was ongoing, it's just that you didn't shout about it because it was dangerous to shout about it'. At the same time the Ulster Community Action Network (UCAN) was formed to reignite discussion about single-identity community development in Protestant/Unionist/Loyalist areas, arguing that yet again 'the other' community had the available resources sewn up. The debate was to grumble on becoming increasingly politicised and acrimonious towards the end of the decade.

One Unionist politician, then serving as Lord Mayor of Belfast, had other things on his mind. He travelled to Cong, in Belgium, to open a memorial garden for soldiers killed in the First World War: 'I got on the train and it was full of mental patients going down to see the D-Day landings, and I sat beside this man who said his name was Napoleon. And I had a whole sort of conversation with him about the Battle of Waterloo, which he said was won by the French, being French you know ... Anyway I said to him "Who told you you were Napoleon?" And he said, "God told me I was Napoleon." And this voice came from the end of the carriage, "I did not." Well I got to the end of that, and my chain (of office) on and so forth, and went to get off the train and the psychiatric social worker started to count the patients getting off the train, and she said, "One, two, three, four –." And it came to me, and she says, "Who are you?" And I says "I'm Lord Mayor of Belfast." And she says, "Five". Just like community infra-structure, peace and resource allocation – all in the eye of the beholder.

CHAPTER 10

The Rollercoaster of Change

The butler in Hillsborough Castle (official residence of Her Majesty the Queen and pied a terre of her Secretary of State), bowing ever so slightly, murmured: 'So nice to see a familiar face', when welcoming a community activist to a function. The developing peace process heralded a change in the political guard by privileging British Government access to elected politicians rather than local activists. In earlier years, community workers had to simply lift the phone when they needed to make contact. If attendance at social soirées offered access this came with a health warning acknowledged by a Northern Ireland Office official: 'What they (NIO officials) did, they were quite cute, quite clever, they actually used proxies ... inviting (individual community activists) to the famous dinners, and you know, they'd milk them basically. They'd set up discussions with them, they'd meet with them, they'd use all sorts of ways to get the information that they needed to be able to take a view to advise Ministers ... And, of course, the other thing about the NIO ... is that they didn't let anyone else near the Ministers'. This approach offered fertile ground for the misinterpretation of a chance remark. As the peace process progressed the game of political messaging became the norm, although not always welcome: 'There was the whole hype around the ceasefires and these Americans were all involved and there was a lot of Americans coming over and visiting, I would have been sent to all these dinners. God, you know, round tables, and you know we'd all talk about the situation'. Political cut and thrust over aperitifs was still the order of the day.

In still contentious areas like North Belfast official visits could be problematic: 'Anytime somebody came to our Centre ... we got a Secretary of State or something, there was a crowd that would picket. One of the best ones was ... (Irish President) McAleese. She asked could she come – no problem, come. But that morning I'll never forget it – I get this phone call, Secretary of State's office – Secretary of State's aware that President McAleese ... do you mind if he pops in? "Aye – well I'm not sure if that would be appropriate." "Oh, but we think it would be great." "I don't think it would be." "Oh, but he'll just pop in anyway." "Right." ... It was hilarious, about two minutes before the Secretary of State arrives the whole Centre (is) surrounded, all these placards and all the rest of it. Secretary of State got in and he was terrified because everybody started to crowd at the door ... So it ended up his security man kept phoning Mary McAleese's car saying "Drive round, drive round, there's a picket." And I'm saying, "No, drive her here." And as soon as she arrived all the placards were taken down. So there you are problem solved'. Handling the intricacies of official visits, whether welcome or not, was an essential element in the job description of any self-respecting community activist alongside that of the security detail. However, when one newly appointed minister suggested to his security man: 'Oh you are the chap who takes a bullet for me', the stony-faced response was: 'Oh no Minister, I'm the chap who gets the bastard that gets you'. Job descriptions had limits.

A visitor that invariably delighted the crowds, despite his invasive secret service shadows who scrutinised everything from sewers to chimneys, was the then President of the United States, Bill Clinton. Switching on the Christmas lights in Belfast and Derry during an initial visit in 1995, his repeated return in subsequent years made the quest for peace his own. He argued the importance of open-mindedness, when politicians were studiously avoiding each other as they entered and left the peace talks; the small UK Unionist Party and bulging Democratic Unionist Party being particularly adept at tactical avoidance. Following Clinton's initial visit the overall level of British troops in Northern Ireland fell to some 17,000. Demilitarisation was linked to decommissioning of weapons, although graffiti in republican areas queried: 'Without arms how can we tie our shoelaces?' The seventeenth-century walls of Derry were even more strident – 'Not a Bullet, Not an Ounce' – imperial weights still applied to semtex.

If the macro-ceasefires were just about holding, there was renewed community controversy over punishment shootings. New acronyms, such as DAAD (Direct Action against Drugs) raised suspicions that paramilitary attacks were either about 'housekeeping', tying up the loose ends of deeply held antagonisms, or maintaining local control over 'anti-social behaviour'. In fourteen months, over 1994 and 1995, there were 223 reported paramilitary 'punishment' beatings, the majority by republicans. Distrust of the RUC meant that local communities still turned to paramilitaries for 'justice' in the politically enforced policing vacuum resulting in many heated meetings: 'Some awful meetings – public meetings that were just looking to beat them (people accused of anti-social behaviour) ... So you had the vigilante stuff going on'. This internal community debate consolidated in the face of perceived 'outsider' condemnation of punishment attacks; particularly when it was interpreted as getting at the IRA. Exposure to a transitional justice framing encouraged attempts to model practical alternatives.

The stars lined up when staff in NIACRO (Northern Ireland Association for the Care and Resettlement of Offenders), who were interested in community-based restorative justice, worked with a republican insider/activist, then employed in Youthlink, a project of local NGO, Extern. After the latter sounded out possibilities, a six week discussion course was designed and delivered to members of the IRA 'Civil and Administration' squad, whose terms of reference included implementing punishment sentences. The issues raised were controversial and hard-hitting regarding the legitimacy of violence: 'Where would you put touting? Oh, very bad. Where would you put torture and all that? ... We ended up at a residential in Co. Donegal and one of the things we did there we did a kind of role play game where the leading fellow (in the IRA team) was the (RUC) Chief Constable and was the most reactionary'. At a certain point the NIACRO facilitators were expelled to walk the sands of a Donegal beach, while the insiders considered the implications of the exercise. The question was whether a community restorative justice approach was a viable alternative to punishment beatings; and if so, whether it could be modelled in practice without having to interface with the police who were suspected of using 'anti-social' elements as informers. Months of silence followed; then those involved in the programme were invited to a Sinn Féin press conference where the full weight of the party was thrown behind the restorative justice approach. This marked political shift, partially due to the trickle-down effect of arguments for alternatives to violence in a post ceasefire context, as well as the less altruistic consideration

of volunteers and weapons put at risk in carrying out the attacks. One of
the civil society facilitators suggested that: '(The) accumulation of protests over a period of time creates atmosphere ... (but) one of the difficulties of republicans is that they live and die within republicanism, within
these circles, and they very rarely get an opportunity to hear an alternative perspective, so everything that they get ... just reaffirms everything
that they hear'. Challenging this situation can be tricky: 'The thing about
republicans was if you're not directly for them, you're opposed to them. If
you're opposed to them you have to be absolutely mad or absolutely bad'.
In these circumstances the role of the questioning outsider needs to be
mediated by the critical insider to create the essential baseline of trust. In
addition, a favourable political context is required to deliver the change
outcome. The process also benefited from constant feedback loops between
the external facilitators and the republican insider to gauge possible fears
and opportunities in advance.

A parallel approach was adopted, with UVF compliance, in the
Greater Shankill area where the critique and validation provided by an
US expert on restorative justice practice was important. Local credibility
with the paramilitaries was provided by a loyalist political ex-prisoner,
although work was necessary to win community acceptance: 'Our reputation started building up and we were able to deliver things and do
things for the community. And then the community seen that this is an
organisation that is doing things for us (the community) as opposed to
doing things for themselves, because there's always this perception that
ex-prisoners that are anyway involved, they must be up to no good ...
Now what we've argued over the years (is that) if you're willing to go to
prison and die for your community, then you should be willing to work
for it ... Try to make it that other young people aren't going through what
we went through'. An advocate of the Greater Shankill Alternatives to
Punishment Beatings outlined the task: 'The reality is that young people
come to the attention of the paramilitaries because people go knocking
on the door of the paramilitaries. What we must do is educate the community that young people who engage in anti-social behaviour do not
come out of a vacuum. It was their own community that, in fact, helped to
shape them'. Although relations between Alternatives and the police were

less toxic than those in republican areas, there was still a need to ensure paramilitary acceptance (in this case, the UVF): 'That whole challenge about punishment beatings and restorative justice coming on line and challenging both the police and different agencies, as well as very much challenging the local paramilitaries with regards to their attitude and how they could deal with things more effectively. And I remember a period when they had come so much on board that they were using it almost as a badge of honour, you know, we support restorative justice, which was great'. A rather more difficult issue was the question of how continuing paramilitary power impacted on inclusive community activism. In the one step forwards, two back, atmosphere of the peace process that was left as a topic for another day.

Onion slicing the peace dividend

As early as spring 1995 the Northern Ireland Economic Council hosted a seminar, 'The Economic Implications of Peace and Prosperity'. The investment potential of 'the peace' was on the agenda, even if some people previously shuddered at the mention of the word 'war'. The MBW-funded Urban Institute in Belfast published a hard hitting report: 'A Tale of One City?', arguing that modern cities were only as strong as their weakest community. A new development axis was proposed to balance investment in city centre regeneration with a strategy to address the needs of deprived communities. Both the centrality of community participation and the sophistication of many community organisations, was recognised, although the report did not shirk from noting the internal animosity that marked the community sector: 'Some can caricature others as strong on rhetoric and weak on practical delivery, as absorbed in victimhood to the point of being unresponsive to the challenge of constructive engagement. Retaliatory claims label such critics as recipients of government biased generosity, who are not rooted in the community, whose operations lack transparency, and who have failed to deliver any substantial community gains for all the resources they have received'. The impact of political vetting was seen as contributing to these divisions.

Ministerial reshuffles and a change in policy emphasis limited MBW ability to champion the approach advocated by the Urban Institute – 'I think all that stuff that Needham (the previous long serving Minister for the Environment) started almost eight or nine years before to attempt to empower ... I think that lost some of its impetus ... In some way a lot of this stuff in the civil service had to do with ministerial drive and commitment; had to do with personalities and where people's agendas were and what they wanted to do'. An added twist was the considerably enhanced power of audit, and an economic appraisal approach to public spending that required the preparation of a 'Green Book' case: 'Very long and bureaucratic and frankly beyond the capacity of any community groups; may I say, beyond the capacity of many of us in the Civil Service. So that led to a change whereby because it was a specialised function, because it was difficult to do, there was a growth in the use of consultants who became very expert in doing this ... So economic appraisals, value for money audit, brought a change in the attitude and culture of dealing with communities in relation to grant applications and to financial support'. Earlier civil service responsiveness was sacrificed to the tyranny of 'keeping the file', causing one insider to reflect: 'Policy got more sophisticated and complicated but not necessarily more empathetic'. – privileging the power of regulation and pro-forma.

At a community level there were notable casualties (such as the North Belfast Community Development Centre) and mounting frustration as the promised 'peace dividend' became more diffuse. Reminders about the overlap between poverty and the impact of the conflict pin-pricked policy-making, as when the North & West Women against Poverty Group issued a report, 'Living with Poverty', that reiterated the fact that 78 per cent of Troubles-related deaths in Belfast had occurred in the North and West of the city. Drawing on interview with women from across the peace lines they concluded: 'The fixation with the Troubles has only served to divert attention away from the burden of living in poverty. Ask any community activist in Protestant or Catholic working-class areas about the main problems they deal with on a daily basis and you would find that "political" ones are well down the list'. Community spirit was cited as essential for resilience, although it was seen as being vulnerable to the working-class phenomenon of 'touting' (informing) on each other rather than campaigning about the rich getting richer. Government commissioned an updated analysis of the geographical distribution of relative deprivation to establish new indicators of social need. The eagerly awaited Noble Report measured deprivation under eight different domains, with the usual areas dominating the list. New TSN (Targeting Social Need) policies were informed by a report that ran to 181 pages, and contained no less than 486 action points under more than 200 headings. Bedtime reading it was not. A spokesperson for the relevant government department assured his audience that: 'There have been significant changes at the margins' – not quite the reassurance that the North and West Belfast women might have hoped for.

To add to the policy mix, the newly configured Department of Social Development held consultations on Urban Development and Neighbourhood Renewal. If consultation was a community sector demand, one activist expressed somewhat jaded views on previous experience: 'They done a whole consultancy thing around the different areas ... and I remember going to several ... and when the report came out I said (to the civil servant involved) "You must have been at different meetings than me, I don't remember any of that." And he said, "Oh, we promised to consult you, but we never said we'd take your ideas on board ..."' However, with consultation again the order of the day, views were being registered with a new political dispensation.

The times they were a changing ...

It was snowing in April 1998 when the Belfast/Good Friday Agreement was agreed, if not signed. The unseasonable weather may have reflected the chill within traditional unionism, with the DUP cast as outsiders and the Ulster Unionist Party fractured. The loyalist parties accepted the Agreement which guaranteed the position of Northern Ireland within the

United Kingdom, subject to the will of the majority, and which ushered in a power-sharing Northern Ireland Executive and Assembly in place of Direct Rule. The Agreement was structured around three strands – strand one dealt with internal arrangements within Northern Ireland; strand two catered for the North-South dimension and strand three addressed relations between the islands of Britain and Ireland. It took the combined political midwifery of British Prime Minister, Tony Blair, Irish Taoiseach, Bertie Ahern, US President, Bill Clinton (on the hotline from Washington DC) and Talks Chairperson, Senator George Mitchell, to get the arrangement over the line. Slated to conclude on the Thursday before Easter Sunday, the delegations were faced with closed canteens and a night of sleeping on office floors as the negotiations nudged into Good Friday. Northern Ireland Secretary of State, Mo Mowlem (who was fighting cancer) prowled the corridors in stockinged feet and threw her wig about in frustration. It was reliably reported that certain pubs on the Shankill Road saw a decline in regular customers that night and the Sinn Féin rooms were packed to bursting point. The awaiting media entertained themselves by interviewing one another.

By Friday morning even the most gregarious of officials expressed consternation as Sinn Féin negotiators worked down their list of fifty plus points of contention. Rumours of imminent political implosion within Ulster Unionism were reflected in the shade of their leader's face; the Northern Ireland Women's Coalition crossed items off its flip chart; loyalism argued its corner while watching its collective back; and the SDLP and Alliance parties exuded a somewhat condescending tolerance for the 'slow learners' that had rejected the 1974 Sunningdale Deal. The final gathering in the conference room to declare a 'sufficiency of consensus' for the Agreement saw tears, high fives, furtive glances to see who was in attendance, and appreciation of symbolism as Provisional IRA founding member, Joe Cahill, placed his hand on Gerry Adams's shoulder. The deal was anointed with a flourish of references to 'reconciliation', 'equality', 'parity of esteem' and 'human rights'. There was even passing reference to the importance of community development, provision for victims of the conflict and the greater participation of women, inserted at the insistence of the Women's Coalition. The weasel issues of decommissioning (of weapons), police reform and demilitarisation were consigned to yet to be established commissions.

Much of the drafting and redrafting was carried out by officialdom, with British Foreign & Commonwealth mandarins meshing with the more ideologically driven NIO officials to cross swords (in the politest possible manner) with the altogether more Machiavellian bon hommé of the Irish Department of Foreign Affairs Anglo-Irish division. One of the latter acknowledged the importance of insights and connections carefully garnered: 'The Irish delegation up to the Good Friday Agreement, I think there were four or five had very strong Northern Ireland backgrounds ... So we had more family connections than a lot of NIO officials ... they lacked the touch on the ground ... Like there was no British official ever went into the Raven (an East Belfast Social Club) as far as I know ... So we would know the local politicians from being around Belfast, even the Unionist ones, we'd know them all personally, and they would know us'.

The very name of the Belfast/Good Friday Agreement proved controversial, with unionists calling it for the place and nationalists for the occasion. Accepted by referenda North and South of the Border, the existing six government departments were reformulated as eleven to accommodate ministerial positions in the new power-sharing Executive. A First and Deputy First Minister were to lead the Executive, although there were those that shook their heads at the over-governance of a region that had eighteen Westminster MPs, three members of the European Parliament, 108 Assembly members and 582 local councillors. Amongst the general relief that something had been finally agreed, there were those who warned that the power-sharing arrangements put in place represented an 'ethnic bargain' which would entrench community divisions. Assembly members had to designate themselves as either nationalist or unionist to facilitate the mechanics of power-sharing.

Although the intention was to get devolution up and running in a matter of months, the planned choreography rapidly came unstuck over the niceties of IRA weapons decommissioning. Ulster Unionists argued that this was the sine que non of Sinn Féin participation in the power-sharing Executive. Sinn Féin, for its part, pointed to its electoral mandate. Direct rule became the default mode of government and 'crisis talks' became the norm, with one such summit coinciding with the British intervention in Kosovo. Prime Minister Blair blanched visibly when a young Ulster Democratic Party member voiced concern at the situation in Moldova. His relief was palpable when told that the cause of anxiety was that the Moldovan soccer team was beating Northern Ireland two goals to one. Irrepressible Secretary of State, Mo Mowlam, went one better, as bustling into the throne room in Hillsborough Castle she instructed the party delegates to gather their papers in preparation for transfer to another venue for fear that DUP protesters would breach the Castle gates. Faced with astonishment, she danced round the room shouting 'April Fool!' – the clock having just turned midnight on 1 April. 'Now for the real fun', she chortled, 'I'm off to tell the Shinners (who were closeted in another room) that the Brits are getting out of Northern Ireland'. The reaction to that announcement went unreported.

Political uncertainty caused by the rollercoaster of implementation offered fertile ground for those unionists who dubbed the Agreement the pinnacle of 'Lundyite treachery' – a reference to seventeenth-century backsliding; or dissident republicans who viewed it as a sell-out of a united Ireland. The devastating Omagh bomb explosion in August 1998 left little room for any uncertainty about dissident intentions. Twenty-nine people died (thirty-one with the addition of unborn twins) and many hundreds of shoppers and passer-byes were left severely injured and traumatised. Although at a much reduced level, killings continued into the next year when a well-known female solicitor died in a car bomb, planted by loyalist dissidents in Portadown. The threat of continuing violence, allied to party political stand-off, leeched popular confidence in the peace process which itself had to absorb redrawn political battle lines over the reform of policing and the decommissioning of armaments.

Doling out 'confidence-building measures' became a daily diet of seeing who would blink first as devolution was either suspended or reinstated depending on incentive bargaining and delivery. Driven by a determined Lord Patten and his Commission team, police reform was one area of remarkable change. Always a contentious issue, the radical shift from the Royal Ulster Constabulary (RUC) to the Police Service of Northern Ireland (PSNI) was finally instituted in November 2001. Rioters despaired when the cry of 'Fuck the Police Service of Northern Ireland' failed to trip off the tongue as easily as the more traditional 'Fuck the RUC!' But despite unionist anger, a police service capable of attracting nationalist recruits was a valuable prize; although the rapid repaint job that reliveried police jeeps from grey to white elicited comments about wolves in sheep's' clothing.

It soon became clear that conflict transformation was not only needed between communities, but within them, as loyalist paramilitary feuding splintered the Greater Shankill and spilled into North Belfast. It was estimated that one family in five had to leave their home in the one square mile that comprised the Lower Shankill, as an anti-peace process alignment of some members of the UFF (Ulster Freedom Fighters) and the LVF (Loyalist Volunteer Force) battled it out with the UVF. A senior policeman described the Shankill as a virtual 'Dodge City'; other people blamed criminality or fighting over control of 'turf', but politics also soured the mix. The feud was finally negotiated to an end with a protocol drawn up as to how to deal with inter-paramilitary tensions in the future. A point of mediation was agreed. A community post mortem reported in 'The Feud and the Fury – The Response of the Community Sector to the Shankill Feud' (2000), concluding that: 'Whilst it is impossible to fully explain the horror, chaos and fear that surrounded the displacements during the Shankill feud, it is clear that the lack of coordination on behalf of statutory organisations contributed to the confusion and the feelings of helplessness experienced by the families'. This seemed a repeat of the findings by the North Belfast Enquiry some years previously. Statutory agencies acknowledged the community anger but pointed to concerns about the safety of their staff. A local Protestant Minister juggled a different issue: 'The only time you would have to be careful at the times of feuds – if you were arranging baptisms. You may have six, seven, maybe eight baptisms, and you had to try to be careful that one group of families from one organisation were not going to be meeting with another group'. A primary school principal in the area also had the additional task of keeping a weather eye on relationships at the school gate in addition to coping with many severely traumatised youngsters.

The turn of the century was still dominated by political crisis management. John Reid, MP, became the first Catholic Secretary of State for Northern Ireland. Gerry Loughran was appointed first Catholic Head of the Northern Ireland Civil Service. Sinn Féin assumed the mantle of the SDLP as the largest party of republican/nationalism in the General Election of 2001, whilst the DUP vote increased at the expense of the Ulster Unionist Party. A succession of crisis talks ran the gamut of the stately homes of England, although it was the extensive parkland of Weston Park that offered Gerry Adams ample opportunity to embrace his psycho-therapy of tree-hugging. By November 2001, John Reid had 'specified' the UDA, UFF and LVF on the basis that to all practical purposes their ceasefires were at an end. The previous month Ulster Unionist ministers resigned their portfolios in frustration at the lack of substantive IRA arms decommissioning. In a tantalising response Adams made a 'significant speech' asking the IRA to address the issue, which resulted in a token decommissioning and a corresponding British gesture. Devolved government resumed in a hesitant fashion.

2002 was a year of covert messages, allegations and tit-for-tat political one-upmanship, reaching a pitch with 'Stormontgate', when armed PSNI officers raided the Sinn Féin offices in the Stormont Parliament, alleging the existence of a spy ring. When it was revealed that one of those arrested was actually a police informer of many years standing, the question became who was spying on who and to what end? Sinn Féin muttered darkly of conspiracies hatched by 'securocrats' to destroy the peace process. An agitated unionism lapped up ever more insulting depictions of the Republic of Ireland, and republicanism generally, coined by its leadership. Perhaps unsurprisingly an opinion poll in February 2003 showed that only 33 per cent of Protestants in Northern Ireland had confidence in the Belfast/ Good Friday Agreement. Interface violence was still occurring across areas of Belfast, although the EU PEACE II programme supported an increasing variety of cross-community initiatives. Contradictions were myriad for those seeking to progress the peace process.

Participative democracy and 'capacity-building'

As politics burnished representative democracy, community and social activists were increasingly dubbed as members of the 'chattering classes'. Political offence sparked if 'participative democracy' was mentioned in the same breath as representative democracy. The Civic Forum championed by the Northern Ireland Women's Coalition, as an advisory second chamber, was a particular irritant, although mezzo-level inter-sectoral partnership models escaped censor. The initial Programme for Government of the Northern Ireland power-sharing Executive endorsed (i) the promotion of partnership between government and the community and voluntary sector by the strategic implementation of the Compact; (ii) development of a strategy on government funding for the voluntary and community sector; (iii) government support for volunteering; and (iv) a review of the role, structure and remit of the Voluntary Activity Unit, now in the Department for Social Development. The implementation of the Compact was monitored by a Joint Forum of government officials and community and voluntary representatives, supported by the Northern Ireland Council for Voluntary Action (NICVA). This Forum contributed to the 'Partnership for Change' strategy (2002), which added meat to the bones of the Compact. The previous year the Forum called for genuine partnership working in practice, supported by adequate resourcing.

'Capacity' became the new catch-cry, linked to effective community and voluntary input into the increasing number and varieties of inter-sectoral partnerships. Designed to inform the delivery of EU PEACE funds, inter-sectoral partnership working was drawn increasingly in line with local authority direction as the powers of the latter were enhanced in terms of the delivery of the EU PEACE II and PEACE III programmes, which were now policed by the new SEUPB (Special EU Programmes Body). The scientology of New Public Management thinking had acknowledged that partnerships, whether 'joined up', 'integrated' or however described, were the in-thing for dealing with complex problems, although the demands of audit, rates of spend and accountability also impacted decision-making.

At the macro Northern Ireland level, the cross-sectoral Concordia (NICVA, representing the community and voluntary sectors) inherited the mantle of the previous G7 (with trade unions, employer and farming interests) to comment on priorities for European funding, the composition of the Local Strategy Partnerships and expressing support for the ongoing peace process. Another strand of European funding (LEADER) promoted partnership in rural communities through LAGs (Local Action Groups).

Such structures were seen as acceptably functional in nature; not so the Civic Forum. Established in 2000, this consultative body had sixty members drawn from the various strands of civic life, including 18 representatives from the community and voluntary sectors. NICVA, Disability Action, the Women's Resource & Development Agency and the Rural Community Network, were called on to manage their selection. Eleven sub-sectoral panels were agreed – older people; youth; women; people with disabilities; ethnic minorities; carers; families and children; community development; community health; community education and environment – with groups registering to vote for specific sub-panels. Each sub-panel organised the nomination and selection procedures. The final selection was equality proofed. After this painstaking process the Civic Forum met twelve times over its two years of existence. A number of reports were issued before the Forum fell victim to the suspension of the Northern Ireland Executive in October 2002. Unlike the Executive, there was little or no political impetus to resurrect it in more settled times. As one elected politician queried – 'Why do we need a Civic Forum when we can come across these people at cocktail parties?'

If participatory democracy proved controversial, the accepted assumption by many politicians and the statutory sector that local communities required 'capacity-building', was rarely challenged. Described by one community trainer as a means of enabling communities, both geographic and thematic, to gain skills to effect positive change by addressing issues of racism, sectarianism, poverty, marginalisation and disadvantage, there was a tendency to apply a 'one size fits all' methodology. With contracts available, capacity-building could be designed by external experts without sufficient clarity regarding capacity-building for what? Activists with years of experience in dealing with political abnormality were caught in the training net, alongside others just starting out. There was little, or no, sense that capacity-building might be a two way process, applicable to civil service resource providers as well as local communities given the unshakable belief in the generalist expertise of the civil service. At least one official remarked on this phenomenon in the Department of Finance & Personnel – 'Suddenly the DFP had to get involved in community organisations and so forth ... The thing that always amused me was that within a very short

period of time they suddenly became experts ... They suddenly were starting to give lectures about partnership ... and they went with frightening
speed from knowing actually bugger all to being an expert'. This state of
affairs was not limited to the DFP.

Capacity-building was also cited in the zero-sum game of community
entitlement, where unionist politicians, in particular, were all too ready to
blame low levels of community capacity in Protestant areas for an apparent
inability to complete funding applications or design fundable programmes.
The argument that parity of esteem could be measured by parity of funding distribution was a potential vote winner in some quarters; equally the
sub-text was clear, not only had power-sharing diluted the political power
base of the community, but there was also the danger that they were being
done out of their rightful share of the peace dividend. The main difficulty
with this scenario was not the increased emphasis on unionist/loyalist
community capacity, but rather the focus on a notion of capacity that
prioritised professionally completed funding applications rather than the
effective delivery of inclusive community development.

The promotion of capacity-building as the cure-all remedy for the
mounting sense of loss in Protestant communities was accentuated by the
political use of increasing community alienation as a negotiation ploy to
draw further concessions from the British Government. With the honour-
able exception of the small Progressive Unionist Party, the ploy may have
had some political traction, but also resulted in the unintended consequence
of confirming local community belief that they had 'lost out' in the peace
process. The contrasting strategy adopted by republicans and nationalists
was to talk up the Agreement, notwithstanding that behind the scenes
Sinn Féin worked through an extensive list of demands, presented on a
'need to know' basis. The self-aggrandisement of a 12 July bonfire placard:
'Carlsberg doesn't do bonfires – but if it did, this would be the Best' – could
only go so far in lifting morale that had already been dealt a hammer blow
by the fall-out of loyalist feuds and repetition of the self-evident truism
that 'we' (the PUL community) have lost, so therefore 'they' (the CNR
community) must have won. Suggestions that the union had never been
safer were met with gloomy predictions about the changing demograph-
ics (which indicated a growth in the Catholic population) and about how

republicans insisted that the Belfast/Good Friday Agreement was 'dynamic' in nature – that is, it did not provide the long-term certainty essential for a sense of unionist security. The commendable efforts of a Community Dialogue initiative, to translate the terms of the various agreements into everyday language, and to circulate these pamphlets throughout communities, could only do so much to counter macro political pessimism.

In an attempt to address the despondency within Protestant areas, two conferences were billed as exploring community relations and the relative lack of confidence in cross-community work. A report, 'Facing our Future with Confidence', produced under the acronym PULSE (Protestant, Unionist, Loyalist Seeking Equality), listed a number of obstacles. There was the under-developed sense of community identity and perceived stripping away of Britishness; the feeling that culture, historical memory and the arts had largely been taken over by an Irish identity; and concerns that community relations was often seen as having an implicit 'united Ireland' agenda. In response, there were calls for the PUL community to learn more about its own history and traditions, rather than simply decrying Irish culture. There was also a plea for an agreed understanding about the nature of 'community relations'; and greater clarification regarding its benefits, if any, for the Protestant community. Inevitably funding was discussed, as demands were made for a 'more equitable distribution of money'; specific funding for 'capacity building' for PUL groups; and that funders should stop 'moving the goalposts' to favour more developed Catholic community groups. It wasn't just about playing the game, but about who was setting the rules.

The politics of the streets ... again

There was little time for reflection on the Ardoyne/Glenbryn interface in North Belfast given the mayhem on the streets. Contested territoriality was alive and well, and the spark of bitter confrontation was all too easily ignited in June 2001. An incident between men putting up flags along the disputed interface resulted in the residents of loyalist Glenbryn organising a rowdy protest against parents and their children that used the disputed Ardoyne Road to attend the Holy Cross Girls' Primary School. The protest, which lasted over eighteen months, consisted of well televised shouting, spitting, clenched fists, sectarian and obscene taunts, as well as bottles, bricks and fireworks being thrown. The children made their way to, and from, school through protective lines of heavily armed police, at a cost of some £100,000 per day. The most frightening occasion, it was reported, was when the massed protestors wore masks.

The antipathy of the protest took most people in Northern Ireland by surprise given that the victims were mainly very young girls, however it did not take long for aspersions to be cast on the parents. Why would they be putting their children through this trauma when they could take the longer back route into the school? Were they deliberately flaunting their presence to provoke loyalist reaction, which was broadcast by the media to the latter's disadvantage? What were the deeper community grievances that caused ordinary men and women to adopt otherwise inexplicable aggressive behaviour? The Concerned Residents of Upper Ardoyne (CRUA), taking their name from the largely republican 'Concerned Residents' groups that mobilised against Orange marches, called for 'reciprocation' and response to their demands before the protests could be ended. A process of inter-community negotiation was designed by government representatives in an attempt to de-escalate the tensions. It was agreed that channels of communication needed to be kept open; that community safety issues had to be addressed; and related community-level priorities identified. A North Belfast Community Action initiative was developed under by a panel consisting of a civil servant, a North Belfast Presbyterian Minister and a Catholic priest. Their report concluded that 'North Belfast has the capacity to absorb resources, destroy people, impoverish children and destabilise other parts of Northern Ireland. The price of failure to address and resolve the issues is high ... It is very important that the North Belfast communities can see that action is planned as a result of the report and that the capacity of malign influences to continue to promote hopelessness is curbed by Government's clear determination to act'. The 'malign influences' referred to went unnamed, although the fears of a dwindling Protestant population who felt themselves 'squeezed out' by an expanding, youthful Catholic population was noted; as was the anger of Catholics, trapped behind 'walls of fear', without access to adequate housing. The inter-generational reality of segregated living fed a mistrust of 'the other side', aggravated by the lack of any shared vision for the area as a whole.

The North Belfast Community Action Initiative recommended a dedicated Unit to build 'community capacity' (defined as the ability and will of people, living in a locality, to act collectively for their common good); develop a long-term strategy for North Belfast; encourage partnerships and take responsibility for addressing issues in interface areas. Community Empowerment Partnerships were to be formed to underpin capacity building. Additional recommendations included developing a Music Action Zone to promote cross-community contact; a Centre for Citizenship; youth provision; and two new Health and Well-being Centres. The ability of statutory agencies to dust existing plans off and insert them for consideration during times of crisis remained amazing. At the neighbourhood level some minor community irritants were acknowledged, such as replacing missing bollards in a local playing field.

A core demand tabled by the Glenbryn Concerned Residents was the extension and heightening of the existing peace wall to prevent stone throwing attacks from the Ardoyne estate. The existing wall that curved between the two communities was known locally as 'the wailing wall', but there were fears that any extension (albeit with a security gate) might inhibit access to the Holy Cross Primary School and could act as a precedent to isolate other schools located near peace lines. Delicate negotiation was needed to nuance the Glenbryn argument that the extension of the wall would be the reciprocal measure for the suspension of the daily protests. Negotiators were conscious of a more general increase in interface violence, as Fr. Aidan Troy, a Catholic priest in Ardoyne, suggested that: 'Riots are a bit like a forest fire. They flare up in different areas and with varying degrees of intensity. It is not easy to predict where a riot will leap next'. The Trade Union Movement organised street rallies to demand an end to sectarian attacks, one of which had claimed the life of a young postal worker.

The fact that community security was found behind corrugated steel fences or aesthetically designed brick walls said much about the impact of the years of violence. Interface Protestant communities all too easily saw the pressure of burgeoning Catholic communities as a process of virtual ethnic cleansing. Their Catholic neighbours responded by pointing to the atavistic sectarianism all too often on display in the street protests and public statements by those on the other side of the peace walls. Policy making was faced with the quandary as to whether to pursue proactive strategies to promote comprehensive urban integration, or whether stability and security necessitated a more pragmatic response with the pace set by local communities. Investment in the revitalisation of 'neutral' urban and town centres suggested the former, whereas the latter was the norm in deprived and fearful interface areas. Change, it was generally felt, had to be rooted in local community buy-in and sense of ownership. As against this, there was the question as to whether single identity territoriality offered a comfortable predictability for both aligned electoral support and paramilitary control; an issue that like Banquo's ghost delivered the subliminal message that street politics had a raison d'etre of its own.

The conceptual framing of inter-community development

Social capital, EDI (Equity, Diversity and Interdependence) and strengthening community infrastructure were some of the many concepts marshalled to explain a community development approach that might more consciously address community division. The Robert Puttnam inspired social capital concept was adopted by CENI (Community Evaluation Northern Ireland) to develop indicators that might interrogate the impact of community action over four added value dimensions: individual capital; organisational capital; community capital and civic capital. Trust-building was named as an essential element in community development, maximising an asset that went far beyond service delivery to 'hard to reach' groups. One long-term community activist was somewhat under-whelmed by the new analytical approach, exclaiming: 'Oh no, not another way of describing what we have always done!' Within the world of local activism new concepts had to be matched with longer term resource commitment if approaches were to be more than academic abstractions.

Puttnam's definition of bonding social capital was seen as being applicable to the internal dynamics of single identity communities that were often strongly bonded in the face of 'the other' community. Bridging social capital was the necessary – although often missing element – to build positive relationships on an inter-community basis, whilst a third dimension, of Linking social capital, was suggested to take account of the essential relationships between local communities and statutory/government decision-makers. The problem, more often than not, was that macro political tensions and uncertainties could undermine the community outreach required for bridging social capital, and even where cross-community networking was effective, there was the danger that community groups feared that they might be defining themselves out of the 'weak infrastructure' category and the funding attached to it. If money was tagged for areas of 'weak community infrastructure' and 'low capacity' then that was the preferred status.

Street tensions provided a sombre backdrop for a review of community relations commissioned by the Office of First Minister/Deputy First Minister. The initial power-sharing Executive Programme for Government seemed, with the benefit of hindsight, overly optimistic in looking forward to 'a peaceful, inclusive, prosperous, stable and fair society, firmly founded on the achievement of reconciliation, tolerance and mutual trust, and the protection and vindication of human rights for all'. In real terms it would prove challenging to shift from seeing community relations as primarily a priority for interface communities, to a policy that examined sectarianism as manifested within Northern Irish society as a whole. In practice any such critique needed to question the self-ascribed neutral functionality of much of society, as well as any idea that funding and capacity-building were sufficient in themselves to secure the outcome of 'harmonious relationships'. This deeper analysis also called into question the somewhat mechanistic understanding of peacebuilding increasingly evident in EU PEACE programme rationale, where a linear connection between funded project work and reconciliation outcomes was expected irrespective of the wider environment.

Academic studies that scrutinised the work of organisations in a divided society, through a framing of Equity, Diversity and Interdependence (EDI), questioned to what extent community and voluntary groups impacted on reconciliation. The EDI thesis argued the importance of critical dialogue within organisations to examine sensitive issues and support more open and honest relationships; in short, shadowing the 'transversal politics' of the women's movement. It was suggested that organisations often survived by ignoring political and community differences rather than addressing them. This could produce workplaces and organisations that were either implicitly partisan (where one community identity predominated, with any attempt to offer a different viewpoint deemed 'the problem'), or where an artificial 'neutrality' predominated (where differences went unacknowledged for the sake of an artificial harmony). The Rural Community Network put EDI into practice when it surveyed its member organisations and staff to capture perceptions as to whether particular political/communal/gender identities dominated, and took steps to interrogate policy positions, but also to build relationships in a conscious manner. The organisational objective was to develop an integrated approach to champion fairness.

Following up on the suggestion that the community and voluntary sectors could do more to address sectarianism, the Northern Ireland Community Relations Council commissioned research which concluded that groups lacked both agreed analysis of the causes of the conflict and clarity concerning their role in promoting accommodation. There were undoubtedly those that believed that conceptual clarity was closely linked to political perspective; while others pointed to the limited resources available to facilitate critical self-reflection outside academia research monies. Organisations often felt that there was pressure enough maintaining operational 'neutrality', particularly where community groups were caught in the single identity circumstances of their location and composition.

It was generally community sector networking organisations that deliberately reached beyond the single-identity restrictions of the local and structured themselves to work on an inter-community basis. Alongside internal reflection, the Rural Community Network (NI) decided to examine the dynamics of living as a minority community within a predominantly single identity area. Two inter-related action-research studies looked at the perceptions of small Protestant communities along the Irish Border; and the position of the Catholic minority in the North Antrim area. The importance of a community development approach that engaged in single identity work, with the ultimate purpose of working towards equitable cross-community relationship building, was flagged up. Evidence showed that where the majority community exceeded 80 per cent, the minority tended to be invisible due to the hegemony exercised by the dominant community. The use of local venues that might be seen to be aligned (such as church or sports halls) could be unquestioned, exuding 'a chill factor' on the minority. Even jokes or the chance remarks between neighbours at meetings could make for uncomfortable circumstances for those coming from a different perspective.

Investment in single identity work was not uncontroversial, with fears expressed that it might serve to support more self-assured bigots who could use enhanced community bonding to marshal negative perceptions of 'the other'. Programmes, such as Communities in Transition (2001–2006), were designed by the Community Foundation for Northern Ireland to offer a counter perspective. Funded by the International Fund for Ireland and the Atlantic Philanthropies, the objectives of this longer-term intervention included building relationships within and between communities; promoting local participation in community development and peacebuilding work; and creating community cohesion by offering opportunities and support in a range of single-identity areas that had not benefited from previous funding programmes. The work offered a more paced, but no less effective, approach to community relations.

The fist of history

When Prime Minister Blair arrived to preside over one of many crisis interventions, he informed the awaiting media that he felt 'the hand of history' on his shoulder. There were many locals who felt the hand of history as a fist. Brendan, from Ardoyne, was a case in point: 'In the early 1970s I had three brothers shot and injured by the British Army. One lost his eyesight, one lost part of his lung and the other one has a limp. These three men were totally innocent of any crimes ... the paratroopers had shot them ... So 1975 comes along and a younger brother went into town and got blew up by a bomb and killed. In 1994, I had a sister who was shot dead ... (and) I had an uncle who was killed in an explosion and a gun attack. In 1995 I had a nephew shot dead and in 1996 I had another nephew shot dead. These people were all killed by different sections of the community, by all different sides claiming they had the right to kill for their cause ... 170 people have been killed in the wee community where I live. The population is 6,600 so everybody has a brother, sister, wife, somebody belonging to them killed. So a lot of hurt'. Brendan set up a centre for victims and survivors in North Belfast, one of the many self-help groups that emerged with early support from the EU PEACE funds; later attracting mainstream statutory resources.

Over the years of the Troubles victims and survivors of the conflict had been largely defined out of the script given the official narrative of normalisation. Even the Disabled Police Officers' Association was seen as off-message when it asserted the needs of its members. An early PEACE grant financed a research study which counted the cost of the Troubles in terms of lost lives. The statistics illustrated a young person's war; young men being particularly at risk. It also showed, to consternation in certain quarters, that more Catholics had been killed by the various republican paramilitaries than by the British Army. A rough calculation of the overall impact of the Troubles showed that some 7,000 parents had lost a child; 14,000 grandparents lost a grandchild; 3,000 people had lost a husband, wife or partner; and a minimum of 15,000 people had lost a sibling. The stark reality of the pain behind the statistics was expressed by a mother from Armagh: 'In 1976 I was three-and-a-half months pregnant with my first child ... I had a friend getting married and she was having a wee do ... We were only through the door (of a bar in Keady) ... and something just happened ... The place was in darkness; there was rubble all over my knees ... I knew then it was an explosion ... I was taken to hospital ... They told my mother then that the good news was that the baby was going to be alright and the bad news was that I was going to lose one eye ... So on 26 January of 1976, Gavin was born. He was seven pounds six, with a big head of blond curls ... Gavin was all into art. He was a very popular boy. He was deputy Head Boy in the High School in Keady ... On Wednesday morning, the 18 May (1994) he left me ... to go to the Technical School in Armagh ... Later Matt (the father) says to me "Maria there's been a shooting in Armagh" ... The next thing the phone rang, it was Father Rice ... He said "Have you got a son at school in Armagh?" I said "I have Father – Oh Father, our Gavin is not caught up in the shooting!" ... Just then the police arrived; Matt and me and Father Rice all went into the house ... and I said, "Father, where did they shoot him?", and he said, "Maria it was one man who put the gun to the child's head and he shot him." I said, "Father did he not see that wee face, he was only a boy, did he not realise?"'. The baby that had survived the bombing was the boy who was murdered. As Maria, his mother, related her story to a conference audience in 1999, she held a photograph of her dead son. Her audience included individuals who were related to members of paramilitary organisations that had been involved in both the bombing and the shooting – individuals who themselves had relatives killed in the Troubles.

Prodded by the peace process, retired civil servant, Sir Kenneth Bloomfield, was appointed by the British Government to prepare a report on the victims of the Troubles. He reflected: 'We encountered feelings of injustice so pronounced that we did not feel that we could leave matters there ... Because bureaucracy, and I was in it myself for years, can be very insensitive'. The government set up a Victims' Liaison Unit and started to allocate mainstream funding to address the needs of victims. The EU PEACE programmes maintained a focus on the reintegration of victims and survivors as a priority theme. While both this, and the increased government funding, was welcome, the ever tighter audit and monitoring requirements often resulted in self-help groups discussing the comparative advantages of reflexology, on the one hand, while verifying rent receipts and travel claims, on the other. A conference for victims and survivor groups organised by the Community Foundation for Northern Ireland in November 2002 heard Direct Rule Minister, Des Browne, acknowledge that his administration was the first to recognise the needs of victims. The conference organisers were preoccupied in trying to avoid a walk out by some of his audience. For a change, this was not in protest at a British Minister, but due to the fact that unwittingly the gathering was held on Remembrance Day – a day with greater resonance for the unionist/loyalist community than for nationalists or republicans. Delicate negotiations were required to reach agreement around which conference participants would stand in memory of what. Nothing was ever simple given contested symbols and memories in support of conflicting narratives.

These same conflicting narratives bedevilled any consensus over the nature of victimhood itself. There were the innocent victims and terrorists, freedom fighters and legitimate targets, all depending on one's political point of view. The intensity of this debate was fuelled by party political interventions which both responded to the views of variously aligned victims' groups, as well as electoral considerations. The official definition of a victim/survivor as anyone that was bereaved and/or injured in the conflict, rapidly descended into a league table of preference. An advocate for the victims/survivors' of state violence argued forcibly that: 'The stark reality is that truth and justice are not universal concepts in the North. These inalienable rights have not been accessible and applicable for all. They are exclusive mostly depending on who you are, which community you come from, and which group is responsible for a particular act of violence. Truth and justice have been sacrificed and are thus casualties of the conflict'. The tectonic plates of clashing perspectives were strengthened in the absence of any agreed and inclusive process of dealing with the past. Within local communities the Troubles remained a kaleidoscope of memories, depending on personal and community experience. What was experienced by a beleaguered Protestant community along the border areas of West Fermanagh was radically different from that in the Catholic Creggan estate in Derry.

Another sizeable community of interest, increasingly evident by the late 1990s, was that of political ex-prisoners. Variably known as prisoners of war, criminals, politically motivated ex-prisoners, perpetrators, terrorists – and in many cases victims themselves – it was estimated that some 25,000–35,000 people fell into this category. Official statistics were not available given the official narrative of 'criminalisation'. However, when calculated, with the addition of direct family members affected, research returned a conservative estimate of between 150,000–200,000 people impacted by politically related imprisonment. Many of these, both republican and loyalist, were concentrated within a relatively small catchment of communities. By 1998 there were over thirty self-help groups providing support services for the political ex-prisoner population, again dependent on funding from the EU PEACE programmes. An activist aligned to the UDA explained: 'If the war's over what do we do now? And for me the natural progression was to mend the community ... So from defending to mending. Basically we got involved in community development ... I think we were the first ex-prisoner group to get involved in interface community stuff ... to try to work out stuff along the interface and work together on interface issues ... It was a bit hard at the start'. The perception of moving from defence of an area to assuming the role of community activist was not uncontroversial, particularly in unionist/loyalist areas.

Interaction Belfast (previously Springfield Inter Community Development Project) developed early programmes to bring together loyalist and republican ex-prisoners and ex-combatants to alleviate violence along the sensitive Springfield interface in West Belfast. A reflective report noted the importance of formative political discussions within the jails as a contributory factor in the peace process. It highlighted the importance of trust-building between people who had previously been enemies. Demystification of the enemy was important, as was finding points of commonality from a shared experience of paramilitarism and imprisonment. The latter was often used as reputational capital to initiate difficult discussions. One loyalist participant recalled: 'I have done things at an inter-community level that I knew was going to stir debate and I knew was going to cause 'ruptions within my own community, but I thought that those debates needed to be brought out and I felt that they needed to be out in the open'. There was a feeling that political ex-prisoners had the credibility that allowed them to exercise leadership, although this often proved more difficult in loyalist communities.

These early seeds grew into a more ambitious programme of conflict transformation both within and between communities. In the case of the former, intra-community dialogue addressed attitudes about the 'other' community; legal and security challenges such as policing and restorative justice; negotiations on paramilitary flags, murals, the siting of bonfires and other symbolic displays of territoriality; alongside a range of pressing social problems. When applied on a cross-community basis, conflict transformation encompassed dialogue between former combatants with a view to encouraging better understanding of differing perceptions; design of specific measures to alleviate interface violence; tentative discussions with victims and survivors; and joint activities to address the legal exclusion of political prisoners from mainstream society. Conflict transformation, it was held, was about changing the paradigm of the conflict, posing questions/positions in different ways and transforming the nature of the relationship between people that had been at war. It was accepted that contested political allegiances would remain, but that these could be addressed within a framework of respect. A number of UVF ex-prisoners were at the leading edge of this thinking, which was captured in a series of pamphlets published by the community-based Farset Community Think Tank Project, and encapsulated in a partnership between loyalist, Billy Mitchell and republican, Liam Maskey, that resulted in the Intercomm initiative in North Belfast. There were those that denounced the rapprochement as tantamount to treachery as well as those who viewed ex-prisoner involvement as a new form of political gatekeeping. Notwithstanding the difficulties the work continued.

The existence, and networking, of political ex-prisoner self-help groups fulfilled another important role – during periods of political uncertainty it allowed a cross-checking of information where doom-laden media headlines invariably reflected the latest political stand-off. The application of conflict transformation in practice, however, was not without its frustrations as when both republican and loyalist ex-prisoners visited Leuvan (Belgium). Two of the delegates were questioned by airport police at London's Heathrow airport. When the organisers queried the delay in releasing the men being held (one UDA and one IRA), concern became exasperation when the police reported that the loyalist insisted on speaking Gaelic which he had learned in prison. This, the organisers felt, was taking conflict transformation one step too far with a plane to catch.

CHAPTER 11

Peacebuilding in Shades of Grey

Times were a-changing when the British and Irish Governments breathed a sigh of relief in 2007 and celebrated 'the chuckle brothers', Sinn Féin's Martin McGuinness and DUP leader, Ian Paisley, representing the two dominant parties in the Northern Ireland Executive and Assembly. The unexpected bon hommé was replaced by a more phlegmatic relationship between McGuinness and Paisley's successor as First Minister, Peter Robinson. Tensions and hard words remained to bobby-trap the developing relationship as serial agreements were negotiated to smooth the path. The St. Andrews Agreement (2006) was followed by the Hillsborough Agreement (2010); the Stormont House Agreement (2014) by the Fresh Start Agreement (2015), and there were still issues too hot to handle. Five political parties, with diametrically opposing policies, accepted ministerial positions in two subsequent power-sharing Executives. The fact that departmental Permanent Secretaries were answerable to their Minister introduced further complexity of governance. Outside the inner workings of the political class the rumblings of loyalist community discontent and unease were evident; while a plethora of 'dissident' republican groups continued to denounce the 'sell out' of a United Ireland, threatening vengeance. Politics was still in prickly offence and counter-offence mode, although zero-sum game calculations sometimes grumbled down into the virtual 'benign apartheid' of back-to-back governance.

A number of weasel words in the Belfast/Good Friday Agreement continued to haunt political stability. Rights, equality and 'parity of esteem' jostled for attention, represented as either a 'republican demand' or 'backdoor sectarianism'. 'Equality' was branded a republican mantra as was 'human rights'; 'parity of esteem' argued the right of the Loyal Orders to parade on their 'traditional routes', while political thermometers checked out which community felt chilliest in the 'cold house' of Northern Ireland. The

Cultural Traditions' wing of the Northern Ireland Community Relations Council had seen this particular straw in the wind well over two decades previously, but not even their sensitive antennae could have foretold the ructions in Stormont over which colour lilies could, and should, be included in floral displays. White lilies were associated with the Irish 1916 Rebellion; orange lilies with the Orange Order 12 July celebrations. Nothing was simple, and thinking around corners remained an essential skill.

With 'parity of esteem' a code for the politics of warring identities, local community organising continued as a mix of motivation, priorities and politics. One inner city loyalist area saw that: 'Former UVF prisoners coincided with a lot of community activism ... so you would have seen the same people out on protests, doing the white line protests (along the middle of the road over traffic congestion); you would have seen the same people protesting around parades and marches; you would have seen the same people involved in community festivals'. When the woman in question was approached to join the PUP (Progressive Unionist Party) her immediate response was 'No, no, me Ma would kill me!', although she eventually agreed. The heightened expectations of nationalists and republicans left little room for appreciation of the apprehension within Protestant communities: 'I think on the ground people had very high expectations of what was going to happen, that there would be work done on – well policing obviously was clearly going to be one ... The flags and emblems became much more a thing and the republican community became much more confident about complaining about marches. They saw that those were rights issues and they began to understand that you could use legislation and the frameworks ... They just became more aware of it as a result of the Agreement; and the things that were very cleverly put into the Agreement are still highly contested and not delivered'. There had been little, or no, thought given to the management of expectations, let alone agreement over a timetable for the implementation of the details of the Belfast/Good Friday Agreement.

The issue of parades, marches, flags and symbols of cultural identity remained largely unresolved despite a number of successful civil society interventions. One of the earliest examples took place in Derry where a negotiated settlement was brokered by business and community interests, supported by the local authority and religious and political leaders. When proximity talks between the Apprentice Boys of Derry and community groups stuttered into disagreement, a new talks initiative was co-chaired by local businessman, Garbhan O'Doherty, and representative of the Town Centre Management Group, Brendan Duddy. Subsequent agreements were hailed as a model of negotiated compromise with the parades rebranded as a tourist attraction. A later Maiden City Accord, hammered out in 2014 after five months of confidential meetings chaired by the Londonderry Bands' Forum, set out the responsibilities of the single identity groups that were involved in parading to counter what was described as deliberate negativity.

Events in Belfast were not as manageable and were exacerbated by the 'Flags protest'. This flared in December 2012 from a Belfast City Council vote to only fly the Union flag on the eighteen days officially set out in government guidelines. The anger that followed was both an inter-generational struggle for power within loyalism as well as a beacon of loyalist feelings of dispossession. A cynical party political spin aggravated the issue given the loss of a DUP Westminster seat to the Alliance Party in East Belfast in the previous election. The protests were in marked contrast to the earlier progress that had been made over parades and interface tension along the Springfield Road in West Belfast. There, after years of careful work, there had been a breakthrough: 'It was about 2005 or 2006, and what happened was a woman had arrived late to the (cross-community) meeting, and she said ... "Why didn't anyone ring me last night, there was something in Lanark Way?" ... And one of the guys from the nationalist side said "Ah X, that was a crowd from our side, they came up to the (interface) gates and there was a couple of land rovers there and they attacked the police." And somebody else from the other (unionist) side said, "No, no, that was ours. A couple of ours had a mad party and afterwards they went out drunk and attacked." I thought, that's it'. This was the point when people started taking responsibility rather than finger pointing at 'the other side'. As the facilitator noted: 'It's all about building trust. It's not even about facing the tragedies or facing the difficult parts, it's facing the difficult parts with integrity and then taking responsibility for it'. Trust was still at a premium six years later.

Supporting police reform

Policing and community safety had long been top of a change agenda that saw the transformation of the RUC (Royal Ulster Constabulary) into the PSNI (Police Service of Northern Ireland). The Independent Patten Commission undertook extensive consultation and produced a report with 175 recommendations. Two priorities were clear, the first to normalise the police service and secondly, to ensure, through affirmative action measures, that it became more reflective of Northern Irish society. Monitored by an Oversight Commissioner, it was reported in 2007 that 82 per cent of the recommendations had been implemented, with good progress being made to meet the recruitment target of 30 per cent Catholic police officers. Accountability was structured to be broadly based, including a Northern Ireland Policing Board, a Police Ombudsman and area-based partnerships. Acrimonious tussles over the name, badge and symbols of the new service took up much political air time, but change was distinctly in the air when Sinn Féin eventually signed up to the new policing arrangements, despite declared reservations about the machinations of shadowy 'securicrats'.

Forward looking community level efforts to build confidence in the PSNI received less attention. Interaction Belfast became involved through its work to alleviate interface violence. After bringing republican and loyalist groups together from North and West Belfast, a key issue emerging from the facilitated four-day process was that of parades: 'Loyalists said to republicans ... "Look we acknowledge that the Orange Order doesn't talk to local residents, and we got to find a way that we can get that", and that was then the North & West Belfast Parades Forum came out of that. "But equally ... you don't talk to the police"'. The discussions were recorded in what became known as the Farset Minute, which formed the basis for future meetings: 'So out of that what we did was we set action plans and then we brought the groups together every three months, and then it just worked, the process worked'. Translating the process into practice was never easy in West Belfast, but fell by the wayside in fractured North Belfast. It was agreed that the Interaction Director act as a conduit between republicans, loyalists and the police with regard to the choreography of a contentious local Loyal Order parade across the interface. The details were worked out: 'I typed it up, I'm very conscientious about writing things. So I wrote out point 1.1., at 3.00pm such and such will happen ... I went to the police and they signed it; I went to the republicans, they signed it and I went to the loyalists ... who signed it – so that everyone knew what they were getting into'. Four witnesses from civil society, the NIO and the Irish Government were tasked to oversee adherence of all parties to the agreement. There was no violence: 'After that it was a dream, we had half a page of an agreement the next year'.

The next issue on the agenda was policing. Work commenced in 2004 when Sinn Féin was still opposing the new policing arrangements. Having undertaken a community safety project, Interaction Belfast was convinced that there was a need to address the issue, but recognised that open engagement with the PSNI was still frowned on in nationalist/republican areas despite quiet communication at times: 'I used to bring messages backwards and forwards (between the PSNI and local people associated with republicanism) ... So I said to X one day, look is there any chance of you actually meeting? So he said, "Look I need to clear it ... could you write me a letter saying that you're involved in this?" So I wrote this big, fanciful letter ... So Peter (PSNI) and him met ... and they hit it off straight away ... and it was really more of a trust building process'. The personal contacts became more formal when, on the basis of initial work around the perceptions of police officers in West Belfast, the community activists involved were invited to make a presentation to the PSNI Chief Constables' Forum: 'We went up and did the presentation – this is what your officers feel – and it was pretty damning ... I'd agreed with different sergeants that I'd met (in West Belfast) that their statements would go to the top ... and it was things like these guys in Armani suits are terrorists, and the Catholic education system gives nationalists a victim mentality; all these very, very stereotypical and prejudiced statements'. This model of engagement and discussion was further tested in the Border areas of Newry and Crossmaglen: 'So we went down and they (the police) were still at war ... They literally were still at war, and this was 2005'. A confidential report was drawn up entitled 'Managing Change'.

The PSNI Chief Constable agreed to a three year programme of work-shops to bring police officers across the district command teams together with republican and loyalist representatives. South African mediator, Brian Currin, helped design a seminar approach called 'Past, Present and Future' – 'So we always had the two days where the first bit was about the past; then the afternoon was about the present and the following day was about the future'. Initial group work was undertaken with the police, who nominated a representative to present their views. Sinn Féin representatives presented their experience of policing in the afternoon, followed by facilitated dis-cussion: 'We would do an afternoon session that I would always have to facilitate ... and it was probably the most difficult session where it was about my friends were killed'. A number of independent perspectives were intro-duced in the evening, often Nuala O'Loan (the Police Ombudsperson) or Denis Bradley (Co-chair of the Dealing with the Past Commission). The morning of the second day was given over to representatives of loyalist groups, with a sharing of perspectives between them and the police offic-ers. The session concluded with a Northern Ireland Office update on the devolution of policing and justice. 'And then it was press re-wind, and we'd do the same thing in the next district and the next district and the next'. The programme only hit the buffers when it came to the participation of Special Branch/C3 officers: 'It was a step too far for the Republicans' at that time.

Despite this quiet programme of work local community activists in nationalist/republican areas were often still uncertain about engaging with the PSNI. Interaction Belfast was working at a number of levels simultane-ously; a process that required transparency – without going overboard: 'So we were having a meeting of the Mobile Phone Network and I remember he (PSNI District Commander of West Belfast) came in ... so I went into the room and said, "I just want to let you know if some of you want to leave, the District Commander is coming into my office next door, and if any of you want to leave, leave" ... Because I never give the other option of he won't come'. Uncertainty about what, and when, people felt they had the permission to do things hung in the air until the endorsement of policing by Sinn Féin in 2007. It was to take another three years before the devolu-tion of policing and justice to a Northern Ireland Minister – Alliance Party,

David Ford – given DUP reservations. If unionists experienced a crisis of confidence, republicans critical of the Good Friday Agreement saw Sinn Féin acceptance of policing as a signifier of acceptance of the Northern Ireland state. For them, police officers remained 'legitimate targets', with a number paying the ultimate price. Meanwhile discussions continued apace to build positive relationships between police and community, as 'community safety' became a mobilising issue. In May 2013, the North Belfast based Intercomm hosted facilitated round table conversations about policing and security with community representatives. Discussion covered the nature of community-based models of policing and security; the characteristics of public order policing; and the lessons to be drawn from the Northern Irish experience for other contested societies. One lesson was the long term nature of change given that community policing still seemed aspirational.

Building bridges at the grassroots

If the' big issues' predominated in political debate, the need to address local community divisions remained important, although influenced by macro-level developments. A long contentious interface between the small Protestant area of Suffolk and the much larger Catholic housing estates of Lenadoon attracted attention for its cross-community initiative. In the mid-1980s a community worker took the risk to mediate joint action to demand traffic lights on the busy interface, Stewartstown Road. By the mid-1990s back-to-back area surveys identified shared issues, which sparked dual single identity interest. Cross-interface contact and communication was supported by having both the single-identity Lenadoon Community Forum and the Protestant Suffolk Community Forum as focal points. An activist from Lenadoon felt that the sharing of area survey data was very effective: 'Chris O'Halloran of the Belfast Interface Project did a scoping exercise ... He actually did single identity interviews with Lenadoon Community Forum, single identity interviews with Suffolk, and he exchanged the notes. And actually that went on for the guts of a year ... I found it started dispelling some of the myths – there was little or no contact for twenty years, from the '70s, and the myths that had grown up. Actually coming towards the end of that year it was like ... what's this crap? All the things we have in common, we should meet. So we actually met that December'. The one day meeting was designed to address shared issues during the morning and contentious issues that afternoon. Initial ground rules were agreed: 'That we would be honest; that each culture was equally valued and each belief system was equally valued; and speak your mind'. The Suffolk-Lenadoon Interface Group (SLIG) was established to take forward the relationship, agreeing that it was important to continue to meet during periods of tension.

Meeting monthly, SLIG established a mobile phone network to keep activists in communication and to explore the potential to develop a 'shared space' initiative. Initial financial support was provided under the Community Bridges programme of the International Fund for Ireland. A protocol was agreed to cover relationships during periods of political tension. When the Northern Ireland Housing Executive decided to demolish a number of buildings facing on to the Stewartstown Road, which included the Suffolk Community Forum office, it prompted the formation of the Stewartstown Road Regeneration Project in 1998. A management board was composed of four representatives from Suffolk and Lenadoon respectively, together with four external members. The 'shared space' project planned was to build a two-storey block of shops and offices. Realising these plans proved time-consuming: 'The process which brought our Company into being was one of the longest, most painstaking processes I have ever experienced. We even spent six months in mediation as part of it ... We had to analyse every possible aspect of the building: its non-political use, flags and emblems, who could come into the building and who couldn't. We had to devise criteria for use, under every conceivable scenario' – in addition to learning how to run the company and assume the roles as board members. SLIG also faced the challenge of bringing the broader community on board, with reservations being expressed at meetings on both sides of the interface. It was women that drove the idea forward in Suffolk; in Lenadoon there was a qualified mandate given; both areas stressed the importance of transparency and local ownership rather than any fait accompli project design.

Accessing funding for a physical regeneration plan proved complex. Initial support provided by the International Fund for Ireland, EU PEACE monies and the Housing Executive was insufficient to overcome the scepticism of civil servants. When funding was eventually released officials were keen to invite a government minister to attend the launch. There was little thought about the likely impact in loyalist Suffolk if the ministerial visit required an invitation to the then MP for West Belfast, Gerry Adams. A Suffolk representative despaired at the lack of sensitivity and consultation with local people, arguing that if the civil service proposal had gone ahead all the patient work undertaken would have been undone. Over the period 2006–2014, The Atlantic Philanthropies, provided a major investment to underpin the work, emphasising a model of peacebuilding and regeneration rooted in community leadership. The 'shared space' regeneration project delivered local facilities including a new Day-care Centre and community outreach programmes. It also supported the reconstruction of the Glen Community Complex. Peacebuilding remained a conscious dimension of the work, although it was acknowledged that an emphasis on peacebuilding in isolation is insufficient in areas of high deprivation.

Unlike the SLIG model, the Communities in Transition Programme designed by the Community Foundation for Northern Ireland was an externally driven initiative which recognised the importance of working in areas that lacked pre-existing community infrastructure. It also replaced previous descriptors such as 'areas of weak infrastructure', or 'lack of capacity', with the more neutral appellation of 'transition', to allow a focus on challenges, opportunities and assets. Words were important. Prioritising ten disadvantaged single identity communities (drawn from both the main communal identities) the programme supported local communities to engage in inclusive community organising; to identify and address causes of community alienation and community tensions; to influence policy makers; and to seek to influence politicians with regard to the potential contribution of community development processes. The Communities in Transition acknowledged that communities affected by the residual features of political conflict were less amenable to cross-community contact, however, instead of attempting to marginalise local people that were seen as associated with paramilitarism (past or current), an emphasis was placed on inclusive community participation. The reality was accepted that, as one loyalist ex-prisoner suggested, paramilitaries did not come down from the mountains at night and retreat back up in the morning – they lived next door. The trick for community organising was balancing community interests rather than privileging the leadership of either 'safe hands' or 'community gatekeepers'. Uncomfortable internal community conversations, facilitated by CFNI staff and mentors, were par for the course. This was particularly contentious in rural Protestant communities where the CFNI Programme Manager described how: 'In the PUL community the process was very different because it meant more public engagement, more letting people talk and be angry and get their issues out on the table. Call each other murderers, call each other this, call each other that, but it had to be done because otherwise that civic society was never going to come back round the table, and the danger there was that the paramilitaries would run absolutely everything. And somewhere in between there needed to be a compromise, because the same paramilitaries are part of that community. But it's working with them and getting them to see their impact and the power that they are bringing to the table, and how that was creating fear and people walking away … and that has been a slower process, but in some ways more grounded and broader'. The issue of timing and pace was essential for a bottom-up process to develop, whereby local people could become involved; build trust and confidence; identify local needs and opportunities; and agree priorities. Any external support provided had to be responsive to this process.

The community dynamics in nationalist/republican areas was different given the growing Sinn Féin political dominance that could serve to exclude those community members holding different political views and allegiances: 'Those that are outside it find it tough. They find it tough to have voice and also find it tough to have access to resources. In the (past) when I suppose there would have been attempts by civil servants or Council workers to deal with that, and be more open and more fair … that space has closed down there quite considerably and it will take an enormous amount of energy to turn that dynamic around and open it up again'. Faced with this challenge the approach adopted was to ask questions and introduce new ideas: 'Talking to people about who is round the table – who is not round the table? How is that right? Why is it right? Is this just your political strategy or can we be broader than that so other people do engage? Slowly breaking down gatekeeping and trying to get more people involved'. Alongside the questioning of inclusive community representation, the importance of effective local communication to boost engagement, and the availability of accessible and flexible small amounts of funding, was recognised as essential.

With a growth in local confidence, together with trust in the development workers, it proved possible to move from single identity work to create the framework to enable single identity community representatives to meet with those from different areas on the basis of shared interests, and often a leavening of curiosity. The ability to integrate community development and peacebuilding practices was a distinctive element of the Communities in Transition objectives and outcomes. Political gatekeeping, sectarianism, antisocial behaviour, racism, paramilitary influences and (violent) splits within communities were all themes that resonated on all sides, alongside the capacity of the peace process to 'deliver' at local level. The clustering of community issues enabled the CIT workers to invite activists from a variety of backgrounds to meet over a cup of coffee or in small seminars. It was important that everyone was made aware of who the other participants would be and what they were committing themselves to. Over time cross-community engagement became more ambitious: 'Sometimes you could get cover for a much bigger event, like a conference of 100 or 120 people, and groups quietly preparing to meet each other for the first time in the room. Then hearing each other speak, but they were speaking to the platform (speakers), they weren't speaking to each other, and eventually starting to break that down as well'. Topics such as community policing, drug and alcohol abuse, community safety, etc. were selected to allow people to hear what others were saying and to listen to alternate views and suggestions that might have relevance to all.

With a repertoire of larger conferences, smaller seminars, workshops and quiet informal discussions, the bonding social capital of single-identity community development could be broadened by the bridging social capital of inter-community engagement. A focus on social issues morphed into the more political: 'We did some oral history projects where the republican and loyalist participants shared each other's stories of the conflict and the various roles they had actively played in the security forces and the various paramilitary groups and, in some instances, in both at the same time and they were absolutely brilliant, but you know we needed to have a lot of work under the belt before we got to that stage'. The exchange of experiences came to a hushed stop on the republican side one occasion when one of the loyalist participants declared himself as having been in the SAS (acronym for the British Army Special Air Services regiment) – only to go on to explain that 'in my case this was a complete putdown because it meant that was the Saturdays and Sundays, as I was only in the TA (Territorial Army)!'. The support work necessary to encourage people to develop levels of trust in order to speak honestly about potentially divisive issues needed political awareness of nuances, a lot of patience, a listening ear and flexibility in relation to time, venue and travel. Evening and week-end working was the norm.

One of a number of structured inter-community partnerships emerging from the programme was FORWARD, between the Carson Project (Harryville, Ballymena) and Leafair Community Association (Galliagh, Derry). Standing for 'Focus on Reconciliation Working to Achieve Real Dialogue', these two very different groups agreed ground rules as to how they would work together. The rules included agreement that any issue would be open for discussion except details about the past of the individuals involved; meetings would include former political prisoners and combatants from both sides; and initial meetings would be confidential. Those involved reflected on their early fears about travelling into each other's area and how the meetings might be perceived by people within their own community. Mounting confidence, over time, allowed the number of people involved in the exchanges to be broadened around three streams of joint work – work with young people; inter-generational work and dialogue between ex-combatants (both paramilitaries and security forces). FORWARD was structured with a management committee composed of activists from both areas. The joint work continued even after a member of the group had an explosive device planted under his car. The group discussed how best to avoid such attacks in the future, but also how they might engage with those who had planted the device. By 2012, FORWARD was hosted by OFMDFM (Office of First Minister, Deputy First Minister) in Stormont as a flagship peacebuilding programme. The patient early investment of respect for local people and responsive pump-priming funding, within a framework of searching for the pulse points of common issues to progress peacebuilding, served to bring bonding, bridging and linking social capital together.

The Communities in Transition programme focused its work on communities outside of the Greater Belfast area given the number of support programmes that Belfast attracted. It actively looked for areas that were increasingly described as 'hard to reach', and quickly concluded that 'reach' requires a physical presence rather than desk research. It also recognised that the policy trend of adopting an exclusively 'evidenced' social need approach (i.e. targeting the top 10 per cent of communities experiencing multiple deprivation) can result in a concentration on certain communities that have been relatively well served by social interventions over the years, while 'by-passing' others whose problems may be reflected in community tensions and a strong paramilitary presence, rather than solely that of poverty. The Manager of both the Communities in Transition programme, and a subsequent Peace Impact Programme (funded by the International Fund for Ireland) noted: 'Something like 72 per cent of the groups and projects targeted are new, and the people involved have never had funding, which seems incredible when you look at the number of community groups there are across Northern Ireland'. Linking community development and peacebuilding, she concluded that post-conflict issues need to be named and addressed rather than avoided. Consequently, while community development is vital, it is not in itself always sufficient to deal with the challenges of peacebuilding, without a clear focus on the needs of the latter. 'An Introduction to Peacebuilding for Community Groups' was drawn together from the programme learning; illustrated in cartoon form.

Moving the peace process forward

The role and contribution of political ex-prisoners was increasingly visible within local communities in the years following the ceasefires and after the implementation of the Early Release provisions under the 1998 Agreement. Paramilitary ex-combatants and prisoners were quick to compare the hefty financial arrangements put in place to cover the severance pay and compensation for security personnel and prison officers, with the lack of any mainstream provision for reintegration and resettlement. Apart from the EU PEACE funds there was little support for the self-help centres that were being set up by groups aligned with the various paramilitary allegiances. Much of the work of the groups focused on supporting individuals and their families and advocacy over issues of discrimination and exclusion. The fact that politically motivated ex-prisoners were still tagged with a general criminal conviction designation made DDR (Demilitarisation, Demobilisation and Reintegration) difficult. Considerable employment, financial and personal obstacles flowed from the label. Despite this, the community standing and self-perception of many political ex-prisoners made them a lynch-pin in conflict transformation. This was generally held to be a more acceptable role in republican communities than the situation experienced by loyalists of different hues.

Regular meetings under the auspices of the Community Foundation for Northern Ireland helped to build relationships between different groups. One specific initiative delivered a 'Prison to Peace' schools pack, drawing on the stories of both loyalist and republican ex-prisoners to explain why they had moved from violence to supporting the peace process. One of the loyalists involved commented: 'We don't shirk away from the hard issues, or the hard question. We sit with our republican colleagues now, and we've a line of contact where we can talk to each other. We're on the phone with each other if certain areas happen to have problems ... we use our influence with our own community activists to try and quell things'. An INLA ex-prisoner agreed: 'We've been away on weekends with people who would have shot each other ... We can phone if there's problems on the interface'. A range of the ex-prisoner groups came together with the Falls Community Council and Intercomm in 2007 to establish the Belfast Conflict Resolution Consortium to structure aspects of this work. With a focus on alleviating interface tensions, the BCRC organised meetings to explore the relationship between grassroots conflict resolution and the ongoing political process. Work over subsequent years continued around community-level interventions to develop a citywide approach to conflict transformation.

Individual ex-prisoner constituencies had their own priorities. Many republican ex-prisoners were active in Sinn Féin, whilst their umbrella organisation, Coiste na n-Iarchímí designed a 'Processes of Nation Building' initiative to reach out to those who found the republican aspiration for an united Ireland either alienating or suspect. The UVF constituency, while retaining links with the Progressive Unionist Party, addressed the challenge of resettlement through a community lens. Its ACT (Action for Community Transformation) initiative developed from earlier experience drawn from community-based activism in North-East Antrim and North Belfast. The ACT programme adopted a more comprehensive approach seeking to support former combatants to reflect on a changing Northern Ireland and to 'embrace new, positive leadership roles within their local communities'. The self-reflection encouraged, allied to the training provided, sought to civilianise former combatants into members of Area Action Groups rooted in community development principles. The latter, in turn, would tailor their voluntary efforts to the specific needs of a given locality. Programmes such as ACT required the space provided by a supportive UVF leadership. Once established, they also provided points of contact with policing and statutory structures through mechanisms such as Interface Monitoring Groups and Community Safety Forums that were working in various areas.

Prior to a settling of the political structures and relationships in Stormont, it was often political ex-prisoners and combatants that had the credibility to engage in cross-community contact. Local activists without these connections could be held back by official party fatwas on meeting with 'the other'. One politically active individual recognised the difficulties – 'I suppose it was reflected in the politics at the time, because I remember ... people really opposed to any dealing with Sinn Féin ... It was like "Oh, you've been doing that, well as long as you're doing it". And it was the same with the political parties, you know. "Oh no, I won't talk to them, I won't talk to them." ... But as soon as you sat down – "What are they like?" You know, there was always this curiosity'. Uncertainty continued until the political circumstances cleared, with a continuing loyalist concern that the perceived Catholic, nationalist or republican monolith extended to community action.

If demilitarisation and civilianisation were tentative processes, the move to achieve decommissioning of weaponry was even more difficult. International facilitation and monitoring of the processes offered an important aspect of independent oversight, although the contribution of quiet civil society diplomacy also played a part. One individual who supported discussions within a republican organisation referred to the importance of building up trust and respecting the views of those involved: 'It was also about possibly giving them other examples internationally of people moving from conflict to peaceful scenarios ... It was important to engage ex-combatants'. The role of what were termed 'critical friends' drew in individuals from both the community and the Trade Union Movement, resulting in the paramilitary organisation in question first announcing its commitment to an 'exclusively peaceful political struggle' and then agreeing to 'put weapons beyond use'. The fact that the organisation felt in control of the decision to decommission, and that the process was implemented on its own terms, was vital. A set of questions prompted internal discussion – (i) How long should their ceasefire be maintained? (ii) Why should the movement continue to hold arms if the ceasefire was to be long-term? (iii) What role is there for armed struggle after the people of Ireland (North and South) had voted for the Good Friday Agreement? And (iv) Was it possible to build a political party if arms were retained? The decommissioning took place through a third party so that the organisation was not seen to have direct dealings with the security forces. The third party would then have the responsibility of disposing the arms and explosives as he thought appropriate. Handing over the armaments to the International Committee on Decommissioning was itself a drama. A token hand-over was arranged at night, in a rural area, with the members of the International Committee arriving in blacked out vehicles. As the designated third party waited anxiously a small moped spluttered to a stop and 'a wee box' containing guns was handed over. The helmeted moped rider puttered off as the box was ceremoniously presented to Canadian General De Chastelain and his team. When it came to the full scale decommissioning it was found that some of the explosives were so unstable that they had to be dealt with by the British Army rather than being delivered south of the Border as originally agreed. Words remained important; decommissioning was re-framed as 'putting arms beyond use'.

Three important elements in the decommissioning process described was the extension of consultation and involvement to the organisation's currently serving prisoners; ensuring channels for regular dialogue with representatives of the British and Irish Governments; and the political context within which those involved saw their future. The importance of all parties delivering on their commitments was stressed, although it was questionable whether this applied in practice to the two governments. One of the civil society intermediaries commented on the level of access they were given when the prospect of decommissioning was on the table, but as a loyalist leader often reflected where officials used to send a chauffeur driven Mercedes to bring him to meetings, after decommissioning had been achieved the doors closed. The event of decommissioning could over-shadow the need for recognition of the process-driven demilitarisation and conflict transformation. For the civil society activists involved this made it even more important to keep faith with the process.

Working within shades of grey

The looming issue that politicians found it difficult to address was the large elephant in the room – the past. The intricacies of the Belfast/Good Friday Agreement were still matters of dispute when Dr Alex Boraine was invited to visit Northern Ireland by NIACRO (Northern Ireland Association of the Care & Resettlement of Offenders) and Victim Support (NI). As Vice-Chairperson of the South African Truth & Reconciliation Commission, Alex Boraine was acutely aware of how that process had worked and whether there was learning to be drawn. There were many in Northern Ireland at that stage that saw discussion of the past as endangering an already beleaguered peace process; however, others felt that: 'We needed to do something to show things aren't black and white'. Such was the interest shown locally, that Dr Boraine was asked to return some months later in March 2000. A report, 'All Truth is Bitter', was published, identifying the need for space to explore what people thought and what they meant. An ad hoc committee came together on a voluntary basis to engage in extensive consultation around how the past might be examined, recorded and dealt with. A founder committee member described the motivation as being: 'Rather than talk about people, talk with people'. The initiative was so sensitive that even membership of the committee itself was tentative, with meeting agendas being shredded after each gathering. It took nine months before it was formally agreed to go forward with Healing Through Remembering (HTR).

If talking with people from the full range of diverse backgrounds was important, so too was the manner of how the talking was conducted; and how listening took place. One of the organisers emphasised: 'Little things made a big difference; that affected how people engaged with us'. One of the 'little things' was asking how people wanted to be described in the consultation report; among the nomenclatures listed were 'Name with-held for fear of attack from your murderous board'; 'Father of an English soldier killed by PIRA'; and 'From an innocent victim's widow'. Although the sensitivities and complexities were already on show, HTR identified a set of priorities – Commemoration and remembering projects; a Day of Reflection; Collective Storytelling and Archiving; a permanent Living Memorial Museum; Acknowledgement and the development of a Healing through Remembering initiative. It was felt to be reassuring for people that – 'We'd shown that we weren't going to run at this wildly'. It was accepted that the initiative had to be membership led, with the organisation being one step ahead, but not more than one step ahead. Within the membership itself, diversity was a core requirement. HTR adopted the view that: 'The way you mirror diversity is if there is anyone that cannot speak to one of you'; the board, and later working groups, were constructed accordingly.

Healing Through Remembering quickly accepted that process – how it walked the road – was what would make or break it. Adopting the hardy whin/gorse flower as its logo, it tipped its hat to the future, while acknowl-edging that peacebuilding tends to be about shades of grey. One of its most protracted discussions was on the use of words. Rather than speaking about victims and survivors, with the inevitable battle over who might be described as such, it spoke about 'those involved in, and affected by, the conflict'. It developed core values and principles for dealing with the past which included societal principles – commitment to a better future; not forgetting; healing and not inflicting unintentional harm; the centrality of truth; and realistic and hopeful goals. These were complemented by the principle of an inclusive, diverse, participative and empowering approach to individuals; and a number of process principles – recognition of language and terminology; flexibility; independence and political commitment; recognition and appreciation of existing work; a structured and holistic approach; and the importance of trust, transparency and engagement. It was concluded that approaches to dealing with the past need to be multi-faceted and risk-taking, but delivered in a spirit of tolerance and respect.

By the Stormont House Agreement (2014) there was hope that approaches to dealing with the past might be taken forward; although prospects dimmed somewhat over the course of the following year. An impressive report had been produced by the Consultative Committee on the Past in 2009, but its recommendations were side-lined as failing to attract political consensus. In a parallel development, a Historical Enquiries Team was established within the Police Service to re-examine over 3,000 cases from between 1968–1998 and a Tribunal of Inquiry, under Lord Saville, reported on 'Bloody Sunday'. This drew criticism from unionist politicians that this one event was being privileged over others, but was described by the then chairperson of the Bloody Sunday Trust as a 'momentus and landmark day for the city'. The widow of one of those killed on Bloody Sunday remarked: 'The heavens wept when Barney was buried. The sun shone when his name was cleared'. Other promised official enquiries were not honoured, and a sense of grievance over the balance between attention to state violence and paramilitary killings, festered.

Parallel developments in designing support for victims and survivors of the conflict (who over fifteen years had become 'a sector') fared better. An Interim Commissioner for Victims and Survivors, appointed in 2005, transmogrified into four commissioners some years later, due to Executive failure to agree on the appointment of one. In a review of Executive policy, measures taken were described as reactive rather than proactive, but by 2015 there was sufficient agreement to appoint a single commissioner. Things were looking up. Although it was difficult to see how overall consensus would be achieved among the many politically splintered self-help groups that had formed, it proved possible to form a twenty-two-person Victims and Survivors Forum in 2012, in circumstances where there was less party political capital to be made in manipulating hurt and anger. A wide range of community-based initiatives seeking to create space for a diversity of stories and views attracted EU PEACE funding across Northern Ireland, ranging from the individual storytelling focus of Towards Understanding and Healing in Derry, to dramas staged in community halls and centres. The amateur actor (a PSNI officer) in one such production, 'We Carried Your Secrets', created by the Theatre of Witness, recalled a member of the audience describing the experience as 'like open-heart surgery for Derry'.

A plethora of policies

In and between, and up and around, the complex politics of conflict transformation there was the general busyness of policy making. Children and Young People's Strategies, Gender Equality strategies, Community Safety strategies, Racial Equality strategies all jostled for consultative attention, as did policies for economic and rural development, inward investment and a multiplicity of others. Hard pressed community and voluntary organisations submitted funding applications to employ Policy Officers to keep ahead of the decision-making curve, although there may have been those within the system who muttered, 'You asked for a voice in decision-making, well now you've got it'. As provided for under the terms of the Belfast/ Good Friday Agreement, all policies had to be 'equality impact proofed' – an exercise that some departments found more bewildering than others. Community development remained housed in the Department of Social Development (established in 1999), where the Voluntary & Community Unit (successor to the Voluntary Activity Unit) was responsible for strengthening the relationship between government and voluntary and community organisations by 'creating an environment in which an enterprising and sustainable voluntary and community sector can thrive, contributing to the government's purposes in tackling disadvantage'. While there may have been general agreement about the shared challenge of tackling disadvantage, the shift in emphasis to 'enterprising', 'sustainable' and 'contributing to government's purposes', did not go without comment. Nor did the fact that the underpinning strategies related to generalist advice services; enterprise and innovation of the 'Third Sector'; faith-based engagement and volunteering. While the Department shuttled between Direct Rule and devolved Executive oversight, local ministers were drawn from the DUP and SDLP parties, with the Department later rebranded as the Department for Communities.

The Department for Social Development devised a seven-ten year strategy for 'Neighbourhood Renewal'. A needs-based approach was adopted in the thirty-four (later thirty-six) urban neighbourhoods exhibiting highest levels of multiple deprivation, with the declared intention of empowering communities to shape, and drive, regeneration initiatives. After four months of consultative workshops it was confirmed that the plans would be delivered through partnerships and integrated working. Workshop participants did query whether sufficient had been learnt from past programmes and made reference to the lack of baseline information available from which to assess success. One commented: 'If you're interested in neighbourhood renewal, if you're genuinely interested in empowering people, then it means giving up some of your control ... The cynic in me says that wouldn't happen; the optimist says it should happen, but I can't see it'. One complaint expressed by a number of community activists involved was that the policy was never strategic and much depended on the civil service understanding of how 'community empowerment' was to be implemented in practice.

One of the success stories of the Neighbourhood Renewal Partnerships that were established was their ability to meet during periods of community tension, acting as a mechanism for communication. Frustration kicked in when the effort to turn the requested long-term community vision into action plans was bobby-trapped by the need for budgets to be agreed on an annual, or bi-annual basis, resulting in delays and layers of decision-making. As in years past there were allegations of lack of statutory buy-in, which restricted action plan implementation and sustainability. Two insightful evaluation reports argued for greater flexibility in implementation and an objective selection of areas that evidenced need, but also demonstrated the potential to achieve maximum impact. The well-worded recommendations were cast in more graphic terms by a Northern Ireland Assembly member: 'Even organisations that have been speaking out about the different pots of funding have said it's just a complete carve up – OFM (DUP) and DFM (Sinn Féin) can fund their own wee groups … and it doesn't bode well, I think, for the future of community development … I think community development now is more about chasing a buck'. There were dark mutterings about the power of 'the SPADS' (Special Political Advisors) from those outside the gilded circle, while others countered by arguing the rightful decision-making power of representative democracy.

Whatever its strengths and weaknesses, Neighbourhood Renewal was a dream away from the 'wicked' policy challenges of community relations. Here too, aspirations were high in the wake of the 1998 Agreement, but fourteen years later the Institute of Conflict Research (ICR) counted ninety-nine security barriers and 'defensive architecture' across Belfast and a Northern Ireland Community Relations Council Peace Monitoring Report (2014) noted that the absence of trust had resulted in an absence of progress. The first Programme for Government committed the Northern Ireland Executive to 'improving community relations and tackling divisions'. A subsequent review by respected retired civil servant, Jeremy Harbison, emphasised the challenge of sectarianism, while warning of decreasing levels of tolerance and trust due to political instability. Direct Rule Minister, Des Browne, issued the unambiguously titled 'Shared Future' policy document in 2005, which stated that 'Separate but equal is not an option. Parallel living and the provision of parallel services are unsustainable both morally and economically'. The Alliance Party fulminated against the cost of segregation, with a study on the economics of division underlining the point. In 2006, the International Fund for Ireland ratcheted up its contribution with a 'Sharing this Space' strategy, and EU PEACE funding continued to focus on five peacebuilding criteria, with an inter-dependent society, being primes inter pares. Within at least some political parties there were signs of unease – would the emphasis on a shared future dilute the equality agenda that had become associated with republicans? Was there a danger of the stereotypical 'NIO man', devoid of identity? Was the proposed culture of tolerance and 'understanding' another step towards a united Ireland?

The draft Programme for Government issued in 2008 made no reference to a shared future or community relations until a late amendment. Two years later, a sharp nudge by the Alliance Party delivered a consultation on a CSI (Cohesion, Sharing and Integration) strategy, which adopted the tone of mutual accommodation. After 'could do better' redrafting the clumsily entitled TBUC (Together Building a United Community) policy was issued in 2013, calling for 'A united community based on equality of opportunity, the desirability of good relations and reconciliation – one which is strengthened by its diversity, where cultural expression is celebrated and embraced and where everyone can live, learn, work and socialise together, free from prejudice, hate and intolerance'. The political parsing highlighted words with a resonance for all concerned. As the previous Director of the Northern Ireland Community Relations Council, Duncan Morrow, constantly reiterated reconciliation in politics is a process, not an event.

Despite the narrowing of differentials in terms of inequalities between the two main communities, issues of intolerance and mistrust remained. A comparison between the Northern Ireland Life and Times Surveys in 1998 and 2013 showed that the Catholics view of relations between the two communities had become more pessimistic, while Protestants, starting from a lower level of optimism in 1998, were still sceptical. Although a modest decline in residential segregation was noted over the period, a study by Queens University academics, Peter Shirlow & Brendan Murtagh (2008) returned depressing evidence that 67 per cent of Catholics and 73 per cent of Protestants were still living in areas that were 80 per cent or more single identity. TBUC with its eleven principles and four key priorities (Children & Young People; Shared Community; Safe Community and Cultural Expression) had its work cut out. The challenge of translating policy vision statements into action remained, with at least one insider exasperated by the: 'slightly surreal world' of senior civil servants being summoned by 'their Grade 3' to come up with implementation ideas, rather than contacting people outside the civil service that were working on the issue. Belief in the value of the generalist expertise of civil servants still held sway.

Development of an integrated community development and good relations practice was still challenging. The earlier 'Shared Future' policy saw it as 'imperative' that community development should seek to 'build relationships between the communities and to work to reduce tension and violence associated with sectarianism and segregation', demanding that single identity work keep a close eye on the promotion of good relations. A long experienced community development practitioner offered a more nuanced approach: 'If dealing with single identity issues initially to build capacity does lead to peacebuilding and reconciliation, and that's part of what your strategy is, then it has a longer and much better chance of success than doing good relations work in isolation. Because if it's not grounded and owned it's always going to be peripheral to what people are thinking'. Another activist argued the need to abandon the 'phantom moral high ground' in order to engage in strategic single identity work: 'It's about what you're doing and how that ties in to what you're going to be doing next; and who is going to be there, and whose going to transmit what's taking place within their community ... I think there's a lot of work that needs to be done on both sides with regard to single identity'. The ability to bridge the divide between those undertaking neighbourhood level work and people behind desks and closed doors remained a challenge, although a North Belfast activist saw appearance as being as important as experience when dealing with officialdom: 'Be prepared to bring a briefcase, even if it's only a sandwich in it'.

Reflecting on how government works, a retired senior civil servant pointed out: 'I've always said government has three roles – you can try and persuade people to do it; you can legislate for it; or you can bribe them to do it, that's how government works'. A current policy maker criticised MOG (machinery of government) for the hierarchy of bureaucracy whereby a Staff Officer drafts an initial paper, which goes to a Deputy Principal, who tweaks it, which then goes back to the Staff Officer to be amended, which then goes to the Grade 7 civil servant, then the Grade 5, then the Grade 3, then to the SPAD (political adviser), and if it passes this level, finally to the Minister. Notwithstanding the: 'Wee chinks of absolutely brilliant practice', the system is not seen as particularly responsive or integrated. Outcome indicators are identified for policies such as TBUC, but: 'The first thing they do is hand out indicators across the departments ... completely missing the point. Things are then siloed'. With departments answerable to individual ministers, drawn from very different political parties, coordination can be a challenge. If there are any political misgivings about the nature of policies, the default response can be to defer it: 'If they don't like anything they just sit on it ... or process it to death'. For those in the system cursed with a social conscience the only alternative is to keep going in an effort to identify policy niches.

The new 'normal'

One of the contradictions facing policy makers was that statistical returns continued to show Catholic areas experiencing higher levels of multiple deprivation, whereas feelings of loss and marginalisation were consistently higher in Protestant areas. Putting this in a political context, a Methodist church Minister explained: 'Looking at this from a loyalist perspective, republicans have a narrative, they have a political goal that's not going to shift, and I think loyalism needs to accept that'. There were, however, few signs of any such acceptance. Concerns focused on the educational under-achievement of socially disadvantaged young Protestant men, and corresponding unemployment levels. Efforts to develop community strategies all too often hit the blockage of 'whataboutery': 'What they do is they give an emotional response, and the emotional response is very genuinely look what's happening to us; look what's happening to us ... And they keep repeating that over and over and over ... (And I argue that) sometimes they should stop and say "Yeah that's happening to us, but you know sometimes we have to take responsibility and do something about it." Whereas it's an outward thing – it's everybody else's fault'. The extent of dependence on individuals to take the community forward was remarked on by a loyalist activist, who accepted that a small number of more experienced practitioners found themselves so busy: 'There wasn't the time to do the other strategic stuff with regards to the people coming behind'. Another community development worker in a loyalist area admitted: 'The Shinners are brilliant ... on the ground. They deliver for people, but they have their thought police ... Once the Prods think that they've got something beat then they walk away, but when you're in development you need to build on it ... I often say to people it's a bit like a football team, it's easier to win the league than to maintain winning it'.

The thought police referred to within republican areas could work to marginalise critical voices, despite pleas that marginalisation rarely worked in the past. Community activists working for dialogue with those that rejected the peace progress were all too easily tarred with the brush of being 'spoilers'. An activist that experienced the sharp edge of being out of step commented on: 'How quickly people who moved into peacebuilding and peacebuilding roles themselves came to be the dominant voice. People were then excluded and demonised'. The call for doors to be left open rather than slammed could receive short shrift, although a range of community dialogue initiatives refused to be corralled by newly burnished community gatekeeping. Layered on top of the politics was a demand on both sides for politicians to be seen to be delivering for 'their' communities.

As governance shuffled towards normality there was less space for community inventiveness given an increased emphasis on a contract culture which saw the community and voluntary sectors as essentially delivery mechanisms for government policies and services. The required form-filling that accompanied contract delivery was ruefully noted: 'I mean even my own experience, 70 per cent of your time would have been spent doing funding applications; doing quarterly returns; it was just madness. I mean literally, you'd be saying 30 per cent of my time doing what I was supposed to be doing ... It stopped a lot of spontaneity ... It's not healthy in terms of that type of challenge or advocacy that community organisations should be doing'. Official codes of practice, that multiplied with alarming rapidity, could hide the fact that effective community action often started with three or four highly motivated people who were prepared to bring others in. This was is in marked contrast to the new dispensation where – 'I mean we can't have an activity unless we have done a risk assessment'. It is questionable if the more courageous cross-community initiatives would have passed the assessment test. For one community activist turned funder game-keeper there was only one option: 'God, there is so much red tape, rules and regulations, and I found it very, very hard. But I stuck with it anyway, and if you don't break the rules you could bend them to help groups'. The question was how many people were prepared to take this approach?

In an attempt to think beyond the box of the restrictions of the contract culture, efforts were made to reframe community action in the context of rights and social justice. The promised Bill of Rights for Northern Ireland, specified in the Belfast/Good Friday Agreement, fell victim to a political failure to reach a consensus as to whether it should encompass social and economic rights or be defined by the narrower considerations arising from the conflict. Despite valiant efforts by the Northern Ireland Human Rights Commission, and long standing Human Rights NGOs, such as CAJ (Committee for the Administration of Justice), the Bill also ran the risk of being pigeon-holed as a republican demand. In marked contrast to this the Human Rights Consortium brought together over 120 community and voluntary sector organisations united around the issue of rights, which the British Government still refused to progress. However, as income inequality increased between the wealthiest 20 per cent and the poorest households over the period 2003 to 2009, issues of social justice could speak to both communities. A number of small grants, with added value community mentoring, were allocated by the Community Foundation for Northern Ireland to model work within both single identity communities and communities of interest, around social justice issues. In one funded project the LGBT support organisation, Foyle Friend in Derry negotiated the right to paint the iconic 'Free Derry' wall in the Bogside, bright pink to raise awareness about LGBT rights. Equally, the Participation and Practice of Rights (PPR) organisation framed mental health, housing and other issues in a participative rights lens. While social justice became particularly relevant to communities of interest that had all too often been ignored over the years of the Troubles, it was still frustrating for civil society proponents of a human rights agenda in Northern Ireland to see foundational concepts being re-messaged by political parties in terms of zero-sum politics. The wasteland of 'lack of political consensus' was becoming increasingly cluttered.

The issue of rights, cultural identity, political divisions that reinforce divisive community narrative and an inability to deal with the past remain obstacles on the path to the new normal. But while it remains true that any death is a death too many, the period 2009–2014 saw seventeen deaths as a result of political violence, compared to 1,892 during the period 1969–1978. It took political accommodation to move to this point, with individuals and groups active at community level making an important contribution to ensure that people could not only survive the Troubles but also feel a sense of ownership of the peace. The space, voice and presence that were carved out made a difference for those most in need. The question remains whether there is still the imagination and energy to move beyond the frame of division and conflict. As one long-term activist reflected on the period: 'The wonderful business of overthrowing the local corporation, overthrowing the State – holy shit, an impossible dream, but a much more difficult dream was what sort of state would we create'. It is clearly still a work-in-progress.

CHAPTER 12

Drawing the Lessons: Community Action in Troubled Times

Protracted violence creates a context that requires specific skills and strategies, but more importantly needs the ability to think in terms of politics, power and narrative – how things are seen and interpreted in contested frames of understanding. Community narratives capture and encompass dominant community memories that shape explanations of the unruly past as well as influencing future relationships and aspirations. Community action can both strengthen these narratives, but at its best, can also question them. It can contribute to building local resilience, but can also promote conflict transformation by humanising 'the other' through questioning stereotypes. It can draw on grounded experience to challenge official state narratives and assert the centrality of human rights and social justice. As experience in Northern Ireland has shown small steps at the community level are often important in modelling the potential for peacebuilding. The creation of space for social and political inclusion is crucial to facilitate progress.

Understanding politics and power is essential if community action is to reach beyond immediate local issues to impact on longer term change. Power is experienced not only on a top-down basis, but also within and between communities. This study has touched on the roles of the Northern Irish and British Governments, as well as the increasing influence of the Irish Government. However, explicit power was also exercised by politicians and political parties, paramilitary organisations and the state forces (army, police and intelligence agencies), either individually or in combination. Less visible is the implicit power of bureaucracy, established institutions (including the churches, judiciary, etc.) and those that managed a divided society through the operation of rules, procedures, the interpretation of regulations and attitudes which mesh together in a 'common-sense' framing for official 'truth-claims'. The most powerful of these was the British Government meta-narrative of 'normalisation, criminalisation and Ulsterisation', which provoked community narratives that begged to differ given their lived experience. Community activists often dismiss the idea that they exercise power, preferring to speak in terms of influence, but arguably this is to under-estimate the importance of the vibrant collective activity, and the understandings drawn from this, that marked the years of the Troubles and subsequent period of peacebuilding.

Whether community action developed out of necessity, as described by a woman intimidated out of two homes during the early conflict: 'We met in each other's houses, there was nothing structured ... The majority of the people in the Residents' Association were squatters. They'd been burnt out of their homes in '69, '70 and '71 ...', or whether community leadership was consciously catalytic, decisions were taken to engage in collective action. As the conflict continued initiatives were also designed to both seed peacebuilding and foster it over the years of tentative political progress. A Derry community activist spoke in terms of community leadership that was both collective in nature and consciously sought the power to question accepted norms.

The ability to reflect on these norms, and to offer alternate paradigms, was also an important exercise of power. In societies affected by violent conflict it is all too often the case that the meta truth-claim disseminated by the state frames what is thinkable, sayable and doable in polite society. In the case of Northern Ireland this even proved embarrassing to civil servants, as recalled by a Northern Ireland Office official: 'I mean for years I was writing answers to parliamentary questions saying that the RUC is normally an unarmed force but in certain circumstances officers are required to carry guns, when you had Inspectors running around with bazookas'. The official truth claim could become overly stretched in the telling, fuelling the alternative community narratives that were developing. The latter became an art form in remembering, in part, packaged to make sense of local experiences as to what happened; why it happened and what the future implications might be. However in circumstances where single-identity communities developed conflicting community narratives, the ability of activists to reach across to understand the experience of 'the other' marked the point where community development embraced peacebuilding.

Community action and development in practice

Although much community development and local activism took place within single identity communities across Northern Ireland, there were key elements of practice that are applicable to any society. Many of these echo the five core values and processes noted in the European Community Development Network (EuCDN) statement on 'Community Development in Europe: Towards a Common Framework and Understanding' (2014) – (i) collective learning to build confidence and solidarity; (ii) empowerment to enhance capacity for involvement, analysis and action; (iii) meaningful participation that is inclusive in nature; (iv) collective action for outcomes that benefit the community as a whole; and (v) an emphasis on equality, which entails challenge to attitudes and practices that discriminate against individuals or groups. While described in different language, the values and processes outlined were not out of kilter with those developed by the Community Development Review Group in Northern Ireland in the early 1990s.

The European Framework made the point that communities can be understood as both geographical communities, but also as communities of interest, identity or thematic. Northern Ireland has experienced an increase in new minority ethnic communities over the past two decades, but with its focus on the impact of the Troubles this study has primarily considered geographic communities, with the exception of the Women's Sector which was thematic. However defined, community development invariably prioritises those communities seen as disadvantaged or marginalised in order to build collective action for transformative change. In principle the nature of that change should be informed by a commitment to a more equal, just and tolerant society; in practice, these values were often contested. Despite this the 'Strategic Framework for Community Development for Northern Ireland', produced in 2011, echoed many of the principles and practice noted in both the European statement and in the UK Community Development Occupational Standards (2015), arguing that 'community development is a long term value based process which aims to address imbalance in power and bring about change founded on social justice, equality and inclusion'.

As re-iterated in the Strategic Framework, community development practice in Northern Ireland that has general applicability includes the importance of listening to local people and respecting (if not always agreeing with) their priorities and insights. If collective action is to develop then local people must be part of the core process of identifying challenges and opportunities and deciding on strategies to effect change. A commitment to community participation means reaching out to those individuals, or groups, that are not in the community mainstream, whether due to difference or exclusion. As seen in the early years of the Falls Community Council, outreach can take many forms, including referral through people that are in regular contact with community residents, or through local information hubs (whether a sports club, a church, a local school, hairdresser, etc.). It remains important to identify and engage with those particular points of contact that are relevant to marginalised groups in order to encourage participation. Once achieved, involvement needs to be maintained, with regular forms of communication being essential. Participation may also be supported by community empowerment approaches that are responsive to local needs rather than the requirements of external agencies. Building individual confidence and skills (such as managing and recording meetings); drawing on peer learning experiences from other communities; using external support mechanisms and expertise to enhance community analysis and opportunities; understanding policy-making; and engaging in decision-making have all played a part in effective community empowerment in Northern Ireland, as elsewhere.

The importance of local communities having a sense of control over the objectives, processes and pace of development has been emphasised. All too often funders and external agencies can dictate a top-down linear process whereby a needs analysis can be followed by a dollop of capacity-building, resulting in a local group devising, agreeing and implementing an action-plan (complemented by a business plan) and, hey presto, agreed outcomes are achieved to a pre-determined budget and timetable, resulting in sustainable development which allows the funder or agency to move on. Even when herded by external consultants, this is simply neither realistic nor realisable in the majority of cases. Community development workers employed to work with local communities can play a useful role in reality checking their agencies. Expectations about the nature and pace of development need to be nuanced given local conditions and the time required for an inclusive community process.

Where community activism is either voluntary in nature, or where local groups employ their own development workers, it is clear that accountability is to the community organisation in question; but in situations where community development workers are employed by an external agency difficulties can be experienced. Many such individuals in Northern Ireland spoke of the importance of having 'champions' within agencies and clarity about whether they are primarily accountable to the communities that they are supporting or to their employer organisation. The Centre for Neighbourhood Development highlighted this issue during the 1980s, and a local authority worker put her finger on the quandary: 'It was about risk-taking ... But half of us were out, you know, being active in the community, walking in another person's shoes, trying to do that ... You did get a wee adverse bit of reaction, can't say we didn't'. The adverse reaction was particularly marked in situations where the community development worker was employed by agencies with a specific focus, such as health or education. Another worker concluded – 'Once you go down the specialisms you cease to see the community as the community'. It is important to be aware of the possible difficulties and to think through the implications.

Other general practice points include the need to ensure access to information and knowledge about systems, procedures and decision-making processes, together with an awareness of tactics and strategy. While knowledge is required to facilitate community strategising, tactics are also important. The art of identifying achievable community objectives that are well understood and have popular appeal was seen as an essential aspect of community action to build both community participation and confidence. The judicious balancing of responsive service provision, action-research and analysis, direct action and advocacy helped to maintain involvement over time.

The fillip and celebration of 'quick wins' further encouraged community participation and was often closely aligned to accessible funding that could offer small amounts of money in a responsive, timely and flexible manner. Local community activists also need to think through their relationship with professional community development workers, while the latter equally need to guard against being seen by external agencies as 'the safe hands' or natural point of contact. An experienced community development practitioner warned: 'Once you become that buffer (between the community and decision-makers) and not an enabler, you know, you might as well give up'.

Moving from the short-term to the longer-tem perspective, the question of engagement with policy makers and partnership working was also an issue. In Northern Ireland the focus of partnership was primarily two-fold – (i) participative and inclusive of different social partners (community and voluntary sectors, employers, trade unions, elected politicians, etc.) a format supported by the European Union; and (ii) an approach that could, at times, span community divisions. Much has been written about the potential and experience of partnership working, with a variety of views expressed by community activists that were involved. Partnership working can be an effective mechanism for policy discussion and delivery, but when related to community development must be grounded in community consultation and shared information. This is particularly important where trust is in relatively short supply.

Community development in a contested society

While community action is valuable in any society there are a number of lessons to be drawn from its specific operation in a violently divided society. Not only has community action to carve out the space to survive, but as many contested societies have witnessed community work practice has to take account of the hurts and anger that both violence and the experience of injustice give rise to. Community work is also impacted by the societal divisions that are often deepened by both the violence and the uncertainties associated with peacebuilding.

If community empowerment and inclusive participation lie at the heart of community development, putting this into practice is not always easy when there is political jostling for control, and dissenting voices within communities are effectively silenced. The need for constant attention on how to keep doors open to encourage inclusive community action is critically important, even in the face of political pressures. Trust needs to be built in order to challenge attitudes and practices that exclude others, whether consciously or unconsciously. Putting the challenging question of 'Who is not at local meetings, or at the table – and why?' also requires a sense of pace and timing as one funder found out when she challenged a group in Co. Fermanagh about the lack of women on their committee: 'The management committee were all men ... and I said to them you need to get some women on the management committee. And he said "Women, women, we have Catholics and Protestants on this management committee" – one at a time, take it easy'. The one step at a time approach may sometimes be necessary. Another Fermanagh group adopted a different approach when they were divided as a result of warring elected representatives. Finding these were all men, they created a women only committee in order to reduce political tensions. What is important is local analysis to identify community fault-lines in order to address them both tactically and strategically. The Community Foundation (NI) Communities in Transition programme focused on this challenge in a 'Power Analysis' toolkit, drawn from practice. Questions were posed about how community groups organised themselves and worked internally, as well as how they were perceived both in their area and externally. Groups were encouraged to address issues of church, political party or paramilitary influence, and how these might affect relations both within, and between, communities. External facilitators helped groups work through these issues, with small grants being available to support local action plans to effect change.

The need to pay attention to differential levels of development within areas of competing community identity is a recurrent theme. It can often be difficult to untangle the nature of, and reasons for, these differences (identified in Northern Ireland as a difference in community identification with the state), but if they are overlooked it can feed a sense of political grievance. This is particularly apparent where an effective community development infrastructure attracts resources. If funding is allocated on the basis of objective socio-economic need, the lack of a community infrastructure might be taken as one such indicator of need, although there also needs to be a balance between addressing deficits and the potential to build community assets. The unfortunate terminology of 'weak community infrastructure' had negative connotations, but its underlying principles were solid. However, equally, communities cannot be allowed to luxuriate in their own self-perceived weakness or in declarations that they are so lacking in confidence that they should not be expected to engage with 'the other' community. Support and challenge go hand in hand. This takes judicious programme planning that is long-term in nature. Programme application needs to be rooted in knowledge of local realities and possibilities. Generalisations that 'they' have everything sown up and 'we' lack the capacity to engage in effective community action also need to be interrogated.

The reality is that everything is potentially political in a contested society and must be treated as such where the power of perception rules. Decisions on where to build community facilities or housing send out signals that will be interpreted as demonstrating partiality to one community or another, where communities are physically divided. The allocation of resources, including attention, support and money, will be scrupulously examined to check whether 'the other side' is being privileged. Even apparently technical issues, such as the siting of a business park or a road, are fraught with perceptions of win-lose territoriality; while the siting of schools or places of worship, is a stamp of control. There needs to be clear information available to explain the rationale for such decisions in order to minimise the inevitable rumours and community interpretation that tends towards worst case scenarios. Consequently it is essential for local communities to be brought into decision-making forums; the various partnership arrangements in Northern Ireland, notwithstanding criticism, moved to address this point.

The range of skills required of community activists themselves in promoting activism in both periods of violence and transition varied across the spectrum of responding to emergencies or improving conditions within the community as a whole. At the height of the conflict individuals volunteered to meet immediate needs. A check list of essential community assets such as transport, communications, contacts, technical skills – and even involvement in early vigilantism – identified people who later often became the back bone of local activism. Changing conditions needed activists who could think through how to structure community development in such a way that it responded to local needs and took account of community representation. There was also the pressure to consider the politics of relations with the state, the British Army and local political forces. Strategies to enhance and maintain community participation had to be considered in conditions where it took courage to be visible. In later years there was a need to recognise, and respond to the fact, that the composition of communities themselves was changing over time. Finally, while activists continued to make a major contribution within their own communities, there was the additional challenge of networking with other communities, whether to build alliances around shared issues or to explore the possibility of designing community approaches to peacebuilding.

If times were difficult during periods of violence, political change also threw up uncertainties as to the balance of power within communities and the nature of community representation. Elected politicians were acutely aware of power, position and privilege as they moved centre-stage in the peace process. It was not unusual for community activists to be brought into formal politics, as seen in many societies emerging from conflict. While this can have benefits it can also have a down-side as noted by a community development worker who reported the new dynamic as: 'Go get a life and be political and you'll be in with the in crowd'. This, in effect, closed down space for civic discourse, with the fate of the Civic Forum in Northern Ireland being a case in point as newly ascendant politicians garnered and guarded political power seeing 'the chattering classes' of deliberative democracy being a distraction. Critics within the community sphere can all too easily be characterised as 'spoilers', with community activists needing to reflect on their relationship with the new politics. The touchstone is to ensure that community issues and priorities neither disappear nor fall victim to the zero-sum game of a still divided political dispensation, while recognising the legitimacy of peace process politics.

The community development survival kit

The community development practitioner's first principle of survival in circumstances of political violence is to keep the ear to the ground and the head down. The second principle is a good understanding of the local politics, including a mental note of who's who; and the third is a well-honed sixth sense for possible trouble. The importance of active listening to what is said, and what is hinted at, within communities was explained by a loyalist community activist: 'The point is you had to be careful. There were wee messages you got when you went into a room. You learnt at the end of the day how far you could push things like anything else'. Sensitivity to both what is said, and what may not be explicitly stated, is essential.

The importance of knowledge about who's who has been referred to by many community activists. This needs to be both internal within a community, but also applies across the community divide. It is good practice for community workers and activists to walk the streets in any case to be seen and to get to know local residents; this becomes essential if working in a potentially tense situation. As one noted: 'You can only drive so far from behind a desk!', and those community workers that see their job as primarily desk-bound will be less effective. Developing a rapport with individuals from all sections of the community stands both activists and workers in good stead, but is particularly important for the latter where their credibility may be questioned. A broad range of contacts also allows for triangulation to check out political developments and community views, given that no community is homogeneous, and diverse communities are just that – diverse.

The role of the 'insider-outsider', or 'insider-partial', has been noted as being able to smooth paths for community initiatives. When part of the community worker's contact list these trusted intermediaries can help assess what is feasible at a particular point in time and sound out proposals. Experience in Northern Ireland has often cast political ex-prisoners or political activists in this role which has created space for others to undertake often sensitive work, as was the case with community restorative justice projects. Although the need for caution was found frustrating by some: 'I suppose you were always under the pressure that while you wanted to do all these things there were these people who could at any time change it ... I mean I've had running battles with paramilitaries for years ...', it was critical for others. The ability to survive local power struggles differs depending on the status and credibility for those involved. An external community development worker can be disadvantaged in this regard unless they have access to networks and connections.

Examples abound of where such networking was formalised through structures and regular meetings. In the early years of the Troubles, community activists and workers met quietly in the North-West in an attempt to alleviate the impact of violence, while the East Belfast Forum came together in an effort to reduce tensions in the mid-2000s: 'We put together a group of people, police, clergy, paramilitaries – all representatives across the three organisations – different community workers ... Thirty people, the first Monday of every month. And we would talk ... And I often said, look we're not all in agreement here, let's be honest about what we're doing so we can make sure there's no duplication. We can even work together'. Such networks facilitated internal community dialogue but could also take account of cross-community issues, organising meetings on this basis. The regularity of communication enhanced the effectiveness of this approach and the personalities involved were important.

At local community level having a broad base of community representation on association and resource centre management committees was also referenced as standing community action in good stead. Although at times controversial, as in the case of the Bogside and Ardoyne Assemblies, it built inclusive community participation albeit within the restrictions of single identity communities. Where outside agencies tried to dictate the composition of such structures, there was invariably the unforeseen consequence of communities reacting against these efforts, even in situations of local political disagreement. Community workers caught in the middle could find such situations uncomfortable, but at the end of the day it was the community itself that had to own the decisions taken.

An often unspoken issue in contested societies is where individual workers hold specific political views and/or affiliations, as is their right. There are multiple examples of interview panels treading gingerly around this question (including one example of a political ex-prisoner group speci-fying in a job advertisement that applicants had to have had prison experi-ence – only for a prison warder to apply!). Evidence shows that particularly where workers are external to the community, openness and honesty is the best policy in a situation where identity and politics will be ascribed if not acknowledged. There must be clarity, however, that any personal views will not colour the work undertaken with the local community; and that information gleaned will be treated in a confidential manner. The issue of access and use of information also applies to agencies and funders given the understandable sensitivities about what data is collected, for what purpose and how it is stored. The Northern Ireland Community Relations Commission debate over the 'community relations' role of the security forces highlighted this issue during the early Troubles, while information gathered on people involved in cross-community meetings during the peace process resulted in police warnings on security grounds.

Then there are those tactics used to address situations of community tension. Disruptive bonfires can be turned into manageable beacons, if there are local negotiations and the will to do so; programmes of youth activities can be planned to take account of known periods of tension. Community workers in North Belfast went one further when they realised that paramilitaries were intimidating local residents by standing at the back of community meetings: 'The caretaker understood these things well and was under instruction to keep putting chairs out ... not to have them out, but to keep putting them out (as people came into the hall) so that the paramilitaries ended up in the middle of them rather than at the back of the room. And we had the politicians all at the front of the room so that they had to lead and didn't (just) follow'. Account needs to be taken of local dynamics with plans made accordingly.

When questioned about staff safety during periods of community ten-sion, a Community Programme Manager paused before answering: 'Really it's about people who get the work and understand it and really want to do it. And you know they will take calculated risks with their safety. Now that is always something that has to be watched and monitored, but ... sometimes people will put themselves in silly situations and, you know, it takes a lot of common sense and a lot of understanding'. Taking the time to reflect on the risks is never time wasted, although it can be difficult to capture common sense in yet another procedure document.

Pushing the cross-community boundaries

If the Northern Ireland Peace Monitoring Report (2014) was glum about the low levels of trust, it celebrated the fact that reconciliation was apparently stronger at the grass roots than at the 'top' of society, citing a number of examples of community outreach and interaction with 'the other'. The 'Strategic Framework for Community Development for Northern Ireland' also made reference to the role of community action in achieving political stability, and although not named, women's groups have long recognised the importance of being able to work on common issues without surrendering personal political positions. Even in the worst of times individual community activists retained connections across the peace walls and interfaces. Issues of shared concern or interest were regularly used as 'cover' to bring people together, in some cases to discuss the issue, in others to examine political differences and opportunities. This was achieved by well-tested and trusted relationships that lasted over time. Movement from reliance on the individual to more structured interactions, such as those between the Greater Shankill and the Springfield in West Belfast in the early 1990s, were particularly important in glossing social and economic concerns, with supportive political communication. Less formal interventions, such as the Mobile Phone Network, also allowed essential cross-community engagement in often difficult circumstances. For this to work in practice, however, there needed to be the political space and acceptance, often mediated through politically connected intermediaries at community level.

Community workers active in cross-community work were acutely aware of the importance of humanising 'the other' community. It was recognised from an early stage that cross-community engagement works best if it is rooted in self-confident communities coming together on the basis of clearly identified objectives. Where an articulate single identity community meets less confident community activists from 'the other' community, the latter may feel overwhelmed and alienated. Conscious of this, a Community Programme Manager adopted an initial indirect contact approach. Activists from the various communities that she was working with were invited a conference to ask questions of a panel of external speakers, rather than of each other. In this manner people could get a sense of the priorities of others without having to engage with them directly. Having broken the ice, the community activists involved felt more comfortable in participating in subsequent face-to-face meetings. Contact is even more valuable where people can come together on a residential basis, allowing them to mingle socially with music, comedy and community quizzes. The pace of the engagement process always needs to be set by local people themselves rather than being externally driven, given the uncertainties of political context. All too often disadvantaged front-line communities are expected to address difficult issues of sectarianism and violence that other sections of society avoid.

Cross-community activity requires acceptance of the ability of people to change and the need to give them that space. The work of Interaction Belfast in smoothing acceptance of a reformed police service resulted in a formal process of change, but space can also be found in the quiet meetings hosted by organisations like Healing Through Remembering. The strategic space offered through initiatives such as the Opsahl Enquiry and 'Beyond Hate' conference in the early 1990s, was important for both its inclusivity and timeliness. Inclusive space was often more effective when it was not publicly dubbed 'community relations' (which could attract contradictory responses) but community development, with a very conscious peacebuilding agenda. If this approach is adopted it is essential to negotiate clear, agreed ground rules to avoid confusion and misrepresentation.

The need for confidentiality and a sense of integrity has been stressed in situations where peacebuilding or cross-community work takes place in particularly sensitive circumstances. One individual with experience of involvement stressed: 'I mentioned the importance of quiet diplomacy ... I think it was about credibility. I think the other issue was (that) trust was crucial'. Another reflected on his back channel communication role: 'If you're in those kind of roles you need to know when to get out of the room. It's a very hard thing to do you know'. Integrity needed to be allied to being 'street-wise' where parties to discussions could adopt diametrically different positions in public. Community-based activity on politically sensitive issues often benefitted from peer learning from other divided societies, with reassuring validation from people with practical experience of conflict transformation and peacebuilding. The most relevant commentators were those that had lived the experience themselves.

And words matter

There is nothing neutral about words in a contested society. How issues are named and framed can create both barriers and opportunities even before any engagement with either local communities and/or the state. In Northern Ireland even the naming of the state, or a major city, is a signifier of political alignment. More importantly, ill-tempered words or political hyperbola have nudged people towards involvement in violence and have fed divisive community perceptions. The words of those deemed 'to be in the know' are particularly powerful and quickly ripple through community hubs and networks. The 'no smoke without fire' syndrome is pervasive.

Experience shows that community development workers need to be conscious of the words used and views expressed; thinking through how these might be interpreted, or deliberately misinterpreted. Although it may be inviting to speak out about certain issues, it is sensible to reflect on what can be achieved as compared to who it can alienate. A quiet word with relevant people can be more effective in the long-term than public statements if doors are to remain open for future engagement. Statements of condemnation need to be particularly well considered, with the credibility of the messenger being as important as what is said.

In Northern Ireland the crafting of community press releases became an art form of balance. The ability to link positions taken with stated values, such as respect for human rights, proved important; although not necessarily sufficient to avoid challenge.

Words, pictures and symbols used were also examined in minute detail, rummaging out any perceived preference for one community over another that might indicate political bias. Such analysis is honed to scalpel sharpness when it comes to calculating where funders allocate resources. Words are seldom allowed to speak for themselves where they are tempered by the power of perception. This even extends to the perceived ownership of concepts. 'Human rights' and 'equality' fall within a Catholic/republican frame, whilst 'parity of esteem' and 'civil liberties' are more often associated with unionism. One exasperated funder fell back on social justice as a more inclusive, if not strictly accurate, descriptor. As to 'community development' – this runs the risk of the zero-sum game of which community we are talking about.

Policies are rarely neutral

If community action is a practice minefield where communities are still divided and contested, the self-perception of policy makers as neutral, objective functionaries is equally open to question. At the macro-political level it proved very challenging for individual senior civil servants to come to terms with leading members of Sinn Féin for the first time. For its part, Sinn Féin did little to make things comfortable: 'The first time government was meeting Sinn Féin officially and Sinn Féin brought people who'd be seen to be prominent in the paramilitary side, again to show that this is what you have to accept ... One prominent member from North Belfast was sat at the table, with the trench coat, just simply to say nothing'. The perceptions of policy makers were critically important in both fuelling the official narrative and in the exercise of power through regulations, explanatory memos and the way in which 'the file' was recorded and maintained. Notwithstanding having to face the pressure of maintaining a degree of functional normality in abnormal circumstances, they were guardians of how systems of thought became legitimate, dominant and controlling. Alternate community narratives, inevitably tinged with mistrust, developed in response.

The physical disconnection of senior policy makers from the realities of life in frontline communities undoubtedly aggravated the situation where policy making is removed from grounded experience and blunted by the 'normalising' influences of a hierarchical system. A number of measures were taken to address this issue, although undermined by an apparent inability to acknowledge the expertise of local activists. Over the most difficult years it was often those individuals within the system that were prepared to think outside the proverbial policy box; maintain lines of communication with local activists; and translate activist experience into policy options that the system could understand, who made the most important contribution. They argued the inter-play between deprivation, political violence, equality and community relations. As far as possible they challenged the framing of policies that were minimalist, such as focusing on poor relations between interface neighbourhoods rather than a more comprehensive analysis of sectarianism in society as a whole. There were whole areas of policy making – such as support for the victims and survivors of violence – that were ignored due to the official narrative of 'normalisation and criminalisation'. In many cases independent Trusts and Foundations were left to resource these policy gaps and to support the development of peacebuilding initiatives. The EU Special Support Programme for Peace & Reconciliation (1995–1999), and subsequent EU PEACE programmes, were also important in this regard.

If policy making was constrained, there was a plethora of approaches to policy implementation. Concepts such as integrated strategies, partnerships, capacity-building, and a multiplicity of others, could slip off the pen to be interpreted by either public servants seconded to work in local areas or their department-confined colleagues. A retired private sector consultant, turned community insider reflected: 'I think if you fit what they're trying to do, how they're trying to do it, then they're a great ally. If there's anything at odds with their objectives then don't talk to me about community needs, or working with the community or making tough decisions ... They're quite clear on what they want, or what they think they know they want, but if it doesn't fit their agenda, forget it'. For its part, as community action became the community sector there were quandaries to be pondered as to how to secure statutory resources while still maintaining a smidgeon of local control and independence. There was also the challenge of how to celebrate community assets in a situation where resources were more often allocated on the basis of need and deficits, giving rise to what has been aptly described as the MOPE syndrome – the downward spiral of who are the most oppressed people/communities ever? With the public sector insulated by an established assumption of implicit generic expertise, community development is still challenged to express its unique contribution to local development and peacebuilding.

And then there was the politics ...

With the benefit of hindsight a community development worker reflected: 'We lived in an abnormal society – there's no comparison with where we are now, but unfortunately we are living with the legacy'. In short, the politics of the situation was inescapable. The lessons from the early years of the Troubles underlined the fact that reforms introduced in a reluctant and tardy manner can effectively alienate one section of a politically divided society, while failing to satisfy the demands of the other. Claims of 'neutral' military intervention or 'anti-radicalisation' policies have to be scrutinised in terms of their outcomes in situations where there is a disproportionate impact on specific sections of the community. The argument for non-violent change can become increasingly difficult where politics is driven by a primary focus on violence and security. Even in these less than auspicious circumstances, however, broader civil society found the space to question the rationale for violence and breaches of human rights. As one ex-civil servant, turned civil society leader, Sir George Quigley, argued: 'Old problems needed new questions asked of them'. Such questions were particularly powerful when asked within local communities.

Reflecting on time served in Northern Ireland, two British Secretaries of State spoke about the post Belfast/Good Friday Agreement challenges. John Reid described a region where Catholics felt not quite at home, but where Protestants felt under threat from an alliance between the vibrant Catholic minority within the state, the Republic of Ireland and a 'spineless, ungrateful and even perfidious parent across the Irish Sea' (Britain). A successor, Peter Hain (2007), admitted that the official narrative of 'Ulsterisation' had entrenched inter-communal bitterness and identified one of the success factors of the peace process as being to develop and encourage dialogue within society. Tony Blair's adviser, Jonathan Powell, enumerated a number of sharper lessons – the 'security delusion' of a purely military victory; the need to communicate with paramilitary organisations recognising that they will simply not surrender; the importance of political leadership; the positive contribution of third parties; and the long-term nature of peacebuilding. There is still limited official recognition of the contribution of the community dimension to peacebuilding.

If the new normal is considerably better than the past, there is still an important role for considered and reflective community action that is value-based. The opportunities remain: 'There's a whole range of (areas) like urban, semi-rural and rural areas where there's a huge appetite to learn about why we're being treated like this; why what's happening to us – why these things? Why we can't have more control over our lives in a small society like this? And what is leading to people coming together to talk about these issues, and often for the first time. Hard to believe forty years on'. As in in many societies emerging from conflict, sustainable peacebuilding requires an open door for those that are finding their voice for the first time, that may be critical of the process, or that feel left behind in the wake of a rapidly changing politics. For more established activists there is still the challenge of finding a defined place for community development in government policy that can play with the concept, but dilutes independent practice. On a broader basis there is the need for both established and new community development practitioners to reimagine relations in order to reconcile conflicting community narratives through an inclusive and honest discussion of the past as well as of the future. In the words of one woman, who cut her activist teeth in the disputed border area of South Armagh: 'Don't forget – remember, learn from the past and move on'.

Further References

By necessity this study makes only passing reference to a number of important events, for those interested in the history of Northern Ireland, and specifically the Troubles, the following books are recommended A. T. Q. Stewart (1989) *The Narrow Ground: The Roots of Conflict in Ulster*: London, Faber; J. Whyte (1991) *Interpreting Northern Ireland*: Oxford, Clarendon Press; D. McKittrick (2000) *Making Sense of the Troubles: The Story of the Conflict in Northern Ireland*: Belfast, Blackstaff Press; F. Ní Aoláin (2000) *The Politics of Force: Conflict Management and State Violence in Northern Ireland*: Belfast, Blackstaff Press; P. Dixon (2008) *Northern Ireland: The Politics of War and Peace*: Palgrave Macmillan; P. Bew (2007) *Ireland – The Politics of Enmity, 1798–2006*: Oxford, Oxford University Press and J. Bardon (1992) *A History of Ulster*: Belfast, Blackstaff Press. A range of studies that focus more specifically on combatant groups are referred to in this book – these include P. Taylor (1998) *The Provos, the IRA and Sinn Féin*: London, Bloomsbury; P. Taylor (1998) *Loyalists*: London, Bloomsbury; J. Cusack & H. McDonald (1997) *The UVF*: Dublin, Poolbeg Press; R. Evelegh (1978) *Peacekeeping in a Democratic Society – The Lessons of Northern Ireland*: London, Hurst; D. Hamill (1985) *Pig in the Middle – The Army in Northern Ireland*: London, Methuen; H. McDonald & J. Cusack (2004) *UDA: Inside the Heart of Loyalist Terror*: Dublin, Penguin Ireland and S. Nelson: London, Methuen and S. Nelson (1984) *Ulster's Uncertain Defenders: Loyalists and the Northern Ireland Conflict*: Belfast, Appletree Press.

The work drew on a range of autobiographies – G. Adams (1994) *Selected Writings*: Dingle, Brandon Books; K. Bloomfield (1994) *Stormont in Crisis: A Memoir*: Belfast, Blackstaff Press; M. Hayes (1995) *Minority Verdict – Experiences of a Catholic Public Servant*: Belfast, Blackstaff Press; J. Oliver (1978) *Working at Stormont*: Dublin, Institute of Public Administration; D. Hurd (2003) *Memoirs*: London, Little Brown and R. Needham (1998) *Battling for Peace: Northern Ireland's Longest Serving British Minister*: Belfast, Blackstaff Press.

Community studies that informed the study included M. Abbott & H. Frazer (eds) (1985) *Women and Community Work in Northern Ireland*: Belfast, Farset Press; N. Acheson & A. Williamson (eds) (1995) *Voluntary Action and Community Policy in Northern Ireland*: Aldershot, Avebury; Ardoyne Commemmoration Project (2002) *Ardoyne: The Untold Truth*: Belfast, Beyond the Pale Press; T. Blackman (1991) *Planning Belfast*: Aldershot, Avebury; F. Burton (1978) *The Politics of Legitimacy – Struggles in a Belfast Community*: London, Routledge & Kegan Paul; F. Cochrane & S. Dunn (2002) *People Power? The Role of the Voluntary and Community Sector in the Northern Ireland Conflict*: Cork, Cork University Press; J. Conroy (1988) *War as a Way of Life: A Belfast Diary*: London, Heinemann; J. Darby (1986) *Intimidation and the Control of Conflict in Northern Ireland*: Dublin, Gill & Macmillan; C. De Baroid (2000) *Ballymurphy and the Irish War*: London, Pluto Press; E. Deane (ed.) (1989) *Lost Horizons, New Horizons – Community Development in Northern Ireland*: Belfast, Community Development Review Group; M-T. Fay, M. Morrissey & M. Smyth (1999) *Northern Ireland's Troubles: The Human Cost*: London, Pluto Press; H. Frazer (ed.) (1981) *Community Work in a Divided Society*: Belfast, Farset Press; Garvaghy Residents (1999) *Garvaghy – A Community under Siege*: Belfast, Beyond the Pale Press; H. Griffiths (1974) *Community Development in Northern Ireland: A Case Study in Agency Conflict*: Coleraine, New University of Ulster; T. Lovett, N. Gillespie & D. Gunn (1995) *Community Development and Community Relations*: Coleraine, University of Ulster; S. McCready (2001) *Empowering People: Community Development and the Conflict, 1969–1999*: Belfast, The Stationary Office; B. Murtagh (ed) (2002) *The Politics of Territory*: Basingstoke, Palgrave Press; T. Robson (2000) *The State and Community Action*; London, Pluto Press; R. Weiner (1980) *The Rape and Plunder of the Shankill: Community Action – The Belfast Experience*: Belfast, Farset Press and E. Rooney & M. Woods (1995) *Women, Community and Politics in Northern Ireland: A Belfast Study*: Coleraine, University of Ulster.

Other useful books referred to are C. Gebler (1992) *The Glass Curtain: Inside an Ulster Community*: London, Hamish Hamilton; M. FitzDuff (1991) *Approaches to Community Relations Work*: Northern Ireland

Community Relations Council; Community Development Review Group (1991) *Community Development: Perspectives for the Future*: Belfast, WEA; C. Cockburn (1998) *The Space Between Us – Negotiating Gender and National Identities in Conflict*: London, Zed Books, WEA; P. Shirlow & B. Murtagh (2004) *Belfast: Segregation, Violence and the City*: London, Pluto Press; E. Melaugh (2005) *Derry: The Troubled Years*: Derry, Guildhall Press and P. Hegarty (ed) (2001) *Paddy Bogside: Paddy Doherty*: Cork, Mercier Press.

Much of the core material was drawn from official government papers lodged in the Public Records Office, Northern Ireland; local newspapers (*Irish News, Newsletter, Belfast Telegraph* and *Derry Journal*); community reports and publications; copies of *Scope* magazine (Northern Ireland Council of Voluntary Action) and community materials kept by community activists. The series of community studies published by Michael Hall, editor of *Island Pamphlets*: Newtownabbey, Island Publications, offer an insight into community views, which supplemented the original interviews carried out with community activists themselves. Interviews were also conducted with a number of retired civil servants and individuals active in political parties and paramilitary organisations. These were all self-reflective and a mine of information, of which only snippets have been included in this book.

Index

www.ingramcontent.com/pod-product-compliance
Lightning Source LLC
Chambersburg PA
CBHW071834270326
41929CB00013B/1998